Tuning Oracle

 *Oracle Press*

Tuning Oracle

Michael J. Corey,
Michael Abbey,
Dan J. Dechichio, Jr.

Osborne **McGraw-Hill**

Berkeley New York St. Louis San Francisco
Auckland Bogotá Hamburg London Madrid
Mexico City Milan Montreal New Delhi Panama City
Paris São Paulo Singapore Sydney Tokyo Toronto

Osborne **McGraw-Hill**
2600 Tenth Street
Berkeley, California 94710
U.S.A.

For information on translations or book distributors outside of the U.S.A., please write to Osborne McGraw-Hill at the above address.

Tuning Oracle

1234567890 DOC 998765

ISBN 0-07-881181-3

Publisher Lawrence Levitsky	**Quality Control Specialist** Joe Scuderi
Acquisitions Editor Jeff Pepper	**Computer Designer** Jani Beckwith
Project Editor Bob Myren	**Illustrator** Marla Shelasky Rhys Elliott
Copy Editor Kathryn Hashimoto	**Series Design** Jani Beckwith
Proofreader Linda Medoff	

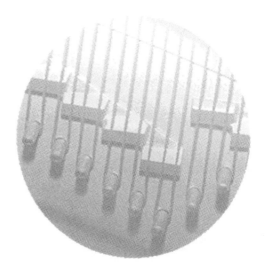

Contents at a Glance

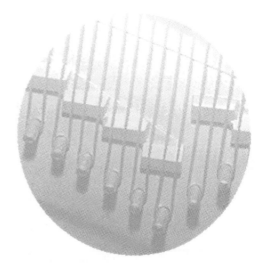

Contents

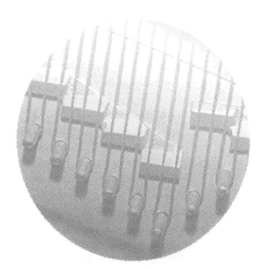

Foreword

The information technology industry is undergoing dramatic change that will result in unprecedented flexibility and economics for corporations and professionals that know how to use it. To prepare itself for this explosive period, Oracle has undergone a dramatic transformation in its products and operations that will establish the company as the leader in enterprise information management. As we face the second half of the decade, there has never been a better time to be an experienced professional in Oracle's technology.

All companies are organic—they are living, breathing organisms that influence corporate and consumer societies. In an ideal world, we want all companies to thrive, throwing off positive contributions to their society in a predictable fashion. Unfortunately, every company is dynamic and exists in a dynamic marketplace. Success and contribution are not predictable and therefore, like life, only few matriculate to the stage where contribution is predictable.

Oracle was founded with the objective of bringing a nascent concept into reality. The concept of storing and managing data in a relational model became manifest in database and tool software for development of corporate applications. Looking back, Oracle's lifecycle has not been unique. Most companies progress through transitional stages as unproven technology progresses through early acceptance, high growth, maturity and decline. In its 17-year history, Oracle has seen every stage, even decline. The resurgence of the last three years is truly remarkable, as few companies are able to reestablish a position of leadership once decline is experienced. Xerox and Ford are two notable exceptions, and now Oracle is proud to be added to this list.

What is not clearly understood, however, is Oracle's contribution to society, because its full lifecycle transpired in such a short period of time, whereas my two former examples took almost a century to experience all stages. Other well known examples of post-matriculation contribution might be Sears or J.C. Penney's development of physical distribution, IBM's development of standardized mainframe computing, and Honda's high quality assembly manufactuing process. I am not aware of any publication that has documented Oracle's contribution to society, largely because one would have to forecast it, but the authors of this book have given me that opportunity while introducing their text written for the sole purpose of using Oracle's products more productively.

Oracle's primary customer base is the development community. We have always tried to place ourselves in the developer's shoes and ask the question, "How can higher quality applications be developed earlier and faster?" As our business expands from development environments to operating environments and prepackaged applications, we are still driven by the challenges of our core customer—the developer. As development technology changes, we must not only change with it, we must lead the advent of this new technology to becoming a productivity standard for our core customers. In the next five years, Oracle's business will evolve into one of mass facilitation of "solution suites" that transform business process in industries for which they are intended. Object technology, multimedia, wireless communications, and client "agent" server architectures will enable Oracle to provide a standard toolkit for multiple technology providers to collaborate on a solution suite, thereby providing a platform for end users and suppliers to accelerate business change. So, (I predict) Oracle's contribution to society is arbitrage—arbitrage for end users that must respond to interindustry business process demands and arbitrage for software providers that need to integrate their technology with others in order to respond to that demand. We will have provided a technology that, when used correctly by experienced developers, provides functionality heretofore unavailable for rapidly addressing the complexity caused by business process change. This will actually create new developers for the ranks of end users and consultants by providing enabling technology that allows industry and functional experts without a deep technical background to develop their own applications. Huge class libraries will be created by a rapidly growing development community that is self-funding through the contribution of objects that are reusable by the whole community.

The authors in this book provide advice and experience that improve the use of our products today. This important step in advancing the contribution I've described will occur before the turn of the decade. The reader will learn and proliferate knowledge about the use of Oracle technology to provide higher quality applications that live up to the challenges of today's complex business problems. If this development community does not evolve, Oracle does not evolve. This book is a supportive step in the evolutionary chain of Oracle and its customers. Oracle is indebted to its authors. Thank you.

Ray Lane
President
Worldwide Operations
Oracle Corporation

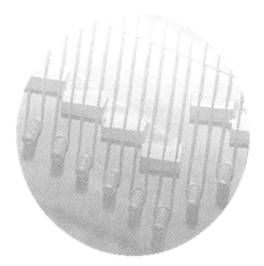

Acknowledgments

I want to thank my wife, Juliann, and my children, John, Annmarie, and Michael. Without their understanding and infinite patience this book would not have been possible. I would also like to thank my partner, David Teplow. While working with David building our consulting business, Database Technologies Inc., I have grown both technically and professionally.

It is very clear to me that at many critical points in my life the people I have had the privilege to interact with have given me the skills needed to accomplish this book. To these many people I would like to give thanks.

To the teacher who allowed me to continue to work with the school's computer after all I had done to the system: Denver Deeter, my high school teacher.

To the people at Honeywell Inc., who introduced me to Oracle: Terry Carlin (Hoser), Fred Powers, and Tom Kenney (a great manager).

To the numerous people at Oracle who have helped me both professionally and technically, a small but incomplete list: Andy Laursen, Mark Porter (alias Video Lad), Scott Martin (inventor of SQL*Trax), Kevin Walsh, Rama Velpuri, David Anderson, Gary Damiano, Ray Lane, Judy Boyle, and John Frazzini (our tech editor).

Over the years, being very active within the Oracle usergroup has helped me tremendously. To those many people who have helped me: David Krienes, Geoffe Girven, Merrilee Nohr, Buff Emisle, Bert Spencer, Warren Capps, Emile Bersin, Tony Zemba, and so many more.

To the people on the CompuServe forum—people Like Chris Wooldridge (WIZOP), Mark Gurry, Peter Corrigan, Jeff Jacobs, and to the many others I have interacted with electronically.

To the people at Osborne/McGraw-Hill who have worked hard to help put this book on the shelves: Jeff Pepper, Ann Wilson, and the staff.

To the many others I have worked with, like B.J. LaChance (my Chapter 5 reviewer), Jim Hussey, Pat Mcdonald, Paul Obyrne, John Allan, Jan Beyen, and many other clients I had the opportunity to work with.

To my coauthors, Michael Abbey and Dan Dechichio, many thanks.

To the founders of Oracle who had a dream that they made a reality. It all started with them.

As you can see it takes a lot of people to make this possible. I hope you enjoy reading the book as I have enjoyed writing it.

Michael J. Corey

The writing of *Tuning Oracle* has been something we have wanted to do for a while. We have over 25 years of combined experience using Oracle over the past several years. Our experience has, for the most part, been enjoyable. We have spent countless hours over those years working with the product and the assortment of tools that run against the Oracle database. There have been many late nights. Time and time again, we have sat in front of a computer screen tearing our hair out trying to get something to work. The work we do with Oracle's software is challenging, sometimes frustrating, enjoyable (most of the time), and has contributed to the successful careers the three of us have embarked on. From UFI all the way to Oracle7 and the Co-operative Development Environment (CDE), we have lived and breathed Oracle for what seems a lifetime.

I wish to thank a number of people who have given me support and helped me work with Oracle and been able to take the time to learn what I have. Thanks to my friend Dianne Henderson who put up with my after-hours work, and encourages me to pursue my Oracle-centered career. Dane Harris of Exocom Systems in Ottawa had an opportunity on some Oracle contracts when I worked for him in 1988. That's where it all started. Thanks Dane! Thanks to Ira Greenblatt and Eric Anttila at the Office of the Auditor General in Ottawa, Canada where I have worked for the past five years. Ira and Eric supported me and eagerly gave the office and me the opportunity to stay current with Oracle's emerging technology. Their trust in my abilities and skills has allowed me to get to the level of expertise I have mastered. Many thanks to my coauthors, Mike Corey and Dan Dechichio, with whom I have produced *Tuning Oracle* over the past number of months. Thanks to Glen McLeod, who has lived up to his image as Mr. Unix. Thanks to David Kreines of ETS with whom I have discussed copious Oracle issues, not to mention the antics of teenage children on a little league baseball diamond. Thanks to Katy Walneuski and Judy Boyle of Oracle, with whom I have worked through the International Oracle Users Group, for the help they have given me in getting to know some of the technical contacts at Oracle whom I have met with over the past few years.

This book is dedicated to my four wonderful children—Benjamin James, Naomi Liba, Nathan Mordecai, and Jordan Noah. I fantasize about how wonderful it is going to be to meet my children's children.

Michael Abbey

There are a number of people that I would like to thank who have given me help and support throughout my career. I would like first to thank my family, my wife Diana and my son Paul, who have given me support and understanding during my long hours and the everyday demands put on a front-line Database Administrator. Charles Amidon, Phil, who has been a true friend and is always there when I needed him. Joseph Noonan, who gave me my first computer-related job where I was first exposed to Oracle. The Database Administration Group at the First National Bank of Boston, especially Jim Hussey, for their welcoming of a new member to their group and making work both challenging and fun. I have been quite fortunate to have met and worked with a number of very talented people throughout my career. There are too many to mention individually, so I would like to thank all the people with whom I have worked, and who have helped me to grow both professionally and personally. A special thanks to my two co-authors: Mike Corey, for initiating the idea of this book, and Michael Abbey, for giving both Mike and myself the push to start this project.

Daniel J. Dechichio, Jr.

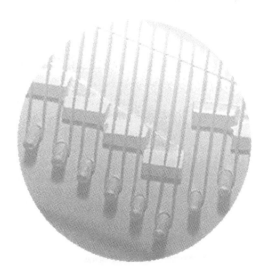

Introduction

For years, the race for market share in the database software business has intensified. Multimedia and *GUI* (graphical user interface) applications have catapulted the major players into billion-dollar companies. Work is progressing on an assortment of media servers to deliver on-demand video services to the living rooms of homes around the world. The most successful company in this environment is Oracle Corporation of Redwood Shores CA, USA. Oracle manufactures a suite of products that support their cooperative server technology. Their server provides accepted standards for a DBMS (database management system). A DBMS must

- Provide a repository for storage of corporate data
- Provide for concurrent user access to that data for the purposes of reporting, information creation, and updating
- Provide efficient security mechanisms to restrict activities on sensitive data
- Provide mechanisms to ensure the integrity of data
- Provide a data access language that conforms to industry standards

- Provide for operations to be segmented between one or more servers (host computers) and many clients (local workstations with no shared storage capabilities).

"The Oracle7 Server has been certified by the U.S. National Institute of Standards and Technology as 100% compliant with Level 2 of the ANSI/ISO SQL89 standard. Oracle7 fully satisfies the requirements of the U.S. Government's FIPS127-1 standard. . ." (**Oracle7 Server Concepts Manual page 1-3**). As of release 7.1, Oracle meets the requirements of ANSI SQL92 (ANSI X3.135-1992 and ISO 1309075:1992)

It is desirable in most installations to provide 24-hour access to a database. Database consumers insist that the investments made in corporate systems are preserved if they choose to move to different hardware platforms and other operating systems.

Tuning Oracle will discuss techniques for tuning the Oracle Server software using off-the-shelf tools provided with the distribution media. Effective system tuning can alleviate the need for new hardware and software purchases. There are many third-party products available to help the DBA optimize the Oracle configuration. We will attempt to highlight the functionality and usage of the Oracle tools to attain a best-case scenario for database support personnel—a system that is reliable and not prone to interruption (hardware, software, or user based). We will discuss Oracle tools used to tune the database. A reliable DBMS provides mechanisms to *backup* (make external copies of data) and *recover* (restore from that external copy). These topics will be addressed in detail.

NOTE

There is a great deal of technical terminology in this book. Readers will find terms defined the first time they are introduced. Acronyms will be spelled out in full when they first occur. Tuning Oracle does not cover the basics of Oracle7 architecture and new mechanisms. Readers are encouraged to consult the *Oracle7 Server Concepts Manual* for in depth discussions of the basics.

Why Tune Oracle?

Optimal performance of an Oracle database translates to:

- Happy clients
- The database responds well
- Throughput of transactions is acceptable to the end-user

- Users can get timely information from their database in a timely manner
- Efficient use of resources
- CPUs (central processing units) can be pushed to the limit with the maximum utilization of memory, disk drives, controllers, and the assortment of other hardware components
- Costly hardware upgrades can be minimized
- Knowledge transfer

Oracle's software becomes increasingly complex and the tips and tricks one picks up through one's own experience can be shared with other technicians.

Components in the Tuning Process

In Tuning Oracle, we look at the big picture with the Oracle database. We have broken the major components into chapters. A high-level summary of each of these components follows.

Installation (Chapter 1)

Optimal installation of Oracle is crucial in the tuning process. The complexity of Oracle is overwhelming at first. Tuning Oracle helps make the complex simpler. Once you start installing the database engine and tools, you will be asked to make a number of decisions. The answers you give determine the file structure and location of the components that make up your Oracle installation. The installation chapter covers

- README files
- Disk space
- Privileges (operating system)
- Privileges (within Oracle)
- SHARED_POOL
- SHARED_POOL_SIZE during installation
- Installation log
- File structure

- CD-ROM vs. tape
- Database creation issues
- Mac data files
- Redo logs
- Tablespace configuration
- Initialization parameter file (init.ora)
- Oracle Reports
- Control files
- Create scripts

Memory (Chapter 2)

Computer memory is measured in *kilobytes,* or more commonly *megabytes.* There are many Oracle-specific structures that reside in main memory including the SGA, the PGA, and an assortment of user, background, and server processes. These segments of memory are allocated when a database is started and remain in use until the database is closed.

The *SGA* (system global area) is a segment of shared memory specific to an Oracle instance (an *instance* is a SGA accompanied by the assortment of processes needed to open and work with an Oracle database). The SGA contains the database buffer cache (database blocks most recently modified), the redo log buffers (information destined for the online redo transaction logs), the shared SQL areas (parsed and compiled SQL statements shared by user applications and Oracle internal support mechanisms), cursors (chunks of memory associated with a specific statement), and the data dictionary cache.

The *PGA* (program global area) is associated with an Oracle server process and holds some data and statistical control information. The nature of the information in the PGA depends on how Oracle is configured. Usage of the *multi-threaded server* as discussed in Chapter 2 affects what is in the PGA.

The Oracle background processes support operations of the instance. For example, these processes take care of:

- Instance recovery on startup
- Cleanup of buffers when a user process aborts
- Archiving of redo log information when running the instance in ARCHIVELOG mode

■ Writing of data block information to disk

■ Writing of redo log information to online redo transaction logs

The memory chapters covers

■ Background processes

■ Trace and instance alert files

■ The SGA

■ Paging and swapping

■ Memory requirements

■ How much memory is enough

■ The Shared pool

■ The database buffer cache

■ The redo log buffer cache

■ Multithreaded server

■ SORT_AREA_SIZE

■ The memory-conserving Oracle7 feature referred to as MTS

I/O (Chapter 3)

All of the files that support an Oracle instance (except the initialization parameter file solely read during startup) are accessed for various reasons during user and system support activities. Efficient use of available disk drives helps the tuning process. The I/O chapter of this book covers

■ Table and index segments

■ Table and index splitting

■ Table and index striping

■ Rollback segments

■ Temporary segments

■ Redo logs

■ Disk controllers

- Hot spots

- Proper table and index sizing—what is really being used

CPU (Chapter 4)

Since the processing power of computers relates to the size of the CPU, ensuring adequate CPU size contributes to the tuning process. Some bottlenecks in running Oracle systems can be attributed to a CPU that is too small. Tuning Oracle outlines some ways to detect when your CPU is not big enough. The CPU chapter of this book covers:

- Favoring CPU

- Parallel query option

- How busy is your CPU

- Maximizing CPU power

- Session control

Other Database Issues (Chapter 5)

Experience working with Oracle has raised on-going issues for all of us. You keep revisiting many performance tuning areas. The other database issue covers:

- The initialization parameter file (INIT.ORA)

- UTLBstat.sql and UTLEstat.sql

- Miscellaneous tuning considerations

Show Stoppers (Chapter 6)

Certain aspects of Oracle continue to mystify even experienced DBA's. Chapter 6 covers the following issues:

- Number of database files

- Recreating a database

- Free list contention

- Do you really have 999 extents

- Runaway size
- Free space indexes
- Transaction space
- DUAL table
- ARCHIVELOG destination flow
- Restricted database access
- Getting locked up by locks

Application Tuning (Chapter 7)

Oracle developers are responsible for ensuring the code they write conforms to accepted tuning standards. The management of the assortment of buffer caches in memory ensures that as much information necessary for application support is read from memory rather than directly from disk. The application chapter of this book covers:

- The shared SQL area
- SQL statement processing
- Using of generic code
- Cost-based optimizing
- Explain plan
- The hints and explain plans toolbox
- tkprof and SQL trace
- Indexing columns
- Locking

Putting It All Together (Chapter 8)

Even though we break up the tuning components into pieces, in this section of *Tuning Oracle* we tie up some loose ends. We introduce the concept that each and every piece in the tuning puzzle can stand on its own as a contributor to the whole process. Chapter 8 covers the following issues:

- Tuning database backups

- Tuning database recovery
- DBA error-trapping routines
- Transaction control features
- Efficient resource management
- Clusters

Scripts and Tips (Chapter 9)

No book on Oracle seems complete without this section. Sharing this information with one another accelerates the learning curve. Why reinvent the wheel? If someone has already done something to enhance the performance of Oracle, spend your valuable time doing something else. Chapter 9 covers:

- Tips on backing up your database
- Space management tips
- Table and index sizing
- User information
- Accessing the V$ and DBA_views
- Sizing the shared pool
- Use of the database blocks in the SGA
- Creating an instance control file
- Renaming a column in a table
- Using SQL to write SQL

Who Tunes Oracle?

The *DBA* (database administrator) is responsible for optimizing the performance of Oracle software. Application developers are partners in this ongoing tuning exercise. As well, the hardware experts play a part by ensuring that hardware is running efficiently. These three key people need to work together to ensure smooth performance of Oracle and the applications it supports.

Database Administrator

The DBA is responsible for ongoing software installation, upgrades, performance tuning, and knowledge transfer to co-DBA personnel and application developers. An Oracle DBA would be expected to be the focal point for all Oracle-related issues and perform duties such as the following:

- Attending technical Oracle events (such as the International Oracle User Week in North America or the European Oracle User Forum in Europe) and staying current with the emerging technology

- Being consulted by management or developers for new product suggestions or questions

- Comparing the amount of free space on all databases against figures for previous periods

- Educating developers on correct use of indexes, space management, and general Oracle technical issues

- Inspecting the miss rate in the data dictionary cache for all active databases

- Inspecting all database alert files for abnormal Oracle errors

- Coding and managing on-going routines to back up and optimize the database

- Logging technical action requests with Oracle support

This list gives a flavor of what the database administrator's job involves. Tuning Oracle will highlight some of the duties of the DBA in the tuning process, and instill an understanding of the off-the-shelf products found on most Oracle distribution media.

Application Developers

Optimization of program code is the primary responsibility of these personnel. With the DBA, developers must attend to performance issues throughout the *SDLC* (system development life cycle). Tuning Oracle will provide the developer with a roadmap to the tools at one's disposal to optimize database program operations. With the buy-in from installation management personnel, developers are encouraged to spend upwards of 25 to 30 percent of their time going over performance issues of their code as they write. Experience dictates that time spent during development on the tuning process pays off many fold down the road.

Hardware Experts

The personnel responsible for maintaining the installation's hardware components play a role in the tuning process as well. Maintenance to computer peripherals and CPU upgrades must be done alongside some Oracle upgrades. For example, when installations are converting from Oracle Version 6 to the Oracle7 Co-operative Server in HP (Hewlett Packard) UNIX, one must pay attention to the operating system version number before proceeding. To illustrate this point, consider the following:

ORACLE VERSION	OPERATING SYSTEM
6.0.36.4	8.0
6.0.36.7.1	8.0
6.0.36.7.1	9.0
7.0.9 (beta)	8.0
7.0.12	9.0
7.0.16	9.0
7.1	9.0

The DBA may need help from system administrators when placing database files on various devices. This can be especially important in UNIX systems (when choosing between file system space and raw devices) but has an impact in all multiuser environments.

Tuning Oracle

The tuning process is a methodical approach where the DBA, developer, and hardware support personnel find the bottlenecks, tune the applications, and provide an adequate hardware environment to optimize the Oracle software. Besides *Tuning Oracle*, there is an assortment of other works on the ins and outs of tuning and performance monitoring. Due to the immense popularity of Oracle software and the expanding install base, you are encouraged to subscribe to technical publications, attend continental Oracle user group conferences, and participate in online communication forums that help users. So without further ado... *let's tune it*!

CHAPTER 1

Installation

You are now in possession of a very complex piece of software and are wondering what to do next. Relax—it's not as bad as you may think. In fact, it's probably better than you could imagine. Whether you have just acquired it or you have used it for some time, you will find that Oracle is a very tunable product once you master the nuances and idiosyncrasies to reach tuning nirvana. It's overwhelming before you get started, but, with this book, tuning is an attainable goal. There is light at the end of the tunnel. Like that little engine that turned "I think I can" into "I thought I could," you can scale that tuning dilemma before it conquers you.

The central purpose of *Tuning Oracle* is to provide database administrators, application developers, and other interested parties with some basic solutions to issues that involve getting the most out of Oracle. Two things we constantly hear are "You know, one of the things I *like* so much about Oracle is that it is so tunable" and "You know, one of the things I *hate* so much about Oracle is that it is so tunable."

We believe both statements reflect where you are at with your knowledge of how Oracle works. When first getting started with Oracle (or any other complex software product), you are barraged with a set of concepts. You then try to weed through those concepts, looking for a theme. When the theme is determined, you can begin to study how the concepts are applied. You find guidance through the following means:

- Reading (or ploughing through) copious amounts of technical documentation received with the product

- Requesting support through contracted support services that the vendor provides

- Rubbing shoulders with coexplorers and learning from your mistakes and successes, as well as those of others

- Devouring the gamut of technical material you find in user group publications and other forms of technical writing

- Trying this, trying that, retrying that another way, back to this, no that...

After a while, you are familiar with how to go about getting what is most important with any software—you want solutions and you want them quickly. Once you know the basic tuning issues, you then embark on the long, winding road to make the most of the knowledge gained on your journey. It's a vicious circle: the more you know, the more you find that you can tune.

Follow the suggestions outlined in *Tuning Oracle.* Take advantage of our collective 25 years of Oracle experience to succeed in real-life problems today. We have focused on areas we know and have had experience in, and our expertise will provide the biggest bang for your tuning investment buck.

Tuning Oracle will provide you with a survival guide to enable quick and competent database and environment tuning. We will present rules to be used as guidelines when tuning Oracle. These rules outline a fundamental tuning methodology, and they are designed to assist you when making tuning decisions. We then provide you with the skills that will get you through the tough times when our rules may not apply. And all you need are the tools that Oracle provides out of the box. You do not need extra hardware or software to take advantage of the information in this book. Just remember: Rome was not built in a day. *Tuning Oracle* will point you in the right direction.

This chapter will deal with the common issues that arise during the installation process. Our goal is to help you avoid some common pitfalls. Many of our suggestions may seem like common sense, but trust us, we see these same mistakes, over and over again. In fact, rumor has it that we have been known to make some of these same mistakes. Just when we think we have a process memorized, Oracle changes it. For example, you may know that with version 6, the default behavior of import was IGNORE=Y (this flag determines how object creation errors are handled; N means report the object creation error before continuing). With Oracle7, however, the default behavior of import has been changed to IGNORE =N. This leads us into our first topic, the README file.

README File

Every Oracle product out of the box contains a README file, which contains a summary of changes and "gotchas" (things that happen to you when you install Oracle and neglect to read this file beforehand). One of the first things you should do during installation is locate all the pertinent README files and review them. Oracle has not yet reached the level of, say, McDonald's, the fast-food restaurant that is standardized around the world (but this may have something to do with the fact that cooking a hamburger is not as complicated as keeping your Oracle database operating). Until Oracle reaches that level of standardization, you must locate README files the old-fashioned way—by looking in every directory. As you can see from the following examples, Oracle places these README files anywhere and calls them most anything:

```
/ora7/sqlreport/README
```

```
/ora7/orainst/README.FIRST
```

```
/ora7/rdbms/doc/README.doc
```

```
/ora7/rdbms/doc/readmeunix.doc
```

What's especially nice about the README files is that they also contain hardware and operating system–specific notes. A list of known bugs are also addressed with the new release of the software. By looking through these README files, you can also learn about new utilities that may make the installation go smoother.

A good example is the utd utility, found during a recent UNIX install. While using the utd utility, we were able to see any escape that was generated for any key struck on the terminal keyboard. This made a very recent installation of SQL*Net go much smoother. It took a lot of the guesswork out of building terminal definition types. You can't imagine how time-consuming it is to look up terminal escape sequences. So the few minutes taken reviewing the README file paid off a hundredfold.

INSTALLATION RULE #1
Read the README files, where Oracle places the most up-to-date information on the product you are about to install. The README files are also where you might learn about useful new utilities or operating system specifics.

Disk Space

Many hours of installation have been lost due to inadequate disk space. Make sure up front that you have the needed disk space. Regardless of what the installation guidelines for disk space needs are, make sure you have additional disk space available. A lot of times, product features, new utilities, and extra README files have been added. Each one of these items is not large in itself, but when added up become a substantial amount. The documentation, on the other hand, may not have been updated to indicate the additional needed space. An hour into the installation process, you find it aborting, due to insufficient disk space.

INSTALLATION RULE #2
Make sure you have enough disk space up front. Many installs fail due to the lack of adequate disk space.

INSTALLATION RULE #3
Overallocate your disk space needs for the installation process (the requirements Oracle suggests plus an extra 20 percent). Many times, the installation guidelines are low. Better to be safe than sorry.

Privileges (O/S Level)

Many Oracle installations fail due to inadequate operating system privileges. To avoid these problems during the installation process, we prefer to install Oracle software with a privilege-rich account. Then after the installation process is complete, we refer to the installation guide and then set privilege levels to those in the installation guide. This may seem backwards to you, but in our many years of Oracle experience, this works. We don't waste time during the installation process struggling with privileges. Calling Oracle support with the statement "I finished installing Oracle with the system account, and all was working until I set my privileges to those listed in the installation guide" gets much quicker resolution.

INSTALLATION RULE #4
When you have the luxury, install Oracle with an account that is overly rich in privileges (i.e., UNIX = root, VMS = SYSTEM). Once you have it working, set the account privileges to those listed in the installation guide for your platform and operating system.

Another common privilege problem concerns file access privileges. To avoid file access issues, it is best to have Oracle own its directories and all its files. It is quite common to see installations having problems writing to the directory, because the system staff forgot to set Oracle as the owner of the entire directory tree. Make sure every directory and file is owned by the account you installed the Oracle software from. In VMS, the command is

```
set file/prot=o:rwed *.*;*
```

whereas in UNIX it is

```
chown oracle *.*
chgrp dba *.*
```

INSTALLATION RULE #5
Oracle should be the owner of its own directory structure. This includes being a member of the same group.

Privileges (Within the Database)

Oracle has two database accounts where all the initial software is loaded: the SYS account and the SYSTEM account. The default password for the SYS account is CHANGE_ON_INSTALL. The default password for the SYSTEM account is MANAGER.

When you begin an install, make sure these database accounts are reset to the original passwords, even though a lot of the newer software asks you for the current passwords for these accounts during the install. Too many installs fail because some old routine used during the install process assumes the password for SYSTEM is MANAGER.

INSTALLATION RULE #6
Reset the SYS account password to CHANGE_ON_INSTALL. Reset the SYSTEM account password to MANAGER. Much of the software still assumes that the passwords are set to these defaults.

INSTALLATION RULE #7
After the installation process, remember to change your SYSTEM and SYS passwords to something other than MANAGER and CHANGE_ON_INSTALL.

SHARED_POOL_SIZE Pitfall

The suggested SHARED_POOL_SIZE is not always adequate. We have had a few occasions where using the default SHARED_POOL_SIZE recommendation has caused the installation to fail. So, based on this experience, we increase the SHARED_POOL_SIZE parameter during installation.

INSTALLATION RULE #8
Increase the default SHARED_POOL_SIZE (an initialization parameter file entry) during the installation process. If it's too small, it will cause your installation to fail. Set it to twice the suggested default.

Installation Log

Every Oracle installation session asks you to specify a log file for the installation session. If the same name is chosen, the installation log is appended to the same file each time. After the installation is completed, even if the installation process informs you that all went well, you must review this log to ensure it finished successfully. Just because the install process told you all was well, don't believe it till you see it for yourself.

In this log, you will typically see the error ORA-00942: Table or view does not exist. This particular error should be ignored. It is just informing you the installation process tried to drop a table, but it could not succeed because the table was not there. This is okay, because the first time you install a product, none of the database objects exist. If you do not have the patience to review the installation logs (this can be a very tedious process), then here is a quick way to search the installation log file for errors. In VMS, the command is

```
search error.log/win=10 error
```

and in UNIX it is

```
more error.log|grep error
```

INSTALLATION RULE #9
Don't assume your installation worked correctly, even if the installation process reports back that it was successful. It is the responsibility of the installer to inspect ALL installation logs to verify all went well.

INSTALLATION RULE #10
To expedite the search, use a system search utility such as more| grep (UNIX) or search/win (VMS).

File Structure

Once you have installed the Oracle software, you should give some thought to the database file layout. This part of the discussion is not about how you separate the database files for performance reasons (that is covered in Chapter 3), but how you name the file structures to make day-to-day maintenance easier.

Remember, when your site's system manager initializes a disk, there are many options. We do not recommend having your system manager merge multiple physical drives into one logical drive, even if your O/S system allows this.

The first important point to make is that one device equals one directory point. For example, if you have three physical disks, we recommend you instruct your site's system manager to allocate the devices as shown in Table 1-1.

DIRECTORY	PHYSICAL DEVICE (SIZE)
/u01 or Disk01:[oracle]	Device01 (2 gigabytes)
/u02 or Disk02:[oracle]	Device02 (2 gigabytes)
/u03 or Disk03:[oracle]	Device03 (2 gigabytes)

TABLE 1-1.   *Disk Layout Example: One Device per Directory*

This is more flexible and optimal than creating one mount point that is a combination of the three drives, as shown in Table 1-2.

INSTALLATION RULE #11
Map your directory structure to physical devices (e.g., if you have five disks, create five directory points). We do not recommend creating large logical drives.

Another situation we see quite often is one where sites take a two-gigabyte device and break it up into three partitions or directories. For example:

```
/sys (500M)
/data (1 gigabyte)
/indexes (500M)
```

It is much simpler and cleaner to have one directory point pointing to the whole physical device. Thus, when placing a file on /u01, obviously it is also being placed on the same physical device as the /data and /indexes directory. We find partitioning disks sometimes limits your view of the world. For disks that are going to be used exclusively to hold Oracle database files, do not partition the disk into separate directories.

INSTALLATION RULE #12
Allocate an entire device to hold Oracle datafiles. Do not partition it into smaller logical devices.

The second point concerns how you allocate space for a large tablespace—one that might take up the entire physical device. For example, if you have a tablespace that is two gigabytes in size and you have a physical device that can hold two gigabytes, then your first instinct may be to allocate space for the tablespace as shown in Figure 1-1. As you can see, the DBA has created a very large tablespace with one datafile of two gigabytes. In theory, this sounds like

DIRECTORY	PHYSICAL DEVICE (SIZE)
/u01 or Disk01:[oracle]	Device01 (2 gigabytes)
	Device 02 (2 gigabytes)
	Device 03 (2 gigabytes)

TABLE 1-2. *Disk Layout Example: Multiple Devices per Directory*

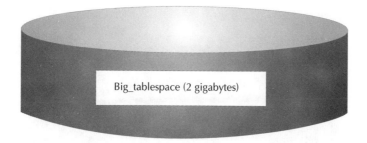

FIGURE 1-1. *Large tablespace in one datafile*

the easiest way to manage the tablespace; in practice, this is not the case. We have a better alternative.

As you can see in Figure 1-2, we allocate space for the tablespace in four datafiles, each 500MB. Compared to Figure 1-1, where the tablespace resides in one datafile of two gigabytes, the setup in Figure 2-2 has numerous advantages:

■ Many UNIX systems still have trouble backing up a single file over one gigabyte in size. Backup recovery issues are always a major concern.

■ When using multiple equal-sized datafiles, you only need to create the first, then add others as your space requirements increase. By creating the first 500MB datafile initially, you save time when backing up the tablespace that resides in that single file.

■ By creating a tablespace in multiple files, you can balance the I/O to that tablespace, if necessary, by moving one datafile to another device. Part of the output of UTLBstat and UTLEstat, as discussed in Chapter 5, reports I/O by database file.

By having the database tablespace in smaller, more manageable pieces, you have the option of separating the tablespace's datafiles onto separate devices. The alternative is the setup shown in Figure 1-1. Using that approach, you are forced to go through detailed analysis to determine which database objects are causing the heavy I/O load. Then you would have to drop and re-create those objects on other devices. This is a very time-consuming process.

INSTALLATION RULE #13
Lay out your large tablespaces into small manageable sections.

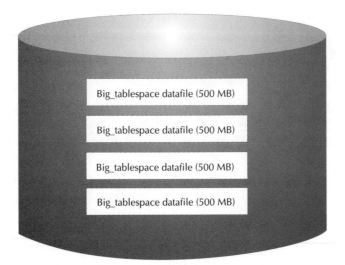

FIGURE 1-2. *Large tablespace in four datafiles*

INSTALLATION RULE #14
Many UNIX backup systems still have problems dealing with datafiles over one gigabyte. We recommend all Oracle datafiles be under one gigabyte (1,024,000,000 bytes).

The third point concerns standardizing your datafile sizes. Make it easy to swap a datafile from one physical device to another. For example, if you have very large tablespaces on two physical devices, make the datafile sizes standard (see Figure 1-3).

Imagine you are tuning the database and you run the UTLBstat/UTLEstat report (discussed in detail in Chapter 5). From that report, you determine that to help balance I/O, you should swap Tablespace A datafile 3 with Tablespace B datafile 4. If your tablespace's datafiles are a standard size, this becomes a very easy task. You know that a datafile from one disk is equal in size to the datafile on another disk.

INSTALLATION RULE #15
Allocate a tablespace's physical datafiles in standard sizes. This will make swapping the datafiles a very easy task when you begin the tuning cycle for I/O balancing.

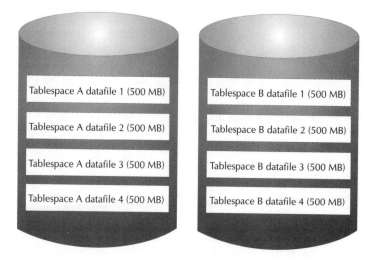

FIGURE 1-3. *Two devices with a standard datafile size*

Our fourth point deals with not complicating your directory structure. For example, many sites have the following:

```
/u01/prod/appl_catscan/catp1.dbf
/u01/prod/appl_nurse/nursep1.dbf
/u01/prod/appl_doctor/doctorp1.dbf
/u01/training/appl_catscan/catt1.dbf
/u01/training/appl_nurse/nurset1.dbf
/u01/test/appl_doctor/doctort1.dbf
```

In this case, on the physical device /u01 a file structure is created based on the type of database application. There are three databases (Production, Test, and Training) and three applications (Catscans, Nurses, and Doctors). Segregating the datafiles this way overly complicates the directory structure and limits your ability to see what's going on. We recommend an alternative approach:

```
/u01/oradbf/catp1.dbf
/u01/oradbf/nursep1.dbf
/u01/oradbf/doctorp1.dbf
/u01/oradbf/catt1.dbf
/u01/oradbf/nurset1.dbf
/u01/oradbf/doctort1.dbf
```

Place all your datafiles into a directory called oradbf. Rather than artificially separating datafiles into separate directories, place them all together. Then, when you move a database file onto that device, you will see every other database file it will be in contention with, regardless of the database. When you are looking for all database files on a particular disk, you have only one location to look at. When you are developing backup schemes, you write a generic backup program that searches every physical device on the system, looking at the oradbf directory.

You can apply the same technique to exports. Create an exports directory; whenever you do an export, it should be placed in the export directory. Then create a generic export job that runs every night, backing up any file that is placed into the export directory.

INSTALLATION RULE #16
A database file is a database file. Place them all on a central directory for that disk.

CD-ROM Versus Tape

We highly recommend that you use CD-ROM for installations. It makes your life easier and it makes installs go quicker. It eliminates the need for a staging area (Oracle places preinstallation copies of all its software in a staging area on disk if a CD-ROM is not used). A CD-ROM drive is well worth the $200 investment.

INSTALLATION RULE #17
Install from CD-ROM whenever possible. Purchase a CD-ROM if you don't have one. It can save space during an Oracle install.

Database Creation Issues

When you create an Oracle database, you need to make a few choices up front that, if done incorrectly, can cost you. The following sections will go over some of these choices.

maxdatafiles

The first and most critical, in our opinion, is the choice you make for the **maxdatafiles** parameter when your database is created (refer to the "Number of Database Files" section in Chapter 6). The maximum setting for this parameter is based upon your operating system. Set this value as high as possible. Over time your database will grow (planned and unplanned), and you will need a lot more datafiles than you ever anticipated. The default setting for this parameter is too low, and the cost to increase it is a larger control file. Here's an example:

```
create database prod
datafile 'disk01:[oradbf]systemp1.dbf' size 50m
maxdatafiles 255;
```

INSTALLATION RULE #18
Set **maxdatafiles** to a very high number. Too many sites use the default and run out. The default is too low.

Redo Logs

You should always mirror your redo logs. Redo logs are a single point of failure. If you lose your redo log, you lose your entire database. So when you create the database, make sure each redo log has a mirror partner.

INSTALLATION RULE #19
Redo logs are a single point of failure for the database: if you lose one, you may lose your entire database and have to restore a copy from a previous backup. To protect yourself, mirror your redo logs.

During database creation, we recommend that you have at least three redo log groups (with Oracle7, we speak of redo log groups that can be made up of one or more members). The following listing shows how to set this up when you create a database. After this code is run, you will have three single-member redo log groups with two members each.

```
create database PROD
logfile group 1 ('dsk1:[oradbf]redo1a.dbf', 'dsk2:[oradbf]redo1b.dbf') size 10M,
logfile group 2 ('dsk1:[oradbf]redo2a.dbf', 'dsk2:[oradbf]redo2b.dbf') size 10M,
logfile group 3 ('dsk1:[oradbf]redo3a.dbf', 'dsk2:[oradbf]redo3b.dbf') size 10M
datafile 'disk01:[oradbf]systemp1.dbf' size 50M
maxdatafiles 255;
```

Tablespace Configuration

Each database should minimally have the following five tablespaces specified:

- SYSTEM: This is where all the information owned by SYS should belong. No other user should have the ability to create objects here.

- ROLLBACK: This is where your rollback segments should be placed. Before all updates can complete, they must be recorded in the rollback segments. Only rollback segments should go in this tablespace. It should have a very generous default storage clause associated with it. For example:

```
create tablespace rollback_segs
datafile '/u01/oradbf/roll.dbf' size 100M
default storage (initial 25K next 75K pctincrease 50);
```

- TEMP: This is where all user temporary space needs are met for **group by** clauses, **order by** clauses, and so on. This tablespace should not contain any objects other than those that Oracle creates and drops internally when processing your SQL statements.

- TOOLS: This is where all your database tool objects should be installed. Typically the tools are objects owned by the system account, for example, the Oracle Forms tables or the Oracle Report tables.

- USERS: This is where users should place their own individual tables. It should have a very low default storage clause. So if a user does not specify a size, we assume they want a very small size. For example:

```
create table space users
 datafile '/u01/oradbf/user.dbf' size 50M
 default storage (initial 10K next 10K pctincrease 0);
```

Set it small by default; if users need more space, they should preallocate it up front.

Use this as the base installation for any Oracle database. From there, you can add additional tablespaces based on need. The point is, no matter how many physical disks you have or how many users, you should still segregate your basic database into this standard design.

Remember, if your SYSTEM tablespace fills up, your database stops. A frozen database is not a tuned database. By segregating the database this way up front, it paves the way for better performance.

Initialization Parameter File Sizing

Oracle does a very good job of giving you a starting point for your initialization parameter file. We go into great detail on fine-tuning your initialization parameter file in Chapter 5. But when you look at the Oracle default initialization parameter file, remember: small is the number of users, not the size of the database.

INSTALLATION RULE #20
In the default initialization parameter file, small means number of users and not database size.

Oracle Reports

When you install Oracle Reports, it asks if you want central table definition or local. Always choose central. You do not want to be in the business of supporting a thousand users' individual copies of these tables.

INSTALLATION RULE #21
Always choose central table support when installing Oracle Reports. Local table support is a DBA nightmare.

Control Files

Control files contain information your database uses to recover itself and maintain its integrity. If you lose your control files, you are in serious trouble. Because the cost of each control file in terms of disk usage is so small, we strongly suggest you create a minimum of three control files on different drives from Day One.

INSTALLATION RULE #22
Each database should have a minimum of three control files. Place the control files on separate physical devices.

With Oracle, you can name most any object any way you want. Use the ability to name objects as a tool. For example, call the control file CONTROL01.DBF, or in the case of multiple databases, CONTROLP1.DBF and CONTROLT1.DBF, where P stands for production and T stands for test.

Scripts

When you install and create a database, do everything through scripts. This includes the creation of all rollback segments, tablespace, indexes, and so on. It will make your life much easier and it will guarantee consistency. All scripts should follow the following format:

```
/* this is the create tablespace script for the production database */
spool script_name.lis
set echo on
create tablespace temp datafile '/u01/oradbf/temp01.dbf' size 50M
default storage (initial 25K next 75K pctincrease 50);
/*  */
create tablespace user datafile '/u02/oradbf/user01.dbf' size 100M
default storage (initial 10K next 10K pctincrease 0);
spool off
```

The spool commands make sure you are able to go back later and see how the file ran. SET ECHO ON makes sure you see every SQL statement run. The use of a script makes database creation much easier.

Let's Tune It

It has been our experience over the years with Oracle, that installing the software can be frustrating at times. We fondly remember the stories we tell one another and problems we have experienced ourselves during installation. Armed with the issues we have discussed in this chapter, we are confident you will make informed decisions when installing Oracle that will pay off down the road. Now that Oracle is properly installed, you are ready to start tuning!

■ Take the time to read the README files Oracle delivers.

■ Ensure that you have an abundance of disk space available during the install—at least the amount you are told to have plus an extra 20 percent.

■ Install from CD-ROM. It offers the most flexible installation environment and does not use as much disk space as tape.

■ Plan the distribution of the database files to take advantage of all the disk drives you have at your disposal.

■ Keep all Oracle database files under 1 gigabyte (1,024,000,000 bytes).

■ Have at least three control files, each placed on a different drive.

■ Your database should minimally consist of a SYSTEM, ROLLBACK, TEMP, TOOLS, and USERS tablespace.

CHAPTER 2

Memory

The amount of computer main memory and its efficient usage by Oracle contribute to the tuning process, and understanding some of the workings of memory will help you tune the database. This section will discuss memory management issues and explain what resides in memory. We will also discuss the assortment of buffers that occupy main memory, and we will provide some hints on buffer sizing.

Oracle loads application and data dictionary data into main memory. One of the goals of Oracle's memory management is trying to get as many requests for information satisfied in memory rather than needing to perform I/O. Oracle's efficient management and use of computer memory requires the we spend some time discussing exactly what is going on as an Oracle instance is running.

Background Processes

Some Oracle server and user processes consume chunks of memory. When an Oracle instance is started, an assortment of background processes are spawned to support the database activities. They run unattended, and take care of resource management and requests for database information as your applications run. The following seven processes reside in memory and support the activities of an Oracle instance.

The *process monitor (PMON)* is the process that performs recovery when a user process fails. PMON cleans up after aborted user processes and signals Oracle of the death of the user process. Resources are freed up after this information is passed to Oracle, and any locks that were held by the process are released.

The *system monitor (SMON)* is responsible for instance recovery (if needed) when the database is started up. SMON releases any resource requests that the user processes no longer require.

The *database writer (DBWR)* takes information out of the buffers and writes it to the database files. (Buffers in the buffer cache are referred to as *dirty* when they contain information that needs to be written to disk by DBWR.) Due to the architecture of the Oracle processes, DBWR ensures that user activities are always able to find free buffers to drop information into. Oracle decides what information to keep in main memory based on least-recently-used, or LRU, logic; blocks containing frequently used information are kept in the buffer cache. Memory access is much faster than disk I/O.

The *log writer process (LGWR)* is responsible for writing information from the redo log buffer to the online redo logs. Oracle writes information about all activity against the database to the online redo logs. Without the checkpoint process (CKPT) discussed next, LGWR is responsible for updating headers in all database files whenever a checkpoint occurs. LGWR writes to the redo log buffers, flushes information to the redo logs when a transaction commits, then reuses the buffers.

The *checkpoint process (CKPT)* can be started to take some of the work away from LGWR. CKPT is responsible for the header updates of all database files. Coding CHECKPOINT_PROCESS=TRUE in the initialization parameter file will bring this process up when the database is started. Most database configurations do not need this stand-alone process to perform the work normally done by LGWR. If your database has a large (more than 20) database files, enabling the checkpoint process may help the throughput of your systems: while the database is performing a checkpoint, system processing can halt until the checkpoint completes.

The *archiver process (ARCH)* is responsible for copying redo logs to an archive destination when a database is running in ARCHIVELOG mode. When using this mode, Oracle makes copies of redo logs in a secondary location before reusing the log file for recording of subsequent transactions. We recommend that you *always* run your database in ARCHIVELOG mode.

If you use the distributed option with Oracle7, you'll find a *recoverer process (RECO)* that handles the resolution of problems with distributed transactions. Oracle7 with the distributed option will support update activities on a remote database and such features as *location transparency,* where tables involved in applications may reside on different nodes of a network. It is brought up by ensuring that the initialization parameter file entry DISTRIBUTED_TRANSACTIONS is set to a value greater than zero.

NOTE
If you set the initialization parameter to 0 while running Oracle7 with the distributed option, you will not be permitted to perform any distributed transactions, and the RECO process will not be started.

Trace Files and Instance Alert Files

Any and all of the background processes, when present in your configuration, will produce trace files. *Trace files* are written by Oracle automatically and contain information about user sessions. At the head of each trace file is information that can be used to identify the instance that produced the file. There are date and time stamps to help match each trace file to the user session that produced it.

Normally, the trace file name is built with the process acronym (e.g., ARCH), the process ID of that background process, and the extension .trc. They are found in the directory specified in the initialization parameter file by the BACKGROUND_DUMP_DEST parameter. DBAs are encouraged to browse these trace files periodically and, especially in the case of the alert logs, to do some cleanup. These alert trace files grow forever until someone manually edits them and reduces their size.

With Oracle7 versions 7.0.16 and up, all logins to the database through connect internal in sqldba are recorded in an audit directory. If the trace files are found in *rdbms/log*, you will find these secure login notification files in *rdbms/audit.* The DBA may want to delete all or some of these files periodically. Other than knowing when a connect internal login occurred using sqldba, we have found no use for keeping these files around.

Oracle writes events to the alert log files. Part of the tuning process involves inspecting these files from time to time and looking for abnormal situations. Deal with these errors before they prevent normal database operations. Periodically, you may want to examine and then delete some or all of these files. The events recorded in them are simply for your information. Some of the messages shown in Figure 2-1 are informative and require no attention.

```
                                HP Prod                           ▼ ▲
  Current log# 5_seq# 37892 mem# 0: /oracle/oracle_aob/log1aob_t5.dbf  ▲
Fri Jun 24 01:02:22 1995
Thread 1 cannot allocate new log, sequence 37893
Checkpoint not complete
  Current log# 5 seq# 37892 mem# 0: /oracle/oracle_aob/log1aob_t5.dbf
Fri Jun 24 01:02:34 1995
Thread 1 advanced to log sequence 37893
  Current log# 1 seq# 37893 mem# 0: /oracle/oracle_aob/log1aob_t1.dbf
Fri Jun 24 01:02:47 1995
Thread 1 advanced to log sequence 37894
  Current log# 2 seq# 37894 mem# 0: /oracle/oracle_aob/log1aob_t2.dbf
Fri Jun 24 01:02:59 1995                                             ▼
◄  ▯                                                              ►
```

FIGURE 2-1.   *Lines from an instance alert log file*

As discussed earlier, Oracle takes information from the log buffers and dumps it to disk. Before Oracle will reuse an online redo log, all information from the buffers destined for that log must be written. If Oracle wants to switch the active redo log group, and LGWR has not done its work, Oracle cannot switch to the new group, and an error message as shown in Figure 2-1 will be written to this alert log file. This situation may require your attention. See the section "The Redo Log Buffer Cache" section later in this chapter for more details.

TIP
Inspect instance alert log files for error messages regarding online redo log groups. It is the easiest way to determine whether you have enough redo log files for your database. If Oracle cannot reuse a redo log because cleanup is not yet completed, you may need more redo logs.

Every time the instance is started, Oracle lists, in the alert file, all nondefault values for initialization parameter file entries. Using this list, along with the discussion in Chapter 5, you can adjust some of these nondefault parameters as part of the tuning process. Nondefault parameters are not necessarily a problem—some of them are there to support your configuration. We suggest that you be aware (using trace file output as illustrated in Figure 2-2) of what initialization parameter file entries are nondefaults.

When you use an existing initialization parameter file as a skeleton to start up a new instance, make sure that the nondefault parameters stay that way for the new database as well. For example, in Figure 2-2, the TIMED_STATISTICS parameter is set

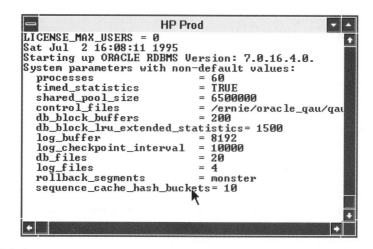

FIGURE 2-2.   *A list of nondefault initialization parameters at startup*

to TRUE to support collection of buffer statistics, as discussed in the section "The Database Buffer Cache" later in this chapter. As well, the ROLLBACK_SEGMENTS parameter is set to MONSTER. Chapters 3 and 5 discuss rollback segments and the initialization parameter file in more detail.

The SGA

The *system global area* (SGA) is a segment of memory allocated to Oracle that contains data and control information particular to an Oracle instance. Sizing of the SGA is partially a hit-and-miss exercise. You will notice that some parameters in the initialization parameter file have a profound effect on the size of the SGA. The initialization parameter file parameters DB_BLOCK_BUFFERS (the number of buffers dedicated to the database buffer cache) and SHARED_POOL_SIZE (the number of bytes allocated to the shared SQL area) are the major contributors to the size of the SGA. Refer to the discussion in Chapter 7 on how to take advantage of the shared SQL area. The amount of memory allocated to the SGA based on the value of DB_BLOCK_BUFFERS depends on the Oracle block size you use. For example, suppose that 32,768 bytes are allocated for these buffers using a 2K (2,048 bytes) block size; if you increase the block size to 4K (4,096 bytes), the database buffer memory requirement will swell to 65,536 bytes without adjusting the DB_BLOCK_BUFFERS entry in the initialization parameter file.

Paging and Swapping

Paging involves moving portions of an application or process out to secondary storage to free up real memory space. *Swapping* involves copying entire processes from memory to secondary storage. Disk drives and an assortment of high-speed storage devices are used for these secondary devices. Your job is to ensure the memory structures used by Oracle can fit into real memory. A number of operating systems require a contiguous chunk of main memory to start Oracle. During the tuning process, you need to monitor the amount of paging and swapping on your system. The operating system may decide to page out portions of the SGA to make room for new processes or existing processes it deems to be in more need of main memory. You may find that without adequate computer memory, the time slice of CPU each user gets may be used up by swapping and paging, and the applications may appear to be doing nothing else. Swap space utilization is assessed using a number of operating system–dependent utilities. For example, in Figure 2-3, notice that 306,608 bytes are configured for swap space, with only 25,400 bytes (swap space configured of 306,608 minus currently free swap space of 281,808) currently in use; this represents an 8 percent swap space usage.

In Figure 2-4, information is shown describing processes and pages swapped in and out of main memory. Compare the number of concurrent processes on your machine, and obtain a ratio of concurrent processes to processes swapped out. Figure 2-4 was created with over 75 concurrent processes on the machine. Of those, only four are presently swapped out or a mere 5.3 percent. This represents a healthy ratio.

```
┌──────────────────────────────── HP Prod ────────────────────────────┐
│ ESOURCE UTILIZATION IN KILOBYTES                                     │
│  Physical memory:           131072   Maximum user memory:    110236  │
│  Free memory:                60580   User memory utilization:    45% │
│  Swap space configured:     306608   Enabled via swapon(1m):  306608 │
│  Currently free swap space: 281208   Swap space utilization:      8% │
│  File system swap available:     0   File system swap utilization: 0%│
│                                                                      │
│ ser CPU:  2%   LAN packets in:   63  Context switches:   139  LOAD AVE│
│ ys CPU:   9%   LAN packets out:  15  Trap calls:          43  1 min: │
│ dle CPU: 89%                         System calls:       576  5 min: │
│ ice CPU:  0%                         Device interrupts:  498  15 min:│
│                                                                      │
│   SWAP DEVICE            KILOBYTES   XFERS   UTIL DISC               │
│   7 0x000001               48560    0        0% 0                    │
└──────────────────────────────────────────────────────────────────────┘
```

FIGURE 2-3. *Swap space utilization method #1*

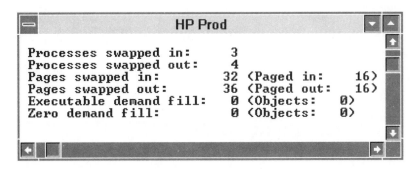

FIGURE 2-4. *Swap space utilization method #2*

Memory Requirements

When tuning memory and ensuring that enough memory resides on your machine, you should ask what the size requirements are of the programs in memory and what they are doing. These are the same questions you ask yourself regardless of the hardware with which you use Oracle. The programs you use to get answers to these hardware-independent questions are hardware-dependent. The example used in this section is based on an HP-UX Series 800 model 897S running HP-UX version 9.0 running the korn shell. This environment uses a two-task architecture with a front-end tool process and a back-end shadow process that does the actual work against the database. Table 2-1 shows the versions of the Oracle components used in this exercise.

Table 2-1 assumes 30 concurrent Oracle sessions. Of those 30, 10 are currently doing something (creating, updating, or querying data) in an SQL*Forms session, 2 are using SQL*Plus, and the remaining 18 are sitting idle in an SQL*Forms session.

CONFIGURATION COMPONENT	VERSION	CONCURRENT ACCESS
Oracle kernel	7.0.16.4	30
SQL*Forms	3.0.16.12.7	28
SQL*Plus	3.1.3.2.1	2

TABLE 2-1. *Sample Users/Application Configuration*

The memory requirements of these 18 idle sessions, as you will see in the output following, are the same as the active sessions. There may indeed be more resources used by the active sessions for locking, acquisition of latches, and disk I/O, but the base memory requirement for these inactive sessions is just about the same as the active ones. The steps in the memory requirement exercise will be outlined, and the examples drawn from the environment shown in Table 2-1.

Step 1: Requirements without Including the SGA

The first step is to assess the memory requirements of the database and tools, excluding the SGA.

Table 2-2 shows the programs running in this sample configuration and their private and shared memory requirements.

PROGRAM	COMPONENT	SHARED MEMORY (BYTES)	PRIVATE MEMORY (BYTES)	TOTAL MEMORY (BYTES)
background processes	archiver(ARCH)	5,304,300	344,064	5,648,364
	database writers (parent plus three writer processes) (DBWR,DB01,DB02,DB03)	including above	741,376	741,376
	process monitor (PMON)	including above	253,952	253,952
	system monitor (SMON)	including above	409,600	409,600
	log writer	including above	225,280	225,280
oracle totals		5,304,300	1,974,272	7,278,572
sqlplus		1,781,760	393,216	393,216
sqlplus shadow		0	217,088	217,088
runform		2,174,976	1,658,880	3,833,856
runform shadow		0	413,696	413,696

TABLE 2-2. *Oracle and Tool Memory Requirements*

Figure 2-5 shows a portion of the screen output from the HP-UX monitor command. Monitor is used to report on the resource utilization on the machine. It displays statistics on memory, disk access, I/O, swapping, and CPU utilization. This section of the screen was used to collect the numbers shown in Table 2-2. The shared memory figures in Table 2-2 were drawn from the TEXT row in the Region column in Figure 2-5. The private memory figures in Table 2-2 were drawn from the DATA and SHMEM rows in the Region column.

Using the information from Table 2-1 and Table 2-2, you can estimate the base amount of main memory required to support this configuration. Table 2-3 shows those requirements broken out by component. For example, the 12,410,880 bytes to support the 30 runform shadow processes is the 413,696 bytes per shadow multiplied by the number of users. The table also includes the SGA memory requirements, which are discussed in the next section.

Step 2: Assessing the SGA Memory Requirements

The simplest way to see the SGA memory requirements is through full-screen sqldba. Issue the command **connect internal** followed by **show sga**. The output is similar to that shown in Figure 2-6.

Based on the information in Table 2-3, this system will consume 49,684,460 bytes, or roughly 48 megabytes of memory. Of course, your configuration and resultant memory requirements will be different. After going through the steps outlined in this section, you will end up with a realistic estimate of your memory requirements. Even though your hardware and configuration may be different, the process will be the same.

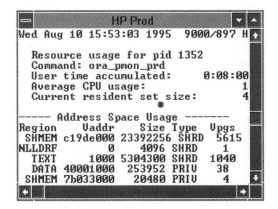

FIGURE 2-5. *Address space usage on the HP-UX monitor*

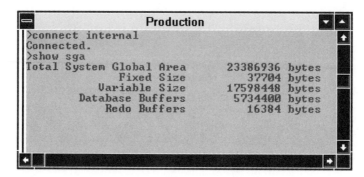

FIGURE 2-6. *Output of show sga command in sqldba*

How Much Memory Is Enough?

Using the figure computed in the previous section, the sample system needs at least 48 megabytes of main memory for itself. When trying to decide memory size, you need to consider the assortment of other memory consumers that live and breathe on your computer. Speak with the person in your office who is responsible for the

COMPONENT	OCCURRENCES	BYTES
Oracle (database)	1	7,278,572
sqlplus (tool)	1	2,174,976
runform (tool)	1	3,833,856
sqlplus (shadow process)	2	434,176
runform (shadow process)	30	12,410,880
Total memory requirement for database engine, tools, and shadow processes		**26,132,460**
Total memory requirement for SGA (see Figure 2-6)		**23,386,936**

TABLE 2-3. *Configuration and SGA Memory Requirements*

computer on which Oracle runs. You must assess the additional space requirements for the following:

- The operating system itself
- The assortment of support mechanisms for that operating system
- The network of operating system buffers
- The software that coexists with Oracle on your machine
- The Oracle databases that coexist on your machine
- The memory overhead per user on the system
- The operating system overhead for supporting the read and write requests of all of those users

A comfortable figure to live with is one that is roughly three times that calculated for the support of your Oracle systems. Given the different combinations of concurrent application software that runs on your machine, you may find the figure for your purposes different. Three times is the suggested minimum, but the figure could be higher with a large number (more than 60) of concurrent users.

The Shared Pool

The shared pool portion of the SGA is made up of the library cache, the dictionary cache, and some user and server session information. When we look at tuning memory with Oracle7, the shared pool is one of the biggest consumers.

The Library Cache

This cache contains parsed and executable SQL statements. For every SQL statement Oracle processes, there is a shared part and a private part. The shared portion of the SGA for every SQL statement is that amount of memory in the shared pool that contains the following components of each statement:

- *Parse tree:* A representation of the results of parsing a SQL statement (the parse phase of statement processing is discussed in Chapter 7)
- *Execution plan:* A roadmap Oracle builds containing the plan of how a statement will be run (it is written after each SQL statement is optimized)

The private part has two components:

- The persistent portion that occupies space in the SGA for the life of every cursor associated with a SQL statement

- The runtime portion that is acquired when a SQL statement executes, and is released when the statement completes

To make efficient use of the space allocated to the SGA, you should close cursors when you are done with them to free up memory allocated for this runtime portion.

An important key to tuning the SGA is ensuring that the library cache is large enough so Oracle can keep parsed and executable statements in the shared pool. You should look in the v$librarycache dictionary view to assess the performance of the library cache at its current size. Figure 2-7 illustrates this operation. A PIN indicates a cache hit (read from memory) and a RELOAD indicates a cache miss (read from disk).

The values in the PINS and RELOADS columns and their relationship in this dynamic performance table is a good indicator of whether the current size may be the optimal size of the library cache in the SGA. The PINS value should be as close to 0 as possible. Any ratio above 1 percent indicates that the library cache hit rate should be increased. Increasing this hit rate is accomplished by increasing the size of the shared pool. Using the information from Figure 2-7, for every 25,009,003 PINS there were 202,131 RELOADS for a ratio of about 0.8 percent. A figure this low indicates a healthy library cache in the SGA.

```
                              HP Prod
SQL> r
  1   select sum(pins) "Pins",sum(reloads) "Reloads",
  2          sum(reloads)/(sum(pins)+sum(reloads))*100
  3          "Percentage"
  4*  from v$librarycache

        Pins     Reloads Percentage
   ----------- ----------- -----------
    25009003      202131 .801752908

SQL> _
```

FIGURE 2-7. *Looking at PINS and RELOADS in v$librarycache*

The Dictionary Cache

The dictionary cache contains data dictionary information pertaining to segments in the database (e.g., indexes, sequences, and tables), file space availability (for acquisition of space by object creation and extension), and object privileges. Dictionary information is moved out of the cache when space is required for newly required information. Looking at the *hit rate* (the ratio of reads satisfied in memory compared to those going to disk) for entries in the dictionary cache gives you an idea of the efficiency of this cache. The following code reports on the dictionary cache by entry. The *miss rate* is calculated as misses divided by the sum of gets and misses and is shown as a percentage.

```
col "Percentage miss" format 990.00
col "Gets" form 999,999,990
col "Misses" form 999,999,990

select unique parameter "Cache entry",
       gets "Gets",                /*Read from memory */
       getmisses "Misses",         /*Read from disk */
       getmisses/(gets+getmisses)*100 "Percentage miss"
  from v$rowcache
 where gets+getmisses <> 0;
```

Parameter	Gets	Misses	Miss rate %
dc_columns	23,531,944	533,293	2.22
dc_constraint_defs	121	63	34.24
dc_constraint_defs	164,065	23,114	12.35
dc_constraints	1,939	792	29.00
dc_database_links	60,395	493	0.81
dc_files	29,809	22	0.07
dc_free_extents	1,640,343	82,436	4.79
dc_indexes	1,428,118	18,191	1.26
dc_object_ids	853	378	30.71
dc_objects	3,465,615	304,367	8.07
dc_rollback_segments	127,899	4	0.00
dc_segments	631,038	30,399	4.60
dc_sequence_grants	10,753	2,921	21.36
dc_sequences	283,069	763	0.27

dc_synonyms	919,519	10,257	1.10
dc_table_grants	11,196,614	421,759	3.63
dc_tables	13,037,675	24,177	0.19
dc_tablespace_quotas	2,655	45	1.67
dc_tablespaces	42,544	60	0.14
dc_tablespaces	158,151	536	0.34
dc_used_extents	84,900	42,729	33.48
dc_user_grants	870,690	8,181	0.93
dc_usernames	1,610,250	9,110	0.56
dc_users	1,703,638	9,070	0.53

A well-tuned database should report an average dictionary cache hit ratio of over 90 percent. The percentages for the entries **dc_table_grants**, **dc_user_grants**, and **dc_users**, used during almost all SQL statement processing, should be well under 5 percent each. Notice in the listing how the values for these three are 3.63 percent, 0.93 percent, and 0.53 percent, respectively. Use a query as illustrated in Figure 2-8 to get the hit ratio as a percentage.

Using version 6 of Oracle, you may remember an assortment of **dc_** initialization parameter file parameters that you adjusted to maximize the usage of slots in the dictionary cache. With Oracle7, the software takes care of that cache management, utilizing space in the shared pool and tuning the dictionary cache. What you have to do during the tuning exercise is ensure that adequate space is available in the pool. You may need to tweak the size of the shared pool for an Oracle7 fresh install to ensure there is adequate space in the shared pool to allow Oracle to fine-tune this cache. This is done by increasing the value in the SHARED_POOL_SIZE entry in the initialization parameter file. When a version 6 database is migrated to Oracle7, an already well-tuned dictionary cache should go up with the Oracle upgrade.

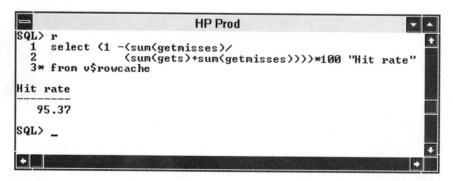

FIGURE 2-8. *Query v$rowcache for dictionary cache efficiency summary*

The Database Buffer Cache

Oracle needs to read and write data to the database buffer cache during operations. A *cache hit* means the information required is already in memory; a *cache miss* means Oracle must perform disk I/O to satisfy a request. The secret when sizing the database buffer cache is to keep the cache misses to a minimum.

The initialization parameter file entry DB_BLOCK_BUFFERS controls the size of the database block buffer cache. You can report on the likelihood of additional cache hits. Ensure the parameter DB_BLOCK_LRU_EXTENDED _STATISTICS has a nonzero value. For each integer value in that parameter, you can report on the increase in hits by adding or taking away one buffer. For example, the integer value of 1,500 means you can report on the addition or removal of up to 1,500 buffers in the database block buffer pool. The x$kcbrbh table provides information on increasing the buffer size parameter, and x$kcbcbh provides information on decreasing the parameter.

The following listing shows how to query x$kcbrbh and shows the effect of adding buffers to the database block buffer cache. The following is used, with the permission of Oracle Corporation, from the *Oracle7 Server Administrator's Guide.*

```
select 250*trunc(indx/250)+1||
       ' to '||250*(trunc(indx/250)+1) "Interval",
       sum(count) "Buffer Cache Hits"
from sys.x$kcbrbh
group by trunc(indx/250);
```

The output from running this query is as follows:

NUMBER OF BUFFERS	CHANGE IN CACHE HITS
1 to 500	1,205
501 to 1,000	1,098
1,001 to 1,500	6,790

Read the output from the top down. The additional cache hits by adding 500 to the buffer cache would be 1,205. By adding 1,000, the increase in hits is 2,303 (1,205 + 1,098). Adding 1,500 buffers, the increase could be as much as 7,093 (1,205 + 1,098 + 6,790).

NOTE
When interpreting output from this query, add the previous row's values to the one you are looking at to get that row's cumulative gained figure.

The following code shows how to look at the loss in cache hits if buffers are removed from the buffer cache. The copy below is used, with the permission of Oracle Corporation, from the *Oracle7 Server Administrator's Guide*.

```
select 25*trunc(indx/25)+1||
       ' to '||25*(trunc(indx/25)+1) "Interval",
       sum(count) "Buffer Cache Hits"
from sys.x$kcbcbh
group by trunc(indx/25);
```

The output from running this query is as follows:

NUMBER OF BUFFERS	CHANGE IN CACHE HITS
1 to 25	3203
26 to 50	56
51 to 75	17

Read the output from the bottom up. Thus, 17 cache hits would be lost if the last 25 buffers (buffers 51 to 75) were removed. By removing the last 50 buffers, 73 (17 + 56) would be lost. The first row returned indicates that the first 25 buffers are responsible for 3,276 (17 + 56 + 3203) cache hits.

After inspecting the output from the queries against x$kcbrbh and x$kcbcbh, you may decide to edit your initialization parameter file and change the value for the DB_BLOCK_BUFFERS entry. Adjustments made to this entry will take effect the next time the instance is shut down and restarted.

NOTE
After adjusting the parameter DB_BLOCK_BUFFERS in the initialization parameter file, the database must be restarted for the new value to take effect.

The Redo Log Buffer Cache

The redo log buffer cache holds information destined for the online redo logs (redo logs were defined at the start of this chapter discussing the LGWR background process). During most database operations, the LGWR background process writes efficiently so that space is always available in this cache for new redo entries. Since the redo log buffer is a segment of shared memory, Oracle manages this buffer cache using latches. Latches are to memory as locks are to data: *latches* are simple, low-level serialization mechanisms to protect shared data structures in the SGA. They are acquired for very short periods of time to work with shared structures in memory. The *redo allocation latch* manages requests for space in the redo log buffer cache. The maximum size of a redo entry that can be copied using this latch is determined by the initialization parameter file parameter LOG_SMALL_ENTRY_MAX_SIZE. On multi-CPU systems, redo entries exceeding this maximum are copied and protected during that copy by a *redo copy latch*. On single-CPU systems, all entries are copied using the redo allocation latch.

It is important to the tuning process to ensure that there are no wait conditions in the movement of information into and out of the redo log buffer cache. Wait situations are detected using the v$latch performance table owned by SYS and should be queried as illustrated in Figure 2-9.

As you see in Figure 2-9, of 3,517,878 willing-to-wait requests to copy entries into the redo log buffer, 999 were not satisfied. No immediate requests were issued during the time slice the query refers to. Oracle decides internally whether to issue a willing-to-wait or an immediate request. If the immediate_misses are more than one percent of the immediate_gets (not the case in Figure 2-9) or the misses are more than one percent of the gets (also not the case in our example), there may be contention for the redo allocation and/or the redo copy latch. The reduction and removal of this contention is part of the memory tuning process. On multiprocessor machines, the initialization parameter file entry LOG_SIMULTANEOUS_COPIES should be set to twice the number of CPUs. This will help reduce any potential contention for the redo copy latch.

```
                              HP Prod
SQL> r
  1   select name "Latch",
  2          sum(gets) "WTW Gets",
  3          sum(misses) "WTW Misses",
  4          sum(immediate_gets) "IMM Gets",
  5          sum(immediate_misses) "IMM Misses"
  6     from v$latch where name like 'redo%'
  7*  group by name

Latch                  WTW Gets WTW Misses    IMM Gets IMM Misses
---------------------- -------- ----------    -------- ----------
redo allocation         3516879        999           0          0
redo copy                     0          0           0          0
```

FIGURE 2-9.   *Inspecting redo latch gets and misses*

Multithreaded Server

In two-task environments where server work is done on behalf of the user by a dedicated process (commonly referred to as the *shadow process*), you can bring up a pool of server processes to be shared by users. This is called a *multithreaded server,* commonly referred to as mts. These shared server processes can conserve main memory. Without mts, a dedicated server process supports the user process, and it sits in limbo until user requests require server process activity. With mts, idle user processes sit alone until server activity is requested. Requests for server actions are routed to the database via a request queue. Responses from that queue are satisfied and the results are sent back to the requesting user process through a response queue. One or more dispatchers take care of the processing of server requests.

Starting MTS

Following are the steps for bringing up the processes to support the multithreaded server. Step 1 ensures an entry is made in an operating system file that lists services running on the machine. Steps 2 and 5 describe some SQL*Net version 2 issues. Steps 3 and 4 change some initialization parameter file entries, then shut down and restart the database to take advantage of these entries' new values.

1. Ensure there is an entry in **/etc/services** that refers to the listener process, protocol, and port as in listener **1521/tcp #oracle V2 listener**. The text following the # is a comment and is optional.

2. Use the configuration tool supplied by Oracle (the SQL*Net V2 Administrator's Guide documents use of this tool) to build your V2 support files listener.ora, tnsnames.ora, and sqlnet.ora. Even though these files are required for using V2 without mts, you will probably not already have these files built. Most people end up starting work with V2 in a two-task environment when first looking at mts.

3. Make necessary entries in the initialization parameter file (see the next section for details).

4. Shut down, then start up the database.

5. Start up the V2 listener using the command **lsnrctl start**.

When steps 1 through 5 are performed successfully, you will have the multithreaded server running and awaiting user connections.

PARAMETER NAME	MEANING AND VALUE(S)
mts_dispatchers	This defines the number of dispatchers to initiate as well as the protocol. The text must be enclosed in double quotes (" "). Example: mts_dispatchers = "tcp,2" mts_dispatchers = "ipc,2"
mts_max_dispatchers	The maximum number of dispatchers the database will support. Using the previous example, you code mts_max_dispatchers = 4
mts_servers	The number of shared server processes to bring up when the database is started.
mts_service	The name of the service. It is recommended that you set it to the same value as the value entered for **db_name** in the initialization parameter file
mts_max_servers	This controls the maximum number of concurrent shared server processes. Oracle spawns shared processes over and above the number in mts_servers up to the number specified here. The default for this parameter is 10.
mts_listener_address	This defines configuration information of the operating system process that awaits user connections using mts.

TABLE 2-4. *MTS Parameters in the Initialization Parameter File*

Changes to the Initialization Parameter File

The mts parameters listed in Table 2-4 need to be entered in your database startup file to bring up the multithreaded server.

When the multithreaded server is running, you should see the dispatcher processes when checking the services being performed by the SQL*Net 2 listener process with the command **lsnrctl services**. The output from this command is shown here:

```
LSNRCTL for HPUX: Version 2.0.15.0.0 - Production on 08-AUG-95 12:37:24
Copyright (c) Oracle Corporation 1993.  All rights reserved.

Connecting to (ADDRESS=(PROTOCOL=IPC)(KEY=dev))
```

```
Services Summary...
tst                     has 3 service handlers
    DEDICATED SERVER established:501 refused:0
    DISPATCHER established:0 refused:0 current:0 max:56 state:ready
      D000 (machine: devel, pid: 23141)
       (ADDRESS=(PROTOCOL=tcp)(DEV=5)(HOST=130.1.0.2)(PORT=3329))
    DISPATCHER established:0 refused:0 current:0 max:56 state:ready
      D001 (machine: devel, pid: 23142)
       (ADDRESS=(PROTOCOL=ipc)(DEV=5)(KEY=#23142.1))
rel                     has 1 service handlers
    DEDICATED SERVER established:1074 refused:0
  usr                     has 1 service handlers
    DEDICATED SERVER established:439 refused:0
  devel                   has 1 service handlers
    DEDICATED SERVER established:2552 refused:0
The command completed successfully
```

Notice the dispatcher processes named D000 and D001 are now running. After the database has been up and users have initiated connections using mts, the connect statistics that follow the dispatcher information will increase. Note as well that even though mts is available, user connections can also use a dedicated server. For a database with mts set in the initialization parameter file, the output reports on all possible methods of connecting to the database. In our example, the output reports three service handlers for the tst database: two of these three use mts, and one uses a dedicated server.

SORT_AREA_SIZE

SORT_AREA_SIZE in the initialization parameter file controls the allocation of chunks of memory for sorting activities. Sorting is explicitly requested by programs or implicitly done by Oracle. It is desirable to do as much sorting as possible in memory—memory sort work is much faster than work done on disk. Index creation and ORDER BY statements in SQL may benefit from an increased value in this parameter. Most environments use a 64K default, but this may be raised by the DBA. You can look at the sort activities of your database using the v$sysstat dynamic performance dictionary view; Figure 2-10 provides an example.

Notice that the first query in Figure 2-10 shows a little less than ten percent of the sorts (1,178 sorts out of 26,140 sorts total) required work done to disk. In the second query, well less than one percent of the sorts (nine sorts out of 24,491 total) required disk access. Your application should be running for a sufficient time (no less than two or three working days at least) to obtain representative counts for normal database activities.

```
┌─────────────────────────── Production ──────────────────────▼─▲─┐
│ SQL> r                                                          ↑│
│   1* select name,value from v$sysstat where name like '%sort%' ││
│                                                                 ││
│ NAME                                                     VALUE   │
│ ─────────────────────────────────────────────────── ─────────  │
│ sorts (memory)                                          24692   │
│ sorts (disk)                                             1178   │
│ sorts (rows)                                         25590319   │
│ SQL> conn /@aob_tcp                                             │
│ Connected.                                                      │
│ SQL> r                                                          │
│   1* select name,value from v$sysstat where name like '%sort%' │
│                                                                 │
│ NAME                                                     VALUE   │
│ ─────────────────────────────────────────────────── ─────────  │
│ sorts (memory)                                          24482   │
│ sorts (disk)                                                9   │
│ sorts (rows)                                           223538   │
│                                                                ▼│
├─┬─────────────────────────────────────────────────────────┬───┤
│◄│█                                                        │ ► │
└─┴───────────────────────────────────────────────────────┴─────┘
```

FIGURE 2-10. *Using v$sysstat to assess sort activities in memory and to disk*

Let's Tune It

Because operations in computer memory are the fastest, ensuring that they are used efficiently contributes to Oracle performance. It is your responsibility to help Oracle manage its memory resources efficiently. The following points summarize the recommendations from this chapter.

- Inspect the instance alert files regularly to be aware of any error conditions being raised by Oracle.

- Become familiar with x$kcbrbh and x$kcbcbh when considering adjusting the DB_BLOCK_BUFFER parameter in the initialization parameter file.

- If the DB_BLOCK_SIZE parameter is changed in the initialization parameter file and the database is recreated, the DB_BLOCK_BUFFER parameter will need adjusting for the database buffers to use the same amount of memory (e.g., if the block size is changed from 2,048 to 4,096, the DB_BLOCK_BUFFER parameter should be halved).

- When inspecting output from the x$kcbrbh table, weigh the additional memory requirements against the added buffer cache hits that additional buffers would create. For example, assuming a block size of 4K, if adding 2,000K of buffers (500 buffers*4K per buffer) increases the hits by 12, then the addition of 500 buffers would not be worth it.

■ When inspecting output from the x$kcbcbh table, weigh the saving in memory requirements against the reduction in buffer cache hits. For example, assuming a block size of 4K, reducing the buffer cache by 100K (25 buffers*4K per buffer) would decrease the hits by 1,200—removal of 25 buffers would be disastrous!

■ In two-task architecture environments, look at the multithreaded server (mts) to conserve memory. You may consider mts as well when users are logged into applications and initiate infrequent server requests due to long periods of terminal inactivity.

■ Monitor the hit rate in the library cache. Adjustments to the SHARED_POOL_SIZE parameter in the initialization parameter file should be considered if the hit ratio is low (less than 80 percent).

■ Monitor the hit rate in the dictionary cache. The SHARED_POOL_SIZE parameter may need adjusting if this hit rate is low (less than 80 percent).

■ Monitor the ratio of misses against gets in the redo log buffer cache by looking at the v$latch dictionary view. If the misses are more than 1 percent of the gets, the result may be contention for the redo latches (copy latch and/or allocation latch, depending on the number of CPUs on your system).

■ When changing the initialization parameter file parameter SORT_AREA_SIZE, weigh the impact of the additional memory requests that will be given for ALL instance sort requests against the reported gain of a larger work space for sorting. With a large SORT_AREA_SIZE, requests for memory work space for sort activities will request the parameter value—for example, 640K—to sort two rows that may be returned from a query.

■ If more than 25 percent of sort requests require disk space (using v$sysstat), consider increasing the initialization parameter file parameter SORT_AREA_SIZE.

■ If possible, leave your database up 24 hours a day. The library cache and dictionary cache must be filled each time the database is restarted. In the midst of filling these caches, the miss ratio will skyrocket. If your database is not up all the time, code some SQL statements to force loading of these caches after the database is brought up.

CHAPTER 3

I/O

I/O (input/output) is one of the most important aspects of a database's performance. If you think about what a database is—an organizer, receiver, and dispenser of information—then obviously the major function of a database will be reading and writing information to disk. Designing the layout and attributes of your database objects (i.e., tablespaces, tables, indexes, redo logs, temporary segments, and rollback segments) to get the fastest reading and writing of information is crucial. In addition, I/O is one of the most expensive tasks a computer can be requested to do. Even though CPUs have become a hundred times faster each year, I/O has not kept up the pace. This chapter will cover these I/O issues.

Table and Index Segments

The first objects in your database that will be discussed are the table and index segments. To start with the basics, data is stored in the database in objects called tables. A *table* can be thought of as a spreadsheet, with rows and columns of information that are called *records* and *fields* in the database. A table holds one type of information in fields that have specific formats. Whenever a request is made to the database to read or write data, a record is either read from a table or written to a table.

The other important object in the database is the index. *Indexes* are objects that contain information from selected field(s) in a table stored in sorted order, plus a pointer to where the actual record of information is stored. Indexes are used for speeding up the reading of information in the tables. Much like the index to a book, the fastest way to locate information is to scan the index and then proceed directly to that page.

It helps to conceptualize an index as a mini copy of the table. The index contains selective column values and pointers to where the data resides. Suppose a STATE table contained 50 records identified by values in the STATE_NAME column. If the STATE_NAME column is not indexed, then a full table scan of all 50 records would be required to find all occurrences of the state name requested. This would involve reading all columns for all records in the table.

If the STATE_NAME column is indexed, then a search would be performed just on the index structure, which only has the STATE_NAME column and a data pointer in it. Less data is read and the index data is sorted. Oracle is intelligent enough to know that when it passes an entry that is alphabetically after the requested name it does not have to search any further. Oracle reads data in 2 kilobyte (2K) blocks, so the number of 2K blocks that have to be read for the index is significantly less than the number of blocks that have to be read for the entire table. The amount of data read at a time (2K in the previous sentence) depends on the Oracle block size that was used when the database was created. The DB_BLOCK_SIZE entry in the initialization parameter file shows your current block size. You may see values there from 512 (one-half K) up to 16,384 (16K). The less blocks read, the faster the dataset is returned.

We will now look at the first example of the processing involved to retrieve a column value from a table using an index. This and subsequent queries refer to the PEOPLE table shown here:

SSN	VARCHAR2(11)
FNAME	VARCHAR2(30)
LNAME	VARCHAR2(30)

and the following ADDRESS sample table:

SSN	VARCHAR2(11)
ADDRESS	VARCHAR2(30)
ADDRESS_TYPE	VARCHAR2(4)

Let us examine the steps when a request is made for a person's name from a table by giving that person's Social Security Number. The Social Security Number has an index on it.

```
select fname, lname from people where ssn = '123-45-6789';
```

Once this SQL statement is issued, the following steps are taken to return the qualifying set of rows.

1. The Oracle server looks in the data dictionary tables to see that the table PEOPLE exists.

2. Data dictionary tables are examined to see if the user making the request has access to read the requested information.

3. Data dictionary tables are examined again to see if the fields FNAME, LNAME, and SSN exist in the PEOPLE table.

4. Data dictionary tables are examined for a third time to see if the field used in the WHERE clause, SSN, is indexed.

5. The index object for the SSN field in the PEOPLE table is read to find a match on the requested SSN.

6. When a match is found, the ROWID of the requested row of data is obtained.

7. The ROWID has the block, row, and file number where the data is and Oracle reads the data row.

As you can see, the process of reading one record of data from the database is decomposed into many steps, and the preceding list of steps is not even complete. Oracle brings all information that it reads into memory in order to use it. Oracle's memory management, as discussed in Chapter 2, operates on two basic principles.

The first principle is that Oracle will keep as much information in memory as there is room for. The second principle is that when Oracle runs out of room in memory and needs to add data, it flushes from its memory the items that have been there the longest without being accessed.

If the PEOPLE table is being accessed constantly and the data dictionary cache is tuned properly, then all the data dictionary reads described earlier are reads from memory and not from disk. Therefore, the only reads that are actually being done from disk in the PEOPLE table example are the index and table reads. The next two sections deal with how to tune the reads from these segments to optimize the speed of disk reads.

Table and Index Splitting

The first rule with table and index objects is to split the indexes from their tables, putting your table data on one disk and your index data on another disk. The way this is accomplished is to always create separate tablespaces for table data and index data. A *tablespace* is one or more data files grouped together to hold Oracle data. When users store data in Oracle, it is placed in a tablespace in which that user has been given the right to occupy space. The *system tablespace* is where Oracle stores all data dictionary information.

I/O RULE #1
Always create separate tablespaces for your tables and indexes and *never* put objects that are not part of the core Oracle system in the system tablespace.

The index tablespace and its corresponding data tablespace should be created on separate disks. Objects (i.e., tables and indexes) are placed in specific tablespaces in the **create** statement. The reasoning is to allow the disk head on one disk to read the index information while the disk head on the other disk reads the table data. Both reads happen faster because one disk head is on the index and the other is on the table data. If the objects were on the same disk, the disk head would need to reposition itself from the index extent to the data extent between the index read and the data read. (An *extent* is a contiguous section of disk space within a tablespace that holds only one object.) This can dramatically decrease the throughput of data in a system.

I/O RULE #2
Ensure that data tablespaces and index tablespaces reside on separate disk drives.

Along with splitting tables and their indexes on separate disks there can also be a need to avoid having different tables on the same disk. For example if two tables are to be accessed at the same time, it would improve performance to have each table on a separate disk. This also applies to indexes where, if an SQL statement would be using two indexes at the same time, it would improve performance to have each index on a separate disk.

The following listing contains three objects that will need to be read from the database. A request is made to display the name and home address of a person whose SSN is known. The name is in one table while the address is in another. The SSN column in the Person table has an index on it.

```
select fname, lname, address from person, address where ssn = '123-45-0269'
and person.ssn = address.ssn and address_type = 'home'
```

The first object is the SSN index on the PEOPLE table, the second object is the PEOPLE table, and the third object is the ADDRESS table. If possible, the three objects that need to be read for one request should be placed on three different disks. In addition, if there is a concatenated index on the SSN and ADDRESS_TYPE from the ADDRESS table, now a fourth object is being read.

Taken to its logical conclusion, you would have only one object in a tablespace and only one tablespace on a disk. Unfortunately, this is neither practical nor totally beneficial. The way the data in your database is to be used must be understood in order to form a comprehensive data placement strategy. Objects that are to be accessed in one statement very frequently should be spread out over separate tablespaces and separate disks to minimize disk contention.

I/O RULE # 3
Know how your data is to be accessed by the end users.

I/O RULE # 4
Whenever possible, place objects that are most often referenced simultaneously and frequently on separate disks.

Table and Index Disk Striping

The previous section assumed only one user accessing the data in the database. When you add to this picture multiple users accessing different data for the same objects, you start running into I/O contention caused by the number of users—not by hardware limitation. *I/O contention* happens when a resource (e.g., a disk head, a specific data block, or an I/O channel) is being used by one process and another process needs to use that resource, but must wait for the first process to finish.

If two users are accessing data from the PEOPLE table and ADDRESS table, both users' disk heads are moving around to access pieces of information. If the object is small, this is not a problem. But if the object is large, then this could increase the read time on each object. When an object in your database is large, it may be useful to place the object on multiple disks. This procedure is called *disk striping*. Disk striping is accomplished by estimating the size of the tablespace that will hold the object and dividing it evenly into multiple datafiles located on different disks. The object is then sized to the datafile size and spread over the files in multiple extents. Disk striping allows the data for one object to be spread over multiple disks, making it possible to simultaneously access different data from an object on different disks.

I/O RULE # 5
When your database contains large objects that will have users concurrently accessing different data elements, striping the object over multiple disks would be helpful.

Rollback Segments

A *rollback segment* is a database object that holds information when a user does a data manipulation action (i.e., **insert**, **update**, or **delete**), so that this action can be rolled back if needed. When an action is *rolled back,* any changes (issued by **update**, **delete**, or **insert** statements) to data are removed and the data is returned to the state it was in before the statement was issued.

If your system is a heavy online transaction system, then the rollback segments are very important. A rollback segment needs to be able to hold enough information so that users can perform the needed data manipulation actions. If your system is multiuser, it must also hold the information for all concurrent actions to avoid user actions interfering with each other.

When an action needs rollback space, it uses the next available rollback segment in your system and uses an extent in that segment. A transaction in Oracle is not allowed to span multiple rollback segments. Therefore, if the rollback segment assigned to your transaction runs out of space, Oracle will attempt to extend that rollback segment in the tablespace where it is located. Because of this, you should never use a rollback segment (besides the system rollback segment) in the system tablespace. If the rollback segment being extended is located in the system tablespace, it can cause fragmentation in that tablespace or it may fill up the system tablespace.

Fragmentation of tablespaces occurs when tables it contains extend themselves, and there are no adjacent blocks to occupy. Oracle allocates space in blocks, and adjacent chunks of blocks are referred to as *contiguous space*. If there is no contiguous space available, Oracle acquires space elsewhere in the datafile(s) associated with the tablespace. When reading data from tables that are fragmented, there can be extra overhead involved since the disk read-write head must move to another spot over the disk platter to perform the operation.

The data dictionary, which is stored in the system tablespace, is read constantly and should be as efficient as possible. When a tablespace runs out of contiguous space, it needs to be expanded (i.e., extra space added with an additional datafile) or reorganized (i.e., the data it contains is moved out, the tablespace re-created, and the data moved back in). This reorganization is not easy to do with the system tablespace. In fact, the **create database** activity followed by re-creation of the data dictionary is the only way to do this for the system tablespace. This difficulty in reorganizing the system tablespace is the biggest reason to keep only system information in the system tablespace.

Rollback tablespaces should be created to hold the rollback segments. If your system is a heavy transaction-based system, you should have at least two rollback tablespaces, and these tablespaces should be located on separate disks. To reduce contention for rollback headers, multiple rollback segments should be in each rollback tablespace. *Contention for rollback headers* occurs when transactions trigger requests for buffers for rollback segment blocks, and those buffers are still busy with previous transaction rollback information.

To control the use of the rollback segments, they must be specified in the initialization parameter file. The order that Oracle assigns rollback segments to transactions is the same as the order that they are listed in the initialization parameter file. For this reason, you should interleaf the order of the rollback segments so that the first one is in one tablespace, the next one is in the other, and so on. In this way, while one transaction is processed the next one uses a rollback segment in the other tablespace located on the other disk, thereby reducing disk head contention and distributing the I/O requests across these disks.

I/O RULE # 6
Create at least two user-defined rollback tablespaces on separate disks to hold your rollback segments.

I/O RULE # 7
Order the rollback segments in the initialization parameter file so that they toggle between multiple disks.

For example, Disk #1 contains one rollback tablespace with the following rollback segments: rbs01, rbs02, rbs03, rbs04. Disk #2 contains another rollback tablespace with the following rollback segments in it: rbs05, rbs06, rbs07, rbs08. Your initial instinct may be to order the rollback segments in the initialization parameter file as the following:

```
rollback_segments = (rbs01, rbs02, rbs03, rbs04, rbs05, rbs06, rbs07, rbs08)
```

This order would not accomplish the interleaving desired of the tablespaces. The statement in the initialization parameter file should be the following instead:

```
rollback_segments = (rbs01, rbs05, rbs02, rbs06...)
```

If you can predict that some transactions will have a large amount of rollback information, you should consider creating one rollback segment larger than all the others. Then, when this type of transaction is about to start, you can specify in the code to use the large rollback segment. This way, you can control the haphazard expansion of rollback segments that can sometimes happen. When a transaction causes arbitrary rollback segments to expand, it will fill up the tablespace that the rollback segment is on and cause the transaction to be aborted.

Temporary Segments

Temporary segments are objects in the database that are used during a transaction in order to complete the transaction. For example, if a query is issued that requires the result set to be sorted, temporary segments may be used to do the sorting. Temporary segments may be used during index creation to sort the index values.

The location of a user's newly created temporary segment is determined by the **create user** statement. In this statement, a user is assigned a tablespace that will hold his or her temporary segments. Do not leave it as the default, which is the system tablespace. You should create at least one temporary tablespace that will be used for the exclusive use of temporary segments. This tablespace should be assigned to users as their temporary tablespace. If you foresee considerable use of temporary segments by many users at the same time, then you would do better to create multiple temporary tablespaces and then distribute the assignment of users to the tablespaces evenly.

I/O RULE # 8
Create at least one tablespace whose exclusive use will be for temporary segments.

Redo Logs

Redo logs are the transaction logs that record every database manipulation action that takes place, as it takes place, indicating if it is committed or rolled back. You need to have at least two redo log groups for your system to work, because when one log group becomes full, Oracle automatically switches to the next redo log group. If the system is a heavy transaction-oriented system, the redo logs are constantly being written to. Oracle's high performance can be partly attributed to the fact that it does not write changes to the database directly to the database but to the redo logs. The information is written to the actual database files by the DBWR process when a checkpoint occurs (refer to discussion of background processes in Chapter 2). The frequency of the checkpoints is determined by the LOG_CHECKPOINT_INTERVAL parameter in the initialization parameter file.

The batch size has a direct correlation to the length of time your Oracle system takes to come up after it closes abnormally. Oracle needs to apply all changes that were committed and roll back any changes that did not get committed since the last checkpoint as a database is starting up.

Since only one redo log group is active at a time, there is not a compelling need to separate your redo log groups on different disks. The one exception is if you have your Oracle database running in ARCHIVELOG mode. What this means is that you are having Oracle make a file copy of the redo log to an archive area when the log becomes full, so that your database can be recovered from the last backup.

But because the redo logs are constantly being written to, they should be separated from your other objects and tablespaces. Therefore, if the hardware exists, your redo logs should be on a disk that contains objects that are not being read or written to often. That is, they should be on a separate disk from all database objects.

I/O RULE # 9
Put your redo logs on a disk that has a low incidence of reads and writes.

Disk Controllers

Many disk systems have *disk controllers,* which are hardware devices that control the actions of one or more disks. These controllers can also create a bottleneck in your system. You must be aware of which disks are controlled by which controllers. A controller can control the I/O of more than one disk, so, for example, requests made to two disks under one controller results in a decrease in performance, while the controller services both disk requests. In addition to putting objects on separate disks being accessed at the same time, you should also make sure that they are on disks controlled by different disk controllers.

If optimal separation for disk controllers is not possible, at least try to distribute the I/O evenly over the controllers. This helps eliminate the degradation of performance due to a heavy request load on a specific disk controller.

Hot Spots

Throughout this chapter, one point cannot be stressed enough: you should distribute your I/O as evenly as possible across as many disks as possible and as many disk controllers as possible. This is easier said than done. The first objective is to know the application(s) that will be using the data. Find out which objects are most likely to be accessed in conjunction with each other. Separate objects out into separate tablespaces from the beginning. Taking the time to separate objects properly at the beginning is easier than having to move objects around later.

Once your system is created and your users have gotten up to speed with the system, Oracle provides a number of tools to look at the I/O by objects, usually files. These tools help point out hot spots. *Hot spots* are the files within the Oracle database that are most heavily read or written to.

Within the sqldba facility is an option to look at the I/O for all selected files. Using this facility, you can observe both the cumulative and current read and write activity by file. By analyzing this information, you can pinpoint which files are used most heavily, making sure that they are on separate disks and separate disk controllers. You must *connect internal* (log on to the database as user SYS) and then issue the command **monitor fileio** to see the contents of the pool. Alternatively, once in sqldba and connected to the database, you may press the MENU key, and select Monitor and then the File I/O option. The latter access mode is shown in Figure 3-1.

Once in the monitor file I/O screen, as shown in Figures 3-2 and 3-3, the Total Blocks Read and Total Blocks Written should assist you in finding your I/O hot spots and ensuring that those files are distirbuted across your disks. Unfortunately, the display is wider than 80 columns. You scroll sideways by placing the cursor in the filename area on the screen and pressing the RIGHT ARROW key. The desired cumulative read and write columns will scroll into view.

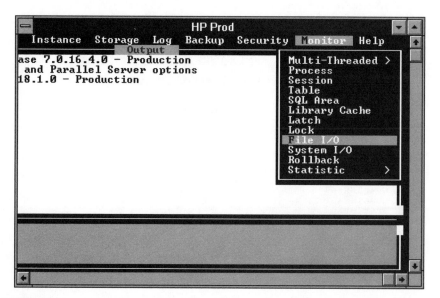

FIGURE 3-1. *Accessing monitor file I/O using the sqldba menu system*

Based on the statistics in Figure 3-3 for the four datafiles with the OracleRaw names, we notice the following:

- The four datafiles are involved in almost ten times more block read than block write activities—there were 17,555 blocks read and only 1,184 blocks written.

- Raw10 and Raw9 have the highest rate of blocks read. Of the 17,555 blocks read, Raw10 had 50.49 percent of all reads and Raw9 had 31.73 percent of all reads.

- Raw1-1 had the highest block write rate as well as the lowest block read rate, with 74.59 percent of the total blocks written and well under 1 percent of all the block read activity.

We can then make the following recommendations and draw the following conclusions about the database we are monitoring in this example.

1. Our applications are heavier on reporting and querying than data entry and transaction processing.

2. Datafiles Raw10 and Raw9 should be placed on different disks.

```
┌─────────────────────────── HP Prod ───────────────── ▼ ▲ ┐
│ File   Edit   Session   Instance   Storage   Log   Backup   Securit │
│ ┌──────────────────────────── Output ────────────────────────────┐ │
│ │                    ORACLE File I/O Monitor                      │ │
│ │ Data File Filter: %%                                           │ │
│ │                                                               R │ │
│ │                      Request Rate       Batch Size             │ │
│ │ ile               Reads/s Writes/s   blks/rd  blks/wt       m │ │
│ │                                                                 │ │
│ │ /dbs/person_pnv.dbf      0       0        0        0            │ │
│ │ rams_production.dbf      0       0        0        0            │ │
│ │ dsk/OracleRaw1-0         0       0        0        0            │ │
│ │ le_prd/sqlopprd.dbf      0       0        0        0            │ │
│ │ e_prd/temp_prd1.dbf      0       0        0        0            │ │
│ │ dsk/OracleRaw10          0       0        0        0            │ │
│ │ dsk/OracleRaw9           0       0        0        0            │ │
│ │ dsk/OracleRaw1-1         0       0        0        0            │ │
│ │ dsk/OracleRaw3           0       0        0        0            │ │
│ │ racle_prd/pdmis.dbf      0       0        0        0            │ │
│ │                                                      ⟨Restart  │ │
│ └─────────────────────────────────────────────────────────────────┘ │
└─────────────────────────────────────────────────────────────────────┘
```

FIGURE 3-2. *Monitor file I/O display part 1*

```
┌─────────────────────────── HP Prod ───────────────── ▼ ▲ ┐
│   Instance   Storage   Log   Backup   Security   Monitor   Help │
│ ┌──────────── Output ────────────────────────────┐             │
│ │           ORACLE File I/O Monitor               │             │
│ │ %%                                             │             │
│ │ te   Batch Size        Response Time    Total Blocks          │
│ │ es/s  blks/rd  blks/wt  ms/rd  ms/wt    Read   Written        │
│ │                                                               │
│ │   0      0        0       0       0      955        0         │
│ │   0      0        0       0       0     1447        2         │
│ │   0      0        0       0       0       11     1059         │
│ │   0      0        0       0       0      890      884         │
│ │   0      0        0       0       0        0     1179         │
│ │   0      0        0       0       0     5570      234         │
│ │   0      0        0       0       0     8863      128         │
│ │   0      0        0       0       0        3     1353         │
│ │   0      0        0       0       0     3119       99         │
│ │   0      0        0       0       0     1498        4         │
│ │                                                               │
│ │                          ⟨Restart⟩   ⟨Hide⟩   ⟨Quit⟩         │
│ └───────────────────────────────────────────────────────────────┘
└─────────────────────────────────────────────────────────────────────┘
```

FIGURE 3-3. *Monitor file I/O display part 2*

3. Raw1-1 preferrably should be placed on its own disk.

4. If we have a pool of disks that are a mixture of speeds, Raw10 and Raw1-1 are the prime candidates for placement on faster disks.

If just one or a few files seem to be seeing a majority of I/O activity, the objects in these files should be looked at closely. If the files contain multiple objects, you should try to separate out these objects either into new files or in existing files that have very low I/O activity on them. If the file contains only one object, then you should consider striping that object. As discussed earlier in this chapter, striping is the process of using multiple files to store an object, in the hope that the I/O can then be distributed among the striped files located on separate disks.

Oracle provides another tool that is of great assistance in determining I/O by file: the UTLBstat/UTLEstat facility (which will be explained in greater detail in Chapter 5). It is mentioned here because of its relevance to I/O. The UTLBstat/UTLEstat facility is actually two scripts that collect database information at different times and compare the two sets of information in a report. Part of this facility is a read/write report by both datafile and tablespace. This report points out hot spots for both reads and writes within your system. Figure 3-4 gives an example of the output from UTLBstat/UTLEstat.

Reading the output from UTLBstat/UTLEstat is similar to the way the output from sqldba monitor file I/O is interpreted. From examining the statistics in the

TABLE_SPACE	FILE_NAME	PHYS READS	PHYS BLKS READS	PHYS READ TIME	PHYS WRTES	PHYS BLKS WRTES	PHYS WRT TIME
SYSTEM	ORA_SYSTEM.DBS	38803	75587	0	1717	1717	0
TBSP_INDEX001	INDEX001.DBS	5309	5309	0	706	706	0
TBSP_DATA001	DATA001.DBS	33723	369685	0	619	619	0
TBSP_INDEX001	INDEX002.DBS	4691	4691	0	2383	2383	0
TBSP_DATA002	DATA002.DBS	68280	792468	0	17387	17387	0
TBSP_DATA003	DATA003.DBS	28	378	0	0	0	0
TBSP_INDEX002	INDEX002.DBS	8748	8748	0	1065	1065	0
TBSP_DATA004	DATA004.DBS	38293	115700	0	1522	1522	0
TBSP_ROLLBACKPROD	ROLLBACK.DBS	81	81	0	20227	20227	0
TBSP_TEMPORARY_PROD	TEMPORARY.DB	0	0	0	3131	3131	0
TBSP_WORKPROD	WORKPROD.DBS	136	2006	0	0	0	0

FIGURE 3-4.   *UTLBstat/UTLEstat file I/O*

PHYS READS (data read from the database files) and PHYS WRITES columns (data written to the database files), we notice the following:

- The four datafiles are involved in nearly four times more read than write activities—there were 198,092 physical reads and only 48,757 physical writes.

- The four datafiles ORA_SYSTEM, DATA001, DATA002, and DATA004 have the highest physical read counts. ORA_SYSTEM shows 19.59 percent of all reads, DATA001 shows 17.02 percent of all reads, DATA002 shows 34.47 percent of all reads, and DATA004 shows 19.33 percent of all reads.

- DATA002 had the highest physical read amount and the second highest physical write amount, with 34.47 percent of all read activity and 35.66 percent of all write activity.

- DATA003 and WORKPROD had no write activity and proportionally little read activity—less than one percent of read activity was against DATA003 and WORKPROD

We can then make the following recommendations and draw the following conclusions about the database we are monitoring in this example. Notice how tablespace TBSP_INDEX001 is made up of the files INDEX001.DBS and INDEX002.DBS and tablespace TBSP_INDEX002 is made up of the file INDEX002.DBS. In point 5, we refer to the three index datafiles as TS1_INDEX001, TS1_INDEX002, and TS2_INDEX002.

1. Our applications are heavier on reporting and querying than data entry and transaction processing.

2. With at least four disks at our disposal, ORA_SYSTEM, DATA001, DATA002, and DATA004 should all be placed on different drives.

3. With only three disks at our disposal, ORA_SYSTEM and DATA002 should be on their own drives, and DATA001 and DATA 004 should be on the same drive.

4. With only two disks at our disposal, ORA_SYSTEM and DATA004 should be placed on the same disk, and DATA001 and DATA002 should be placed on the same disk.

5. If the datafiles TS1_INDEX001, TS1_INDEX002, and TS2_ INDEX002 need to be placed on two drives, it would be best to put TS1_INDEX001 and TS1_INDEX002 together and TS2_INDEX002 by itself. TS1_INDEX001 gets 2.68 percent of read activity and the previous TS1_INDEX002 gets 2.37 percent of read activity, whereas TS2_INDEX002 gets 4.42 percent of read activity.

6. The placement of DATA003 and WORKPROD will have little or no impact on I/O tuning.

Proper Table and Index Sizing

The discussion so far has focused on where to put your database objects, which is very important. But equally important is in what size these table and index objects are created. The size of the tables and indexes determine the needed size of the tablespaces to hold them, which, in turn, determine which tablespaces can physically fit on how many disks and in which combination.

Letting Oracle use its default sizing for your objects is not the way you should determine object sizing for a system of any importance. A proven analytical method is necessary to size your objects properly.

I/O RULE # 10
Use a proven analytical method to size your tables and indexes.

We have used the following formulas over the years, and they have proven to be quite reliable. The following examples assume a 2K (2,048 byte) block size. The first formula estimates the size required to hold a table.

```
greatest(4, ceil(ROW_COUNT /
 ((round(((1958 - (initrans * 23)) *
 ((100-PCT_FREE)/100)) / ADJ_ROW_SIZE)))) * 2)
```

This formula takes into account and uses the following as variables or constants:

- Actual number of bytes available in a block (1958)

- Number of bytes used by each initrans value (23)

- Percent free specified for the table (PCT_FREE)

- Estimated adjusted row size of each row in the table (ADJ_ROW_SIZE)

- Estimated number of rows for the table (ROW_COUNT)

The following formula estimates the size required to hold indexes.

```
greatest(4, ( 1.01 ) * ((ROW_COUNT /
(( floor(((2048 - 113 - (initrans * 23)) * (1-(percent_free/100.))) /
((10+uniqueness)+number_col_index+(total_col_length))))))*2))
```

This formula takes into account and uses the following as variables or constants:

- Estimated number of rows in the table (ROW_COUNT)

- Actual number of bytes available in the block (1935 or 2048–113)

- Bytes used for each initrans (23)

- Percent free specified for the index (percent_free)

- If the index is unique or not, and its effect in bytes (the variable uniqueness is 1 if the index is unique or 0 if it is not)

- Number of columns in the index (number_col_index)

- Estimated length of the index (total_col_length)

We have designed and used for quite some time an index and table sizing SQL*Forms 3.0 form that lets you put in the information requested. A portion of the processing in the index and table sizing form is presented and discussed later in Chapter 9. The form calculates the sizing of the table and indexes within the form. It also allows you to specify the percent of total load of the table that you would like to size, in case you wish to do an incremental sizing of the database, increasing the allocated storage space over time as the objects grow. Because the information is stored in an Oracle database, reports are designed to run off the information, and use the preceding formulas to calculate the table and index sizing for the objects stored in the database.

Another point that should be kept in mind when sizing tables and indexes is the **pctfree** factor, which sets aside a certain percentage of the data block for future use. If the record is to be updated in such a way that NULL fields will be populated or VARCHAR2 fields will have their values updated to a longer value, then a higher **pctfree** factor should be used. But the use of a high **pctfree** factor should be used with caution. The higher the **pctfree**, the fewer data rows that can fit into a block. Because Oracle always reads in block increments, the more data per block, the more data is read in one read. Therefore an accurate determination of the **pctfree** factor of each table and index is important.

Tablespace Sizing Example

If a table has an initial extent of 16K, a next extent of 4K, and a percent increase of 0, the tablespace should be sized at $(16 + 4 * (N – 1)) + 1(K)$, where N is the number of extents of the object the user wants in the tablespace plus 1K as an overhead.

Consistent Tablespace Sizing Example

Tablespace files should be sized as a multiple of a predetermined base size, which will make it easier to move files from one disk to another to distribute the I/O. This base size should also allow for the maximum utilization of disk space.

If the base size is 100K for the tablespaces, then all files should be multiples of 100K. This would make it possible to move a 200K file on a disk and move off two 100K files. The datafiles should be multiples of extent size so that extents will not span datafiles.

Along with the **pctfree** factor, there is a **pctused** factor. This factor determines when a data block that has reached its **pctfree** threshold will become available to store more data. For example, if a table has a **pctfree** set at 15 percent and a **pctused** set at 80 percent, Oracle will stop storing data in a block belonging to this table when it has 15 percent of its space free, but if data is deleted so that 80 percent or less space is used, Oracle will store additional rows in that block.

The sum of the **pctfree** and the **pctused** must always be less than or equal to 100, and must be chosen so that a block does not keep getting switched from available to not available to store data (i.e., on the free block list). This will reduce the performance overhead of moving a block on and off the free block list (see Chapter 6 for more on the free block list).

Along with the proper sizing of your database objects (i.e., tables, indexes, and tablespaces) you should also make an effort to standardize this sizing as best as possible. If a tablespace has only one object in it, the database files in the tablespace should be sized as an even increment of the next extent plus the initial extent and an overhead amount (assuming a percent increase of 0). This way, unusable space won't be left in the tablespace.

Space–What Is Really Being Used?

Not only must database objects be properly sized, but these objects and the space that they are using must be continually monitored. Once an extent in a tablespace is assigned to a table, it would be desirable to know how much of that extent is actually being used by data and how many blocks are empty.

Following are two scripts used to gather statistics about tables and reports on the number of empty blocks. The first SQL statement uses the **analyze table** command with the **compute statistics** qualifier to populate the statistical columns in the dba_tables system table. It takes as a parameter the table name in the form of OWNER.TABLE_NAME:

```
analyze table (owner.table_name) compute statistics;
Select empty_blocks
from sys.dba_tables
where owner||'.'||table_name = (owner.table_name);
```

The second SQL statement selects from the empty_blocks column of the DBA_TABLES system table. It presents the total blocks, percent used, and percent empty for the table identified by the OWNER.TABLE_NAME parameter:

```
select a.blocks "Total Blocks Allocated",
       ((a.blocks - b.empty_blocks)/a.blocks)*100. "%Blocks Used",
       (b.empty_blocks/a.blocks)*100. "%Blocks Empty"
from sys.dba_segments a, sys.dba_tables b
where a.owner||'.'||a.segment_name = b.owner||'.'||b.table_name and
      b.owner||'.'||b.table_name = (owner.table_name)
```

A script can be written that stores this information in Oracle tables along with the date when the data was collected. This would give information that can be used for trend analysis about the growth of the table over time. It also gives useful information relating to proper sizing of tables.

For indexes, Oracle provides the same utility, **analyze**, to see how much space is actually being used. The **analyze index** statement with the **validate structure** qualifier is used to check a particular index for consistency. (Note: This statement is similar to the Version 6 **validate index** statement.) This statement uses the index as its source and can detect the following:

- Invalid index formats or bad index structure

- Index entries that do not match row data, or a bad index (as when an index entry has no matching row)

During this validation process, two tables are populated that hold information about the index. These tables can be queried and statistical information about the index can be reported.

The tables are INDEX_STATS and INDEX_HISTOGRAM. Tables 3-1 and 3-2 list the columns that are in each of these tables and what information is contained in each column.

By querying the two tables, you can determine statistical information about the index. This includes the distribution of the index values and the amount of space that is allocated to the index, how much space is being used by the index, and, most important for tuning purposes, the amount of deleted space in the index. If a large amount of space exists in the index because of deleted values or the **pctused** value for the index is low, then the index needs to be either dropped and recreated to release unusable space or dropped, resized, and recreated.

COLUMN NAME	CONTENTS
NAME	Name of the index
LF_ROWS	Number of leaf rows
LF_BLKS	Number of leaf blocks in BTree
LF_ROW_LEN	Size of all leaf blocks in BTree
LF_BLK_LEN	Usable space in leaf rows
BR_ROWS	Number of branch rows
BR_BLKS	Number of branch blocks in BTree
BR_ROWS_LEN	Size of all branch blocks in BTree
BR_BLK_LEN	Usable space in branch block
DISTINCT_KEYS	Number of distinct keys in index
MOST_REPEATED_KEY	Times most repeated key is repeated
ROWS_PER_KEY	Average number of rows per distinct key
DEL_LF_ROWS	Total length of all deleted rows
DEL_LF_ROWS_LEN	Number of deleted leaf rows in index
BLOCKS	Number of blocks allocated for the index
BTREE_SPACE	Total space that is currently allocated
USED_SPACE	Total space that is currently used
PCT_USED	Percentage of space allocated that is used
HEIGHT	Height of the BTree
BLKS_GETS_PER_ACCESS	Blocks to be read for a random read

TABLE 3-1. *Columns for INDEX_STATS Table*

COLUMN NAME	CONTENTS
REPEAT COUNT	Number of duplicates in the index
KEYS_WITH_REPEAT_COUNT	Number of occurrences for REPEAT COUNT indexes

TABLE 3-2. *Columns for INDEX_HISTOGRAM Table*

Let's Tune It

This chapter dealt with a number of issues relating to I/O for tuning an Oracle database. To summarize, here are the highlights or main points of this chapter.

- Create separate tablespaces for heavily accessed tables and their indexes and put them on separate disks.

- Never put application or user objects in the system tablespace.

- By knowing how your users will be accessing the data, you can plan your data distribution better.

- Place objects that are most often referenced simultaneously and frequently on separate disks.

- Stripe large objects over multiple disks.

- Create user-defined rollback tablespaces to hold rollback segments.

- Put rollback segments in at least two tablespaces and interleaf their order in the initialization parameter file.

- Create at least one tablespace for the exclusive use of temporary segments and assign users this tablespace as their temporary tablespace.

- Put your redo logs on a disk that has a low incidence of reads and writes.

- Distribute your I/O evenly over disk controllers.

- Identify and reduce disk hot spots.

- Properly size your tables, indexes, and tablespaces.

- Monitor the space allocated and used by your tables and indexes and make adjustments when necessary.

CHAPTER 4

CPU

The processing power of your database is strongly influenced by the computer's CPU. In fact, most operations performed by the software running on your machine require work to be done by the CPU. In terms of tuning the Oracle database, the size and processing power of the CPU will affect the job of tending to online systems throughput. In this chapter, we will discuss managing your current CPU, assessing the load on your CPU, and ways to maximize your CPU using some of the new Oracle7 features.

Favoring CPU

The past few years have seen major advances in CPU power. Vendors continue to produce machines with stronger and stronger CPUs; some machines have multiple CPUs working in parallel and sharing the processing. (This should not be confused with the Oracle7 parallel server option, in which loosely coupled computers, such as the DEC VAX cluster, share a disk but have their own memory.) Oracle, along with the other vendors, has realized that the CPU has grown exponentially while some of the other computer components have not. The smart software manufacturers favor CPU, the smart network administrators favor CPU, and therefore smart DBAs favor CPU to ensure that their applications run faster and sooner.

In addition, with products such as the Oracle7 parallel query option with release 7.1, Oracle can partition the processing of a query over a specified number of query processes. The direction of the industry is clear. Why is the bulk of the IBM mainframe environment downsizing today? One reason: economics. Reengineering your applications, buying new hardware, and porting your applications to that new environment is getting cheaper; cost benefits will be realized in two years. This is why the classic legacy systems are disappearing. As system professionals, you strive to get the most out of your applications (at the least cost). The best bang for the buck is by capitalizing on new technology—in the CPU arena for the quickest gain.

CPU technology has produced more and more powerful machines in relatively short time periods. Applications that ran on 386 processors can run twice as fast on the 486—simply by upgrading the CPU. CPU is cheap and getting cheaper. With emerging CPU technology, bigger and better CPUs can get the work done in a fraction of the time. Oracle technology is moving in a direction that takes advantage of parallel processing. Queries run in a fraction of the time using multiple CPUs. A 16-minute query running in under 30 seconds, on a massively parallel processor with a bank of 20 to 30 CPUs, is not unheard of. In light of this, when we speak of CPU in this chapter, the same discussion points apply to computers with more than one CPU.

Computer manufacturers are building the new-generation computers with multiple processors. Manufacturers have two basic ways to build a machine with more than one processor: shared-memory symmetrical multiprocessors and massively parallel processors.

SMP

The *symmetrical multiprocessor* (SMP) architecture involves more than one CPU utilizing common memory and I/O. The operating system runs concurrently as one system image across multiple CPUs. The operating system provides scheduling so that tasks execute on all CPUs in a symmetrical fashion. There is no single control processor. Each processor executes tasks off a common execution queue. State-of-the-art SMP systems have up to 64 processors (e.g., Cray CS6400); the average SMP has 8 to 32 CPUs.

MPP

The *massively parallel processor* (MPP) is somewhat different than the SMP. MPPs are composed of nodes that are connected via a high-speed interconnect mechanism. An MPP node consists of a processor, local memory, and sometimes local I/O. The interprocessor communications and transfers to nonlocally attached I/O is much faster than with SMP machines. Unlike SMP machines, there is no single copy of the operating system controlling work flow or scheduling across nodes. The operating system as such appears to be running independent operating systems on each node. Typically, there is no scheduling provided by the operating system. Task scheduling across nodes is provided by applications or other software that do not exist in the SMP environment. The state-of-the-art MPP can have 4,096 or more processors. Machines with 32 to 512 nodes are commonplace.

The advantage of MPP over SMP is quite simple. Every computer has a piece of hardware called the *system bus,* where interprocess communication takes place. The two-way transfer of information from disk to memory and memory to disk is done on this bus. When you put more than about 32 processors on a common system bus, the bus itself becomes a bottleneck. This means that most SMPs won't be able to take advantage of all of the I/O or CPUs, as they will spend most of their time fighting for the bus. MPPs do not have this problem, because they have local memory as well as global or local high-speed I/O.

Most MPPs also have the characteristic of *scalability,* which means that as you add nodes, each additional node comes with additional memory, additional I/O bandwidth, as well as additional computer horsepower. The machine actually gets faster as you add nodes, with no shared items to become bottlenecks. The same principle applies when operations can be broken down into a set of smaller tasks that can be run independently.

The Parallel Query Option

Oracle's commitment to multiprocessor machines is obvious, based on the new option with release 7.1—the parallel query option. With the parallel query option and multi-CPU machines, you can take advantage of the ability to process queries using many query server processes running against multiple CPUs. Clearly, Oracle, like the other vendors, favors CPU for the reasons described in the previous section. The end result of using the parallel query option with more than one CPU is faster processing. The processing of queries in parallel is referred to as *query parallelization.* We will discuss some of the terminology and theory on this option. For more technical details and the syntax to word queries, refer to Chapter 6 of the *Oracle7 Server Documentation Addendum, Release 7.1*.

Prior to release 7.1 with the parallel query option, a SQL statement was processed by a single server process. SQL statement processing with the parallel query option is handled the following way. (The first step is the same, with or without the parallel query option.)

1. SQL statements are parsed and, if no matching statement is already in the shared pool, an execution plan is determined (for a discussion of SQL statement processing and using the shared pool, refer to Chapter 7).

2. Oracle determines that the statement is a candidate for parallel processing, as long as both of the following conditions are met:

   - The statement must contain a simple **select**, or contain an **update**, **delete**, **insert**, or **create** table using a subquery.

   - One or more full-table scans must be in the execution plan determined for the statement.

3. Once it is determined that the statement can be processed in parallel, a query coordinator server process is invoked to manage the parallel processing.

4. The query coordinator dispatches a number of query servers to handle the processing, the number of query processes being determined by a combination of the following:

   - Hints embedded in the SQL statement (if present)

   - Data dictionary information on the table(s) involved in the parallel process (parallel processing-associated keywords can be used when tables are created or modified)

   - A number of initialization parameter file entries that determine a default degree of parallelism behavior (the number of query server processes used to perform a single operation is referred to as the *degree of parallelism*)

5. The processing to satisfy the parallel query is partitioned among the query server processes, i.e., the workload is shared.

6. The results from the query server processes are merged and returned to the user process in the form of query results.

When parallel query processing is done on multi-CPU machines, the benefits become obvious. The throughput of online queries can increase many times over. Allowing simultaneous processing of portions of a query can dramatically reduce a query's time to completion. Oracle believes the parallel query option will result in the biggest benefits on the following systems (used with permission of Oracle Corporation, from the *Oracle7 Server Documentation Addendum,* Chapter 6):

■ Symmetrical multiprocessor (SMP) or massively parallel processor (MPP) systems

■ Systems with high I/O bandwidth (that is, many datafiles on many different disk drives)

■ Systems with underutilized or intermittently used CPUs (for example, systems where CPU usage is typically less than 30 percent)

■ Systems with sufficient memory to devote to sort space for queries

How Busy Is Your CPU?

One of the goals of this chapter is to show you how to maximize existing CPU and plan for the turnkey gains that will occur with each new generation of CPU. The examples and some of the operating system utilities referred to in this chapter are based on an HP-UX Series 800 model 897S running HP-UX version 9.0 and the korn shell. The sample environment is made up of SQL*Forms–based systems.

A starting point is to assess the load on the machine at various times during the day (or predefined times over a series of days). When you have a handle on who is doing what on your machine and when, you can then proceed to ensure your CPU is doing the most efficient job given its processing power. The ability of your CPU to provide acceptable performance for your systems is fundamental to the tuning process. Your operating environment (the mixture of online and background processing) may require some adjustment to maximize the processing power of your CPU. Some suggestions will follow to get you started on a regimen to use your CPU effectively.

Assessing CPU Busy

First, you need the information to decide if your CPU is large enough to support your configuration. At that point, you can prepare a report card on your CPU and use its recommendations to influence your plans for future upgrades (if and when required). Five components need to be assessed to help you get an idea of how much work your CPU has to do:

1. CPU requirements and utilization during busy time periods

2. CPU requirements and utilization during quiet periods

3. User session idle time

4. CPU requirements to support Oracle

5. The balance between the CPU of the portions dedicated to user and system support services

The following series of exercises you will go through to assess CPU utilization is hardware-independent.

You might think the CPU is not powerful enough to handle the Oracle systems. As we will discuss in Chapter 7, efficient SQL statements run faster than statements that have not been optimized. The results of the following exercise may uncover the need for application tuning. Follow the recommendations in Chapter 7 and follow the steps outlined here to assess CPU performance.

Sample Assessment of CPU Busy

You will now begin to assemble information about your operating environment. One of the steps in the tuning process is finding out how much work your CPU is being asked to do. Application and database tuning are directly linked, because a poorly tuned set of applications will use more CPU and consume more resources. Finding what your CPU has to contend with can be accomplished by gathering statistics on the five components that were introduced in the previous section.

COMPONENT RULE #1
Assess the demands placed on the CPU by the users during busy time periods.

Select a series of times during the day or over a period of a few days. Collect statistics on the number of users on the machine. For our example, Figure 4-1 shows the activity on the machine at the start of the exercise at 11:27 A.M. Late morning is a good time, because the users in both the eastern and western regions have been up for a number of hours. Figure 4-2 shows the activity at 12:27 P.M. The installation used in this sample is a government department with an average of 15 to 20 concurrent users. They will be designated as *usera, userb,* up to *userr.* Interval

```
 ─                          HP Prod                      ▼  ▲
  Who      logged  on          CPU    Doing  what          ▲
 ────────────────────────────────────────────────────────
  usera 11:23:08 ?            0:00 oracleprd P:4096,8,11
  userb 11:07:39 ?            0:02 oracleprd P:4096,8,11
  userc 10:56:32 ?            2:19 oracleprd P:4096,8,11
  userd 10:49:14 ?            1:39 oracleprd P:4096,8,11
  usere 11:22:46 ?            0:00 oracleprd P:4096,8,11
  userf 11:20:03 ?            0:01 oracleprd P:4096,8,11
  userg 11:13:11 ?            0:01 oracleprd P:4096,8,11
  userh 10:30:28 ?            0:03 oracleprd P:4096,8,11
  useri 10:49:01 ?            0:05 oracleprd P:4096,8,11
  userj 11:07:12 ?            0:00 oracleprd P:4096,8,11
  userk 11:22:45 ?            0:00 oracleprd P:4096,8,11
  userl 11:23:22 ?            0:05 oracleprd P:4096,8,11
  userm 11:20:35 ?            0:00 oracleprd P:4096,8,11

  August 11, 1995 @11:27 AM                               ▼
 ◄   █                                                  ►
```

FIGURE 4-1.   *User activity at the start of the exercise*

```
 ─                          HP Prod                      ▼  ▲
                                                          ▲
  Who      logged  on          CPU    Doing  what
 ────────────────────────────────────────────────────────
  usera 11:23:08 ?            0:00 oracleprd P:4096,8,11
  userc 10:56:32 ?           19:28 oracleprd P:4096,8,11
  userd 10:49:14 ?            8:45 oracleprd P:4096,8,11
  userg 11:13:11 ?            0:44 oracleprd P:4096,8,11
  userh 10:30:28 ?            3:23 oracleprd P:4096,8,11
  userj 11:07:12 ?            4:48 oracleprd P:4096,8,11
  userk 11:22:45 ?            0:00 oracleprd P:4096,8,11
  userl 11:23:22 ?            3:25 oracleprd P:4096,8,11
  userm 11:20:35 ?            0:00 oracleprd P:4096,8,11
  userp 12:10:35 ?            4:01 oracleprd P:4096,8,11
  userr 12:00:35 ?            2:14 oracleprd P:4096,8,11

  August 11, 1995 @12:27 PM                               ▼
 ◄   █                                                  ►
```

FIGURE 4-2.   *User activity at the end of interval #1*

#1 is the time period up to 11:27 A.M. Interval #2 is the time period between 11:28 A.M and 12:27 P.M. These screens were collected using the command

```
ps -ef ¦ grep oracleprd ¦ cut -c1-70.
```

From examining the output, we can begin to assess how busy the users are and the amount of resources they are consuming for their server processes. The following assumptions are made for the purpose of this exercise based on the statistics from the listing of Oracle server processes:

- The listing shows Oracle server processes, identified by "oracleprd P:4096,8,11".

- Concurrent user count means persons logged on at the end of the interval.

- Persons not connected at the end of interval #2 are deemed to have disconnected right at the end of the interval #1.

Table 4-1 shows the CPU utilization of the users logged in during the two intervals. Userb, usere, userf, and useri logged off the machine sometime during interval #2. From looking at Figure 4-2, you can see that userp and userr connected during interval #2. The login time is shown beside the single-character user identifier (a, b, c, and so on). For each interval, the time logged on during that interval and the CPU time used in minutes and seconds is shown. The "% CPU" column indicates the relationship between connect time and CPU utilization, expressed as a percentage.

For the 13 concurrent users logged on throughout interval #1, the average CPU busy time to support their server processes was 1.38 percent (the sum of each user's % CPU value from the table, divided by the number 13). For the 11 concurrent users logged on throughout interval #2, the average CPU busy time to support their server processes was 8.51 percent (the sum of each user's % CPU value from the table, divided by the number 11). Keeping in mind the nature of the other activities on your machine, this seems like an insignificant amount, but it can be misleading if you do not look at all other consumers of CPU time. Using your operating system utilities, at predefined periods during the business day, track the output of CPU monitoring.

Findings (Based on This Example)
The user processes use varying amounts of CPU time during peak periods. The consumption is heavily dependent on what the user processes are doing. Given the time slice that concurrent user processes get of CPU time, user connect time far exceeds CPU utilization during busy time periods.

Login		mm:ss	INTERVAL #1 CPU mm:ss	% CPU	mm:ss	INTERVAL #2 CPU mm:ss	% CPU
a	11:23:08	3:52	0:00	0	60:00	0:00	0
b	11:07:39	19:21	0:02	0	***	***	***
c	10:56:32	30:28	2:19	7.60	60:00	17:09	28.58
d	10:49:14	17:46	1:39	9.28	60:00	7:06	11.83
e	11:22:46	4:14	0:00	0	***	***	***
f	11:20:03	6:57	0:01	.24	***	***	***
g	11:13:11	13:49	0:01	.12	60:00	0:43	1.19
h	10:38:28	48:32	0:03	.10	60:00	3:20	5.56
i	10:49:01	27:59	0:05	.30	***	***	***
j	11:07:12	19:48	0:00	0	60:00	4:48	8.00
k	11:22:45	4:15	0:00	0	60:00	0:00	0
l	11:23:22	3:38	0:05	.30	60:00	3:20	5.56
m	11:20:35	6:25	0:00	0	60:00	0:00	0
p	12:10:35	***	***	***	16:25	4:01	24.47
r	12:00:35	***	***	***	26:25	2:14	8.45

TABLE 4-1. *Summary Statistics from Intervals #1 and #2*

COMPONENT RULE #2
Assess the demands placed on the CPU by the users during
not-so-busy time periods (evenings and weekends).

The output in Figures 4-3 and 4-4 was generated at 10:35 P.M. on a quiet
machine. No other users were on the machine, so the whole CPU was at the disposal
of whatever Oracle processes required. Notice how Oracle contributed to the use
of between 29 percent and 100 percent of the available CPU processing power in
Figure 4-3. Oracle contributed to the use of between 29 percent and 67 percent
CPU utilization in Figure 4-4. Not surprisingly, the CPU required to process the query
against the larger table is higher. Bear in mind that these are single table queries.
With the joining of multiple tables, it is realistic to assume that the CPU requirements
for a join between large objects will be higher than between small ones.

Using the command at the top of Figure 4-3 and Figure 4-4, the last three
columns of the output show the CPU consumption by users (the value under *us*),

```
── HP Prod ▼ ▲
vmstat 2 5!cut −c70−200                        ↑
                 faults          cpu
   sr      in      sy      cs    us sy id
    0     113     560      85    21  8 71
    0     247    3257     419    85 16 −1
    0     235    2795     340    89 12 −1
    0     235    3247     412    77 20  2
    0     302    3428     487    76 20  4
  $
  $ _                                          ▼
◄ █                                          ►
```

FIGURE 4-3. *vmstat output while running query #1*

the system (the value under *sy*), and the idle time (the value under *id*). The first command was issued while running a query against a single-indexed column that returned 500,000 rows. The second was issued while running a query against a single-indexed column returning 2,100 rows.

The difference between the outputs from Figure 4-5 and Figure 4-6 is interesting, but expected, as well. The indexed column query contributed to the usage of an average of 72.2 percent of CPU utilization. The unindexed column query contributed to the usage of an average of 86.4 percent of CPU utilization.

The CPU utilization figures were derived by summing the values in the us, sy, and id columns and dividing by the number of rows in the time-slice of the

```
── HP Prod ▼ ▲
$ vmstat 2 5 ¦ cut −c70−200                     ↑

                 faults          cpu
   sr      in      sy      cs    us sy id
    0     113     560      85    21  8 71
    0     183     639     137    59  8 33
    0     204     695     150    45  2 53
    0     219     843     155    54  3 43
    0     218    1059     175    61  6 34
◄ █                                          ►
```

FIGURE 4-4. *vmstat output while running query #2*

```
┌─────────────────────────────────────────────────────────────┐
│ ═                        HP Prod                      ▼ │ ▲ │
├─────────────────────────────────────────────────────────┤───┤
│                 faults           cpu                    │ ▲ │
│   sr      in      sy      cs    us  sy  id               │   │
│    0     113     560      85    21   8  71               │   │
│    0     484    6563     701    41  27  32               │   │
│    0     477    6484     692    48  19  33               │   │
│    0     461    6307     675    47  18  36               │   │
│    0     450    6167     658    47  20  34               │   │
│    0     461    6351     675    59  25  16               │   │
│    0     476    6577     700    62  25  13               │   │
│    0     501    6735     710    65  27   8               │   │
│    0     509    6912     729    65  17  18               │   │
│    0     519    6984     738    58  25  17               │ ▼ │
├─────────────────────────────────────────────────────────┴───┤
│ ◄ │                                                      │ ► │
└─────────────────────────────────────────────────────────────┘
```

FIGURE 4-5.   *Running an indexed column query returning 500,000 rows*

command. The command tells vmstat to report five times with a two-second delay between reports.

Findings (Based on This Example)

During quiet times, Oracle will use as much CPU as is available. When it does not have to share CPU with other consumers, statements in programs are processed

```
┌─────────────────────────────────────────────────────────────┐
│ ═                        HP Prod                      ▼ │ ▲ │
├─────────────────────────────────────────────────────────┤───┤
│   sr      in      sy      cs    us  sy  id               │ ▲ │
│    0     113     560      85    21   8  71               │   │
│    0     295    6339     609    63  32   5               │   │
│    0     311    6335     600    80  11   9               │   │
│    0     292    5666     531    69  19  12               │   │
│    0     325    5754     546    69  30   1               │   │
│    0     335    5967     562    66  29   5               │   │
│    0     346    6076     576    71  18  11               │   │
│    0     369    5968     585    62  32   6               │   │
│    0     436    6109     644    57  31  12               │   │
│    0     472    6241     680    70  26   4               │ ▼ │
├─────────────────────────────────────────────────────────┴───┤
│ ◄ │                                                      │ ► │
└─────────────────────────────────────────────────────────────┘
```

FIGURE 4-6.   *Running an unindexed column query returning 500,000 rows*

according to their efficiency. CPU consumption for Oracle user requirements can run as high as 100 percent when the computer is otherwise idle.

COMPONENT RULE #3
Assess the amount of idle time of user sessions.

Component #3 can be accomplished by taking snapshots of user activity over a representative period of a normal business day. First, you must figure out who the heavy users are and what applications they are running. Second, speak with those people and get an idea of a period they are logged on at the same time. You are then ready to run your experiment. You should ensure that your heaviest users are working during the test as well as a sample of people performing less intensive activity. By having your busiest users logged on, you can get a realistic idea of what goes on when you have a mix of high- and low-level activity persons on the machine. The command shown in Figure 4-7 was used to collect statistics every 10 minutes for a one-hour period.

Tables 4-2 to 4-5 show the number of processes using CPU organized by process type. The three processes inspected are the ones that support the login (ksh), the tool process (iap30x), and the database communication process (shadow).

The command shown in Figure 4-7 is broken up as follows.

■ The ps -ef shows the program status of the machine.

■ The first grep cuts rows from the program status that do not contain the text P:4096 (the Oracle shadow process).

■ The second grep cuts rows from the program status that show no CPU utilization (indicated by 0:00).

■ The wc -l command counts the number of lines displayed by the program status command.

```
echo " "
echo "CPU > 0 shadow \c";ps -ef|grep P:4096|grep -v 0:00|grep -v grep|wc -1
echo "CPU > 0 iap30x \c";ps -ef|grep iap30x|grep -v 0:00|grep -v grep|wc -1
echo "CPU > 0 -ksh  \c";ps -ef|grep ksh|grep -v 0:00|grep -v grep|wc -1
echo " "
echo "CPU = 0 shadow \c";ps -ef|grep P:4096|grep 0:00|grep -v grep|wc -1
echo "CPU = 0 iap30x \c";ps -ef|grep iap30x|grep 0:00|grep -v grep|wc -1
echo "CPU = 0 -ksh  \c";ps -ef|grep ksh|grep 0:00|grep -v grep|wc -1
sleep 600
```

FIGURE 4-7. *Command to collect statistics on program status*

Tables 4-2 through 4-6 summarize the output from the command and present it in a readable format.

USERS CONSUMING CPU		USERS NOT CONSUMING CPU	
shadow	12	shadow	10
iap30x	7	iap30x	14
-ksh	0	-ksh	25
Total:	19	Total:	49

TABLE 4-2.   *Start of Collection at 10:54:11 E.D.T.*

USERS CONSUMING CPU		USERS NOT CONSUMING CPU	
shadow	13	shadow	8
iap30x	7	iap30x	13
-ksh	0	-ksh	25
Total:	20	Total:	46

TABLE 4-3.   *First Interval at 11:04:14 E.D.T.*

USERS CONSUMING CPU		USERS NOT CONSUMING CPU	
shadow	11	shadow	13
iap30x	8	iap30x	15
-ksh	0	-ksh	26
Total:	21	Total:	54

TABLE 4-4.   *Second Interval at 11:14:16 E.D.T.*

USERS CONSUMING CPU		USERS NOT CONSUMING CPU	
shadow	8	shadow	14
iap30x	5	iap30x	16
-ksh	0	-ksh	21
Total:	13	Total:	51

TABLE 4-5.   *End of Sixth Interval at 11:54:24 E.D.T.*

ACTIVITY	% USING CPU	% NOT USING CPU
shadow process	49.4	50.6
iap30x (tool process)	31.8	68.2
user login process	0	100.0

TABLE 4-6. *Process CPU Utilization Percentages*

From the information in Tables 4-2 to 4-5, we can summarize process to CPU utilization activity on the machine (Table 4-6).

Findings (Based on This Example)

The evidence points to a great deal of idle time on the machine. It is possible that a number of users quickly log on to the machine to satisfy one query, then end up sitting there until they exit back to their local environment. Because the measurement can only be done once a process has consumed one second, the CPU figures may be ignoring some very small requests.

Having looked at user process requirements, you should as well inspect the CPU figures for Oracle and its background processes. The machine we are using has two separate instances of Oracle, one running in ARCHIVELOG mode. When a database runs in ARCHIVELOG mode, Oracle keeps copies of online redo logs before it reuses them. One has a single database writer process, the other has three writers.

COMPONENT RULE #4
Assess the ongoing CPU requirements for the Oracle engine.

Figure 4-8 shows information collected on the processes running to support the Oracle configuration on the sample machine.

As you see in Figure 4-8, the CPU requirements for Oracle are easily being met. It indicates that the CPU requirements for the Oracle support processes are small. Oracle is not hogging CPU, and the output indicates there is sufficient time for the CPU to service the Oracle database engine and user process requests. The database was started on August 6 and Figure 4-8 was captured August 12—6 days later. The system monitor process (referred to as SMON in Chapter 2) is the biggest user of CPU—a mere 3 minutes and 16 seconds in six days. Notice how the version 2 listener

```
┌─────────────────────────────────────────────────────────────┐
│ ═                         HP Prod                       ▼ ▲  │
├─────────────────────────────────────────────────────────────┤
│ Net 1 listener - May 29  ?          0:00 orasrv opsoff dbaof▲│
│ Net 2 listener - Jul 25  ?          0:36 /oracle/bin/tnslsnr │
│                                                              │
│ archiver        - Aug  7  ?          0:28 ora_arch_prd       │
│ database writer- Aug  7  ?          1:12 ora_dbwr_prd        │
│ database writer- Aug  7  ?          0:29 ora_db01_prd        │
│ database writer- Aug  7  ?          0:22 ora_db02_prd        │
│ database writer- Aug  7  ?          0:19 ora_db03_prd        │
│ log writer      - Aug  7  ?          1:54 ora_lgwr_prd       │
│ process monitor- Aug  7  ?          0:00 ora_pmon_prd        │
│ system monitor - Aug  7  ?          3:16 ora_smon_prd        │
│                                                              │
│ database writer-23:14:36  ?          1:07 ora_dbwr_aob       │
│ process monitor-23:14:34  ?          0:00 ora_pmon_aob       │
│ log writer      -23:14:38  ?          0:36 ora_lgwr_aob      │
│ system monitor -23:14:40  ?          0:08 ora_smon_aob     ▼ │
├─────────────────────────────────────────────────────────────┤
│ ◄                                                          ► │
└─────────────────────────────────────────────────────────────┘
```

FIGURE 4-8. *Program status for Oracle support processes*

(the SQL*Net 2.0 process that receives incoming requests from the network) has been running over 50 days and requested a mere 36 seconds of CPU time.

COMPONENT RULE #5
Assess the balance between CPU time required to support user processes versus system services.

Because the CPU can only handle either user support or system support one request at a time, knowing the balance between the amount of time dedicated to each is part of the process. In the following listing, CPU usage was reported for a 40-minute period every two minutes. The command used was

vmstat ¦ cut -c70-200 ; sleep 120

		faults		cpu		
sr	in	sy	cs	us	sy	id
0	109	546	80	22	8	70
0	98	553	77	18	8	74
0	122	547	73	43	8	49
0	111	548	83	22	5	73
0	119	546	70	31	9	60
0	108	512	66	28	18	54
0	117	532	69	34	23	44

0	121	538	83	22	15	74
0	109	530	82	32	18	50
0	98	546	82	8	0	92
0	122	527	70	54	11	35
0	111	541	73	22	5	73
0	119	508	80	19	3	79
0	96	554	75	22	15	74
0	108	509	74	41	12	47
0	117	531	59	24	23	54
0	121	534	80	22	15	74
0	109	523	72	29	14	57
0	111	509	70	31	12	57
0	99	542	69	20	8	72

The columns we are paying attention to are the three columns on the right, under the heading "cpu". The "us" column indicates user CPU, the "sy" column indicates the percentage of system CPU, and the "id" column shows the percentage of CPU idle time. These results indicate a healthy balance between user and system utilization. The other four columns can be ignored.

We call this a healthy balance since the percentages in the "us" column continually exceed those in the "sy" column. The CPU is spending more time servicing user requests than system support. Over the 20 reporting intervals, the average user figure is 27.2 percent and the average system figure is 11.5 percent.

Conclusions Drawn from the Example

To summarize the findings of the above exercise, you can draw the following conclusions and make recommendations.

CPU Is More Than Adequate

Based on the output, this machine's CPU is easily meeting the resource requests of the Oracle database engine, Oracle user application processes, and processes supporting non-Oracle activities. During the business day, there are a great deal of users on the machine making little or no CPU resource requests. More users are idle during the day than those doing transactions against or reporting on the database. During quiet times, Oracle uses as much CPU as it can find. This is a healthy situation since a dedicated CPU speeds up processing of requests and maximizes the power of the computer. The operating system configuration easily supports the databases on this machine. The balance between CPU utilization for system support and user support indicates a correctly sized CPU. Do not consider a CPU upgrade. It is not necessary.

Session Monitoring

Monitor CPU utilization on a regular basis and ensure reporting is done during presumed heaviest user access. Because memory and basic support services are required for support of a great deal of idle sessions, a session monitor process should be put in place to kill unnecessary user sessions after a 20-minute period of terminal inactivity. This could be done at the operating system level or by using Oracle7 PROFILEs as discussed in this chapter.

CPU Too Small

Once you go through the exercises described in the preceding sections, you may realize that your results point to a completely different set of findings. The following guidelines are designed to encourage continued attention, to recognize indicators that may point to problems with the size of your CPU.

- More than 50 percent of CPU utilization is dedicated to support of system services as opposed to satisfying user process requests.

- Transactions seem to be never ending. After ensuring your applications are tuned, it is possible that the time slice each user gets of CPU may be performing excessive paging and swapping instead of actual processing.

- There is very little (less than 5 percent) CPU idle time even when the activity level on the machine is low. Even though the users are not doing much processing, the CPU is busy.

- If your memory is limited and your SORT_AREA_SIZE is at the default (usually 64K), a CPU that is too small may be overburdened with the I/O requests necessary to perform sorting to disk. Look at disk and memory sort statistics discussed in Chapter 2.

- Sometime you may be tempted to adjust the priority of the Oracle background processes to compensate for a small CPU. The hope is that if the Oracle processes have a higher priority, the CPU will process user session requests faster due to the increased priority given to Oracle. Increasing the priority of Oracle processes may keep user processes from acquiring an adequate slice of the CPU to get their work accomplished. Reducing the priority of Oracle processes can result in the database writer (for example) never getting an opportunity to write data to disk. Problems may occur when priorities are mismatched between Oracle and user processes.

Maximizing CPU Power

You are encouraged to develop a regimen in which nothing that can run in off-hours is allowed to run during the day. Many installations insist that reports must be produced immediately, and the information contained in them must be 100 percent current. A great deal of reporting that is done with online systems can be canned and run at night. By making this clear to system owners as new systems are developed, you end up giving your CPU a break during its most hectic processing periods—the classic 9:00 to 5:00 working day. You need to convince your users that online data entry systems will perform better when as much reporting work as possible is done at night. The higher up the management chain, the higher the level of summary reporting needed. Summary reporting collects massive amounts of detail transaction data and rolls it up to help management with issues concerning planning, budget control, and resource allocation. Factors that help in tuning CPU utilization are listed at the end of this chapter.

Session Control

Oracle7 permits more system and session control from within Oracle than was ever possible before. Moving more and more session control under Oracle's umbrella allows you to have more tools at your disposal that help you maximize the power of your CPU. Restricting access to the database and removing unwanted sessions, as described in the following sections, have operating system as well as Oracle-based security in place for protection. Note that not every operating system account is able to log into sqldba and issue the command **alter system** as discussed in the following section.

Restricting Access

With Oracle7, you may want to restrict access to the database during special processing periods to allow high-profile jobs to have the machine to themselves. Ensure the scheduling of programs run in off-hours does not interfere with your mission-critical applications.

For example, let's say that you work in a government telecommunications installation that bills clients on the first and fifteenth days of each month. You cannot afford to have the billing detail job abort—no bills translates to lost income. This application needs the CPU's undivided attention. With Version 6, you needed to restrict access to the database by shutting down the instance, then restarting it with the **startup dba** command. While Oracle was running in this mode, you could ensure that only users with the DBA privilege could connect to the database. Unfortunately, the assortment of caches as discussed in Chapter 2 were empty after the startup. The CPU needed to perform the necessary I/O to fill these caches again. It was a shame to have the CPU doing this work simply for the sake of having a database with restricted access.

Oracle7 introduces the concept of restricting access without having to restart the database. Restricting access is accomplished via the command

```
alter system enable restricted session;
```

Restoring the database to normal unrestricted access is accomplished via the command

```
alter system disable restricted session;
```

While the database is operating in restricted mode, users without restricted session access capabilities receive the following error message:

```
ORA-01035: ORACLE only available to users with RESTRICTED SESSION privilege
```

Removing Unwanted Sessions

Periodically, for an assortment of reasons, user sessions are aborted, and the operating system does not clean up when the user signs off. You need to detect the existence of these aborted sessions, then clean up after them to free up any resources they have obtained and still may be using.

Using sqldba or SQL*Plus, runaway sessions can be terminated by issuing the command **alter system kill session**. The command requires two arguments: the session number and the serial number of the process to be killed.

Identify the Owner of the Session

You need to identify the user who owns the process to be killed. The following listing shows that the second fitzpaj session is still using the machine, because you see a -ksh (sign-on), an iap30x (Oracle runform), and a shadow process (the database communication process). On the other hand, the first fitzpaj has been terminated, but the shadow process is still running. It started up at 09:09:22 A.M., and when the listing was created at 01:29:09 P.M., or some 4 hours, 19 minutes, and 31 seconds later, the process had consumed 3 hours, 32 minutes, and 51 seconds of CPU time (212:51). This session is the one to remove using the **alter system kill session** command.

```
fitzpaj  5002    1  0 09:09:22 ?      212:51 oracleprd P4096,8,1
fitzpaj  4223 4222  0 14:01:51 ttyra    0:00 -ksh
fitzpaj  4267 4223  0 14:01:58 ttyra    0:00 iap30x -q -c wpbios:vt220 /usr/
fitzpaj  4268 4267  0 14:01:58 ?        0:00 oracleprd P:4096,8,1
```

Knowing your operating system and configuration is important when deciding which session to kill. In the listing, the first number after the user name is the process ID number of the session component. The next column is the process ID of the parent of each session component. Notice how the parent of the second fitzpaj shadow process (ID 4268) is the iap30x with process ID 4267. Likewise, the iap30x process has a parent ID 4223—the ID of the -ksh component. This relationship is normal on this UNIX machine. However, notice how the parent process ID number of the first fitzpaj session is a process with ID 1. In UNIX, if a shadow process ID belongs to a parent with process ID 1, then that shadow process belonged to a user session that has been terminated.

Killing the Session Using sqldba
Kill a session using sqldba by performing these five steps:

1. Connect to the database.

2. Go to the menu bar at the top of the screen using the MENU key (most environments present a function key help screen when you press CTRL-K).

3. Select the Session option using the arrow keys or pressing s.

4. Select the Kill session option using the arrow key or pressing k.

5. Select the session to kill by pressing the spacebar if on the first line, or using the arrow keys to move around the window.

Looking at the Kill User Session window in Figure 4-9, notice that two sessions belong to the Oracle user name OPS$FITZPAJ. You may need to use operating system commands coupled with sqldba to figure out which session to kill. Complete the kill session activity by pressing the ENTER key when the correct session is highlighted. When this is done, you will be returned to the sqldba screen, and the command that was passed to Oracle to execute the kill statement will be displayed on the screen. Using the window shown in Figure 4-9, the command passed to Oracle in this case would have been

```
ALTER SYSTEM KILL SESSION '41,20898';
```

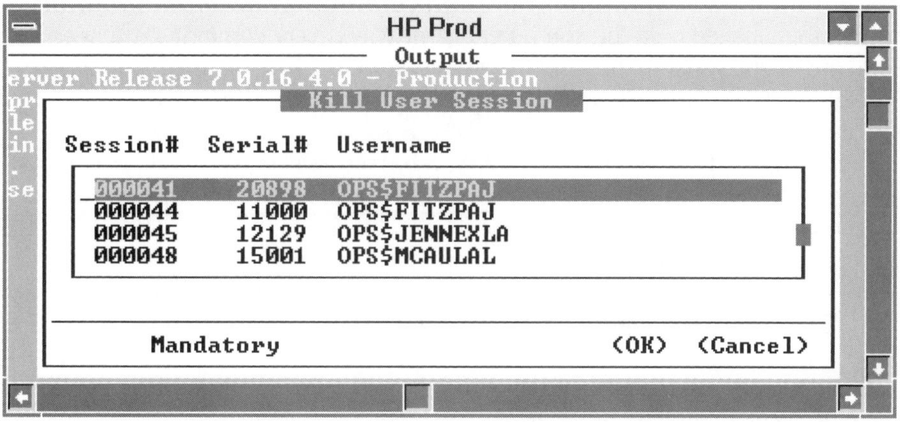

```
┌─────────────────────────────────────────────────────────┐▼│▲│
│ ─                          HP Prod                       │ │▲│
│ ──────────────────────── Output ────────────────────────│ │↑│
│erver Release 7.0.16.4.0 - Production                     │ │ │
│pr ╔══════════════ Kill User Session ══════════════╗      │ │ │
│le ║                                                ║      │ │ │
│in ║  Session#   Serial#    Username                ║      │ │ │
│.  ║ ┌───────────────────────────────────────────┐ ║      │ │ │
│se ║ │ 000041     20898     OPS$FITZPAJ          │ ║      │ │ │
│   ║ │ 000044     11000     OPS$FITZPAJ          │▓║      │ │ │
│   ║ │ 000045     12129     OPS$JENNEXLA         │▓║      │ │ │
│   ║ │ 000048     15001     OPS$MCAULAL          │ ║      │ │ │
│   ║ │                                           │ ║      │ │ │
│   ║ └───────────────────────────────────────────┘ ║      │ │ │
│   ║                                                ║      │ │ │
│   ║     Mandatory                    <OK>  <Cancel>║      │ │▼│
│   ╚════════════════════════════════════════════════╝      │ │ │
││◄│                        │ █ │                      │►│   │
└─────────────────────────────────────────────────────────┘
```

FIGURE 4-9. *Kill User Session dialog box in sqldba*

Killing the Session Using SQL*Plus

Kill a session using SQL*Plus by performing these three steps:

1. Log onto SQL*Plus as the SYSTEM or SYS user.

2. Issue the query to obtain the two arguments required to kill the session.

3. Issue the session kill command.

For our example, following is the query to obtain the session number and serial number (step #2):

```
select sid, serial#
from v$session
where username = 'OPS$FITZPAJ';
```

The output from this query is shown here. As with sqldba, notice the two sessions belonging to the same user were active when this query ran.

```
       SID      SERIAL#
----------- -------------
        41        20898
        44        11000
```

We have shown an example where UNIX user fitzpaj has teminated an Oracle session, then logged onto the computer again. This is very common. You need to figure out which serial number (in this case 20898 or 11000) and which session number (41 or 44) belongs to the first fitzpaj session. The easiest way is using SQL*Plus and the v$session dictionary view as shown in Figure 4-10.

Notice how SID 41 with SERIAL# 20898 has a status of INACTIVE, whereas SID 44 with a SERIAL# of 11000 shows a status of ACTIVE. This confirms the session that should be killed is the one with the 41 and 20898 combination. You may also use sqldba by doing a **connect internal**, pressing the Menu key, then <u>M</u>onitor followed by <u>S</u>ession. The sqldba monitor output shown in Figure 4-11 was taken after OPS$FITZPAJ had logged off the machine. This is why sessions 41 and 44 no longer show.

Now you have the session number and serial number for the session to be killed; proceed to kill the unwanted session as shown here:

```
SQL>  sho user
user is "SYSTEM"
SQL> alter system kill session '41,20898';
System altered.
SQL>
```

```
┌──────────────────────── HP Prod ────────────────────────┐
│SQL> select sid, serial#, status,server from v$session    │
│                                                          │
│        SID   SERIAL# STATUS    SERVER                     │
│     -------- ------- --------  --------                   │
│           1        1 ACTIVE    DEDICATED                  │
│           2        1 ACTIVE    DEDICATED                  │
│           3        1 ACTIVE    DEDICATED                  │
│           4        1 ACTIVE    DEDICATED                  │
│           5        1 ACTIVE    DEDICATED                  │
│           6        1 ACTIVE    DEDICATED                  │
│           7        1 ACTIVE    DEDICATED                  │
│           8        1 ACTIVE    DEDICATED                  │
│           9       21 INACTIVE  DEDICATED                  │
│          13    11098 ACTIVE    DEDICATED                  │
│          15     9843 ACTIVE    DEDICATED                  │
│          18    10032 ACTIVE    DEDICATED                  │
│          33    10078 ACTIVE    DEDICATED                  │
│          41    20898 INACTIVE  DEDICATED                  │
│          44    11000 ACTIVE    DEDICATED                  │
└──────────────────────────────────────────────────────────┘
```

FIGURE 4-10. *Querying user session status using SQL*Plus*

```
╔═══════════════════════════════════════════════════════╗
║  ═  │              HP Prod                   │ ▼ │ ▲  ║
╠═══════════════════════════════════════════════════════╣
║ e Filter: ▓▓▓▓▓▓▓▓                                 ▀  ║
║                                                       ║
║ Serial Process                              Lock      ║
║ Number   ID    Status   Username            Waited    ║
║                                                       ║
║     21   10 INACTIVE OPS$SQLOPPRD                     ║
║  10242   11 ACTIVE   OPS$SQLOPPRD                     ║
║   5836   12 INACTIVE OPS$ORADBA            ▓          ║
║   3336   13 ACTIVE   SYS                              ║
║                                                       ║
║                                                       ║
║                                                       ║
║                                                       ║
║                                            ⟨R⟩  ▼    ║
╠═══════════════════════════════════════════════════════╣
║ ◄ │        │   █     ▲                       │ ► ║
╚═══════════════════════════════════════════════════════╝
```

FIGURE 4-11. *Querying user session status using sqldba*

To summarize, in order to remove unwanted sessions that are robbing CPU and other system resources from users, you need to monitor activity on your computer and intervene, as we have demonstrated in this section.

Using Profiles

With Oracle7, you may use profiles to limit resource utilization for database users. A *profile* is a set of resource limits. Profiles can aid you when maximizing utilization of the CPU. By default, users are assigned the profile DEFAULT when they are first set up as database users. The dictionary view dba_profiles owned by Oracle user SYS contains information about the limits, if any, placed on resource consumption by defined profiles. Profiles can be created using full-screen sqldba or SQL*Plus. Table 4-7 shows what can be controlled using profiles.

Even though the two CPU_ rows in Table 4-7 are the only ones that mention CPU, the other rows have an effect on CPU utilization. To help tune your database, consider setting a nondefault profile for some of your applications. You know your users better than anyone else—your financial application users may have extraordinary processing requirements that dictate the following profile. For

KEYWORD	UNITS	MEANING
SESSIONS_PER_USER	Integer	Maximum number of concurrent user processes per Oracle username
CPU_PER_SESSION	Hundredths of a second	Maximum CPU utilization without reconnecting to Oracle
CPU_PER_CALL	Hundredths of a second	Maximum CPU utilization per call to the database
LOGICAL_READS_PER_SESSION	Integer	Maximum number of database blocks that can be read per session
LOGICAL_READS_PER_CALL	Integer	Maximum number of database blocks that can be read per call
IDLE_TIME	Minutes	Time of no keyboard activity after which user session is terminated
CONNECT_TIME	Minutes	Maximum connect time to Oracle

TABLE 4-7.   *Resource Limits Set Using Profiles*

security reasons, you may restrict them to one concurrent session per user. This is how the FINUSERS profile could be created:

```
CREATE PROFILE FINUSERS LIMIT
    CPU_PER_SESSION       20
    SESSIONS_PER_USER      1
    IDLE_TIME             30;
```

Users assigned the FINUSERS profile will be allowed 20 minutes of CPU time per session, one concurrent session per user, and a keyboard inactivity time of 30 minutes before being logged off Oracle. Because all other resource limits were not mentioned in the statement, they remain the default.

Your personnel application may have short session requirements with very little CPU needs. The human resources profile could be created using this statement:

```
CREATE PROFILE HUMANRES LIMIT
    CPU_PER_SESSION       20
    IDLE_TIME              8;
```

Users assigned the HUMANRES profile will be allowed 20 minutes of CPU time per session and a keyboard inactivity time of 8 minutes before being logged off Oracle. Again, because all other resource limits were not mentioned in the statement, they remain the default.

Tuning the CPU requires limiting who can do what within your applications. The secret is to maximize the efficient utilization of existing CPU.

Let's Tune It

In summary, assess the demands on your existing configuration. See how the CPU is meeting busy and slow time periods processing in your applications. Take advantage of the features highlighted in this chapter and become familiar with the Oracle7 session control mechanisms we have discussed. The first four points below highlight five entries in the intitialization parameter file. Adjusting these entries as suggested can help the CPU tuning exercise.

- Allocate as much real memory as possible to the shared pool and database buffers (SHARED_POOL_SIZE and DB_BLOCK_BUFFERS entries in the initialization parameter file) to permit as much work as possible to be done in memory. Work done in memory rather than disk does not use as much CPU.

- Set the initialization parameter file SEQUENCE_CACHE_ENTRIES high (the default is 10—try setting it to 1,000).

- Allocate more than the default amount of memory to do sorting (SORT_AREA_SIZE entry in the initialization parameter file); memory sorts not requiring I/O use much less CPU.

- On multi-CPU machines, increase the initialization parameter file entry LOG_SIMULTANEOUS_COPIES to allow one process per CPU to copy entries into the redo log buffers (see Chapter 2 for a discussion of the redo log buffer cache).

- Minimize I/O at all costs to free up CPU (e.g., a good number-crunching mainframe that is I/O-bound has no time to do any processing when the CPU is so tied up with I/O requests).

- Maximize availability of CPU power by distributing the load over the business day and night.

- Embark on a methodical assessment of your CPU before considering upgrades.

- Run reporting jobs during quiet hours; perhaps trade enhancements to existing systems for the approval to can jobs to run overnight (the old "enhancements cookie trick").

- If you need to back up your data during the day, try doing it between 11:30 A.M. and 1:00 P.M.—these hours tend to be most quiet during the business day.

- Encourage users to minimize session idle time. Consider implementing a process to kill idle sessions after a predefined time of keyboard inactivity.

- Look at implementing Oracle7 profiles.

- Leave your database up 24 hours a day—precious time is lost when a database has to be closed for system backups.

- Try to keep current with Oracle versions. Performance enhancements are built into each release of the database engine.

- Use governors programmed into some of the Oracle tools to limit CPU consumption of the suite of adhoc end-user query tools (one is built into Data Query 3.0 and later, for example).

- Keep your users out of SQL*Plus, where they can, after mastering the syntax, submit the famous join of two 300,000 row tables without specifying enough join conditions (commonly referred to as the "query from h...").

- Hide the operating system from your users. Implement a captive machine environment where users enter applications at once when logging onto their machine.

CHAPTER 5

Other Database Issues

The preceding chapters of this book have dealt with the basics: memory, I/O, and CPU. This chapter will deal with other database issues that affect the performance of an Oracle database. First, we'll discuss the entries in the initialization parameter (database parameters) file. The parameters within the initialization parameter file allow optimization of memory structures, database-wide defaults, and user and process default limits. Lock contention is an important consideration in multiuser Oracle systems that handle heavy data manipulation; Oracle gives you out-of-the-box tools, such as sqldba, and UTLBstat/UTLEstat will also be discussed. We'll also discuss tuning of the redo logs in some detail. All these tools can be used to tune an Oracle system and investigate what is happening within the database.

The Initialization Parameter (INIT.ORA) File

Over one hundred settable parameters are in the initialization parameter file. Some of these parameters affect performance, while others do not. Appendix A of the *Oracle7 Server Administrator's Guide* provides a comprehensive list of the parameters that you can set in the initialization parameter file. Not all settable parameters in this file will be mentioned in this chapter; the parameters discussed here will be broken into two groups:

- Parameters affecting the entire database limits
- Parameters affecting the user or an individual process

Database-Wide Parameters

Database-wide parameters impose limits (for example, set a maximum number of oranges that can be put in the shopping cart) or define a number of entries that Oracle maintains for you (for example, keep five checkout counters active simultaneously in the store). Let's look at those database-wide parameters that affect performance.

SHARED_POOL_SIZE

This parameter determines the amount of memory that Oracle uses for its library cache and data dictionary cache. The value is expressed in bytes. These caches are discussed in Chapers 2 and 7. Chapter 2 also discusses the Oracle7 multithreaded server (mts). When you use mts, some user process information is in this pool as well.

Library Cache   The library cache contains shared SQL and PL/SQL information. Ideally, caching commonly used preparsed SQL and PL/SQL statements into memory is the goal. A number of statistics are available to help you determine how effectively Oracle is using this cache. Due to the substantial overhead associated with parsing PL/SQL and SQL statements, the goal is to parse once and execute many times. Chapter 7 discusses the phases in the processing of SQL statements (parse, execute, and fetch) and use of the shared pool. Readers who are familiar with Oracle 3GL compilers have probably seen and used the HOLD_CURSOR parameter. Setting the parameter to Y instructs Oracle to keep the precompiler SQL statements in the shared pool. Again, the goal is to make the SQL area large enough to hold frequently used SQL statements in memory to avoid reparsing. Interpretation of these statistics will be covered in the section on UTLBstat and UTLEstat later in this chapter.

The entire tuning process of the shared pool is treated extensively in Chapter 7. If the tuning process determines that the shared pool size needs adjustment, this is done in the initialization parameter file.

Data Dictionary Cache   The data dictionary cache used to be controlled by the **dc_** parameters in Oracle version 6. With Oracle7, this is now combined in the shared pool area of memory. The allocation of space to the different structure types in the shared pool is managed by Oracle internal mechanisms. The data dictionary cache contains data dictionary items in memory. The objective is to keep all needed data dictionary information cached so that physical disk access can be minimized. The data dictionary is where Oracle stores all the information required to monitor itself (that is, who owns it, where is it, how to get it). Before Oracle can return a piece of data to the user, it must first examine the data dictionary. The hit and miss statistics for the data dictionary are presented in the UTLBstat/UTLEstat package that comes with Oracle (see the "UTLBstat.SQL and UTLEstat.SQL" section later in this chapter).

Table 5-1 gives a list of parameters and what items in the data dictionary they affect. Examining the output from UTLBstat/UTLEstat helps to determine if specific data elements are cached effectively.

The occurrence of the objects in memory is not dependent upon the number of specific objects that have been defined within the database. It is dependent upon the number of objects that are referenced by the users. The standards used to implement systems within an organization help determine the number of objects that end up in memory. For example, if you use *public grants* (everyone who can connect to the database has privileges on objects) and *public synonyms* (a central reference name for all users to refer to an object) for your database objects, then the grants and synonyms needed in the dictionary cache are quite small compared to an organization that grants access by individual users and creates private user synonyms for those objects.

Under version 6, substantial performance gains were realized when the dictionary caches (commonly referred to as the *DC cache*) were tuned correctly. In fact, we expected to see a 95 percent hit ratio or better. Now that this area in Oracle7 is tuned by Oracle, we are not seeing such high hit ratios. It is our hope that for seasoned DBAs, Oracle will return to direct tuning of the dictionary cache settable parameters in the future, much like what you have with the cost-based versus rules-based optimizer. For now, we feel it is useful to understand the details of how the DC caches are managed. The bottom line is, if you are not pleased with your hit ratio, then you need to increase the initialization parameter file entry SHARED_POOL_SIZE.

Session Information   Session information is used when the database is running Oracle's multithreaded server. Under this mode, Oracle stores session information in the shared pool rather than in the individual process or user's memory. By

PARAMETER	WHAT INFORMATION IT CONTAINS
DC_COLUMN_GRANTS	Grants that have been given on columns within tables
DC_COLUMNS	The columns that are in the tables in the database
DC_CONTRAINTS	The constraints that have been defined in the database
DC_DATABASE_LINKS	Database links to remote databases that have been defined in the database
DC_FILES	Files that are defined in the database
DC_FREE_EXTENTS	The chunks of free space that can be used in the database
DC_INDEXES	The indexes that exist in the database
DC_OBJECT_IDS	The ID number of objects in the database
DC_OBJECTS	The objects in the database
DC_PROFILES	Profiles that have been set up in the database
DC_ROLLBACK_SEGMENTS	The rollback segments that are usable in the database
DC_SEGMENTS	The segments in the database that are being used
DC_SEQUENCE_GRANTS	Grants that have been given to sequence numbers
DC_SEQUENCES	Sequence numbers that have been defined in the database
DC_SYNONYMS	The synonyms that have been defined in the database
DC_TABLE_GRANTS	The grants that have been given on the tables in the database
DC_TABLES	The tables that are in the database
DC_TABLSPACE_QUOTAS	Quotas that have been applied to specific tablespaces
DC_TABLESPACES	The number of tablespaces
DC_USED_EXTENTS	The chunks of file space in the database that are currently used
DC_USER_GRANTS	The grants that have been given to users in the database
DC_USERNAMES	The usernames that are in the database (i.e., SYS and SYSTEM)
DC_USERS	The users authorized to connect to the database

TABLE 5-1. *The dc_ Information Slots in the Dictionary Cache*

looking at the v$sesstat and v$statname dictionary views, you can measure the size of session information. The number sitting in the VALUE column from v$sesstat shows the number of bytes of memory the process is using. The numbers returned under the VALUE column can be summed to find out the total amount of memory in use by all running processes. The results are in bytes, and their sum can be helpful when making adjustments to the size of the shared pool. In the following listing, we have shown statistics number 15 (session memory) and 16 (max session memory). We introduced the v$statname view to retrieve the NAME of each STATISTIC# from v$sesstat.

```
SQL> select a.sid,b.name,a.value from v$sesstat a, v$statname b
  2 where a.statistic# in (15,16)
  3 and a.statistic# = b.statistic#
  4 order by 1,3;
       SID NAME                                      VALUE
---------- ------------------------------- ----------
         1 session memory                             9116
         1 max session memory                         9116
         2 session memory                             8388
         2 max session memory                         8388
         3 session memory                             8772
         3 max session memory                         8772
         4 session memory                             8460
         4 max session memory                         8460
         5 session memory                            15396
         5 max session memory                        15396
         6 session memory                             9284
         6 max session memory                         9284
         7 session memory                             9284
         7 max session memory                         9284
         8 session memory                             9284
         8 max session memory                         9284
         9 session memory                           185676
         9 max session memory                       202660
        20 session memory                            26212
        20 max session memory                        26212
        38 session memory                            17372
        38 max session memory                        25556
```

ISSUES RULE #1
Make the shared pool large enough to eliminate unnecessary reparsing.

ISSUES RULE #2
The shared pool should be large enough to achieve an 80 percent or greater hit ratio on the data dictionary cache. Since the caches are always empty when the database starts up, measure after the database has been primed.

CHECKPOINT_PROCESS

A *checkpoint* occurs when Oracle writes information from its buffers in memory to the appropriate database files. When this happens, an area in the data files is updated to indicate that a checkpoint has occurred. The writing of this information to the datafiles can either be done by the log writer (LGWR) or a dedicated checkpoint process (CKPT). If the checkpoint process is disabled, it is performed by the log writer. On systems with heavy transaction loads, allowing the log writer process to synchronize these data files may slow down or halt processing momentarily while the header information in the datafiles is updated.

If your system is heavily transaction-oriented so that it frequently checkpoints, then enabling the checkpoint process is extremely beneficial. Keep in mind that enabling this process will add one more process to both your Oracle system and your operating system. The interval at which a checkpoint occurs is determined by two factors. First, whenever the Oracle system switches redo logs, a checkpoint occurs. Second, LOG_CHECKPOINT_INTERVAL and LOG_CHECKPOINT_TIMEOUT discussed in the following sections also trigger checkpoints at regular intervals.

ISSUES RULE #3
Activate the checkpoint process if you have heavy online transaction processing. Too few checkpoints can cause system degradation. When in doubt, enable it.

LOG_CHECKPOINT_INTERVAL

This is the number of newly filled redo log file blocks (based on the size of your operating system blocks, NOT the Oracle block size) that are needed to trigger a checkpoint. If this value is larger than the size of the redo logs, then a checkpoint only occurs when there is a log switch (when the redo log fills up). If the redo logs for your system are large, or the time that Oracle takes to recover using the redo log needs to be shortened, then the value of this parameter should be set to a number smaller than the size of the redo logs.

This value should be set so that checkpoints are spread as evenly as possible through the processing of a redo log. For example, if your redo log is 1,000 blocks, then it would not make sense to set this parameter to 900; the net effect would be a checkpoint once 900 blocks were written, then again when 100 blocks more were written (remember, when a redo log fills up, you have a log switch). If you wish to have checkpoints more often than 1,000 blocks, then, you should set a value that would evenly space checkpoints throughout the redo log. For example if your redo log is 1,000 blocks, and you set LOG_CHECKPOINT_INTERVAL to 250, you would have four checkpoints per redo log file.

Another factor that determines when checkpointing should be done is the speed of the disk drives. If the disk drives are slow, it takes a longer time to recover using the redo logs. The database writer process also takes a longer time to write an entire redo log. Therefore, to reduce these time delays, checkpointing should be more frequent. But be careful, a high frequency of checkpoints in an Oracle system can degrade performance. Too frequent checkpoints diminish the benefits of delayed database file writes in a batch rather than transaction mode.

As with most tunable parameters, there is no exact science to determine appropriate settings. Experimentation with each Oracle system and with each hardware, file distribution, and user activity configuration is necessary.

ISSUES RULE #4
If the redo logs are large, set the checkpoint interval to occur at evenly spaced lengths throughout the logging process. This will reduce the startup time of the system after a crash.

LOG_CHECKPOINT_TIMEOUT
In considering checkpoints, we should not overlook the parameter LOG_CHECKPOINT_TIMEOUT. This parameter works on time. The value forces a checkpoint based on the number of seconds since the last checkpoint. If you want to guarantee a checkpoint every three minutes, for example, you would set the value to 180. This parameter is different than LOG_CHECKPOINT_INTERVAL, which uses the number of buffers filled as its indicator of when to force a checkpoint.

ISSUES RULE #5
If performance is your concern, set LOG_CHECKPOINT_INTERVAL to 0 (the default). Set LOG_CHECKPOINT_INTERVAL to a size greater than the physical redo log file. Then checkpoints will occur only when the redo log file fills up—we like to see that happen once every two hours.

DB_BLOCK_BUFFERS
This parameter is the number of database block buffers that are cached in memory. This is your *data* cache, one of the most important parameters you have in the initialization parameter file. Before the introduction of the SHARED_POOL_SIZE

parameter in Oracle7, this would have been the most important tunable parameter in the initialization parameter file. Now, one could debate as to which is the most important tunable parameter in the parameters file—DB_BLOCK_BUFFERS or the SHARED_POOL_SIZE. Simply stated: Every piece of data a user ever sees first passes through this DB_BLOCK_BUFFERS data cache.

The larger the cache, the more data Oracle can hold in memory; the smaller the cache, the less data Oracle can hold in memory. If the data is not in memory, Oracle issues the needed I/O requests to obtain the data. Remember, I/O is one of the slowest operations a computer can perform. Oracle manages this area using a Least Recently Used (LRU) algorithm. This means that if the buffer cache contains a hot data block (in a trading system, an example of a hot data block would be one containing Oracle stock), then, memory permitting, it stays in the cache. If the buffer cache contains a cold data block (in a trading system, it would be a data block holding Sybase stock), then when additional DB_BLOCK_BUFFERS are needed, Oracle will swap the cold blocks out of memory.

To summarize, the larger number you choose for DB_BLOCK_BUFFERS, the larger your user data cache. A large data cache is very desirable. In fact, in the perfect world, you might want to make your DB_BLOCK_BUFFERS large enough to hold your entire database. In this situation, the need to go to the actual disk might be eliminated.

We know of two situations where this concept was taken to the limit, and both situations had very interesting results. In the first situation, with a very large Oracle database on a pyramid/Nile machine, the DBA had always heard that the larger the System Global Area (SGA), the better. He made changes to the initialization parameter file that caused the SGA to grow to 750 megabytes. It is important that its SHARED_POOL_SIZE and DB_BLOCK_BUFFERS parameters typically account for 90 percent of SGA total size. So in this case we had an enormous DB_BLOCK_BUFFERS setting. It was set to 40,000 (Pyramid is a 16K block, whereas most UNIX boxes are typically 2K blocks). When we began to evaluate this database, we questioned the need for such a large DB_BLOCK_BUFFERS. When we lowered DB_BLOCK_BUFFERS, we saw database performance increase. We wondered why performance would increase when Oracle no longer had to read its data from disk and it could use main memory.

The solution turned out to be quite simple. Oracle itself was constraining the operation of the system, because the SGA was taking up 75 percent of the available memory. We had induced system paging and swapping by requesting too much memory for the SGA. As we discussed in Chapter 2, paging involves moving portions of an application or process out to secondary storage to free up real memory space. Swapping involves copying entire processes from memory to secondary storage.

ISSUES RULE #6

Remember, Oracle is one of many processes that must all live, share, and breathe all available resources. In addition, the SGA should never take over 50 percent of the available memory.

The interesting problem that came out of this situation was how to determine when DB_BLOCK_BUFFERS is set too high. To determine this, we came up with the following SQL statement shown in Figure 5-1. This code must be run from the Oracle SYS account.

By looking at the status of the block header, we can determine what they are doing. If they are free, this means that the DB_BLOCK_BUFFERS value is too large—it has leftover blocks that were never used. In the case of DB_BLOCK_BUFFERS set to 40,000, we found quite a few that were never used. This was an interesting twist to an old rule.

ISSUES RULE #7

Set the DB_BLOCK_BUFFERS as high as possible for your operating environment in order to hold as much data in memory as possible. But don't induce excessive operating system paging and swapping. (This goes to show you that every rule, no matter how good, has its exceptions.)

The second situation involved a very large Oracle database on a Vax/VMS 6450 machine. Because the entire machine was dedicated to a single Oracle application, we had the luxury of tuning the entire machine to benefit Oracle. At that time, we had never heard of a VAX/VMS SGA over 32 megabytes; we decided to look into the pros and cons of doing an SGA larger than 32 megabytes.

The quest for information led us to Mark Porter (rumor has it that Mark is now known as Video LAD), who was then an Oracle kernel developer. We discussed

```
select   decode(state,      0,'Free',
                 1, 'Read and Modified',
                 2, 'Read and Not Modified',
                 3, 'Currently Being Read', 'Other'), Count(*)
from x$bh
group by decode(state,      0,'Free',
                 1, 'Read and Modified',
                 2, 'Read and Not Modified',
                 3, 'Currently Being Read', 'Other');
```

FIGURE 5-1. *Utilization of buffers in DB_BLOCK_BUFFERS*

what we were trying to do, and Mark explained that it was possible because the VMS operating system current at the time supported larger *working set sizes* (the amount of memory a VMS system administrator allocates to a user session). This larger working set size now allowed a VMS installation the ability to increase the SGA size over 32 megabytes. So with Mark's help, we made the necessary system changes to handle a larger SGA and tried it. The most notable improvements were a decrease in the time needed to activate a menu, enter SQL*Plus, and start up a form. After we examined the situation, this made sense. Oracle had to map the requested image to the SGA. The larger the number the SGA was set to, the more work the operating system had to do to invoke SQL*Plus or Oracle Forms.

By making the decision to go to a larger SGA, we had to live with the trade-off that initial image activation would be slower the first time.

ISSUES RULE #8
Tuning is all about trade-offs. As the DBA, you must constantly struggle with all the available resources and decide what the equitable split is for your situation.

In summary, you need to look at your individual situation to decide what is appropriate for your applications and available memory. As a rule of thumb, we recommend making DB_BLOCK_BUFFERS as large as possible. You do this to minimize I/O, which is a very expensive operation. It is a trade-off that you will find usually makes sense. If the system is strictly a data entry system, with little or no query action, then this trade-off would not make sense. On the other hand, if the system is a reporting system that uses few batch or interactive user processes, it would be best to allocate as much available memory as possible to Oracle so that as much data as possible could be stored in memory to reduce the direct system I/O. In most environments, it's a mix, so we still stand by Issues Rule #7 mentioned earlier.

DB_BLOCK_LRU_EXTENDED_STATISTICS
This parameter enables or disables the compilation of statistics in the x$kcbrbh and the x$kcbcbh tables. Using these tables, you can assess the change in the number of disk accesses that would be gained by increasing the allocation of additional buffers or would be lost by the removal of a portion of buffers. Consult the discussion in Chapter 2 for details.

The use of this statistics-gathering tool has, itself, an effect on the performance of the database. This parameter should not be turned on in normal operation. It should only be used in a controlled test environment where the negative performance impact will not adversely affect the normal, necessary operations of the database.

In general, we see very few people using this parameter, because it requires starting and stopping the database so that you can get these statistics. In addition, while this parameter is turned on, your database performance is affected. We recommend you use the SQL statement in Figure 5-1 that references the x$bh table.

The UTLBstat and UTLEstat utility discussed later in this chapter gives information on the ratio of times data was found in memory compared to the number of requests for data needed to be satisfied from disk (i.e., the hit ratio). The sqldba monitor I/O also gives a summary statistic that shows this ratio. These are all excellent ways to determine if DB_BLOCK_BUFFERS is too small.

DB_BLOCK_LRU_STATISTICS

This parameter is set either to TRUE or FALSE. A TRUE setting combined with the DB_BLOCK_LRU_EXTENDED_STATISTICS set to a non-zero value allows monitoring the gain or loss of cache hits from adding or removing buffers from the database block buffer pool. Refer to the discussion in Chapter 2 for details.

ISSUES RULE #9
Only use the DB_BLOCK_LRU_STATISTICS to determine if more or less DB_BLOCKS_BUFFERS should be used, and not during normal operations, because of the negative impact it has on performance.

DML_LOCKS

This parameter is the maximum number of locks that can be placed on all tables by all users at one time. If you have three users updating five tables, you need 15 DML locks to perform the concurrent operation. If you do not have this parameter set high enough, processing stops and an Oracle error is issued.

Our experience has shown that this parameter should be set artificially high from the start. This parameter has no effect on performance—resetting it involves modifying the initialization parameter file and restarting the database. A closed database is not a tuned database—restarting the database will flush all cache information loaded into memory.

ISSUES RULE #10
Estimate over the number of DML_LOCKS that will be needed, because if you run out, it's a show stopper. Better too many than not enough.

LOG_BUFFER

This parameter is the number of bytes that are allocated to the redo log buffer in the SGA. This area is used when a user is executing a transaction that can be rolled back. Once a transaction is committed or rolled back, the information in the log buffer in the SGA is written to the redo log file. If the Oracle system is processing long transactions or if many in-process transactions will be occurring, this parameter should be increased to reduce the I /O to the redo logs.

ISSUES RULE #11
Size the LOG_BUFFER properly to reduce I /O to the redo logs.

PROCESSES

This parameter defines the maximum number of processes that can simultaneously connect to the Oracle database. The default number of 50 is good only for a very limited system. Keep in mind that the background Oracle processes are included in this number and if an application is written that spawns processes recursively, all these spawned processes count.

The conservative setting of the parameter is used to limit the number of users, for a business reason or because of hardware/system capacity issues. If limiting users is not a concern, then it is best to overestimate this parameter value.

ISSUES RULE #12
If the objective is to not limit the number of users on the system, overestimate the number of concurrent processes.

ROLLBACK_SEGMENTS

This parameter is the line in the initialization parameter file where all user-created private rollback segments are referenced. For example, the line may read

```
ROLLBACK_SEGMENTS = (RS1,RS2,RBS_HUGE)
```

We never use public rollback segments. With Oracle, you have the choice between a private or a public rollback segment. A private rollback segment can only be used if referenced in the line above. The advantage to using private is you have complete control over what segments are acquired by the database instance when started. A public rollback segment is there for the taking. You have no control over which public rollback segments the database instance will acquire.

As we suggested in Chapter 3, never put rollback segments in the same tablespace as your data and indexes. You cannot take a tablespace offline that contains rollback information, because rollback segments are always active. In addition, for performance reasons, you should place your private rollback segments in their own tablespace(s).

One of the major performance gains with Oracle version 6 was its ability to break the I/O barrier concerning updates. This was accomplished by breaking the update into two distinct phases: the undo phase and the commit phase. We will illustrate this point using the example of a banking system.

1. Money Grabbers goes to the local automated teller and requests her bank account balance. Using SQL, the request is the following:

```
SELECT NAME, ACCOUNT, BALANCE
FROM ORCL
WHERE NAME     = 'MONEY GRABBERS'
AND     ACCOUNT   = '5002300';
```

Table 5-2 shows what values exist in what areas (SGA, rollback, and redo log) as the above SQL is run.

2. Money Grabbers, noticing a bank error of $200 in her favor, decides to make a withdrawal. Using SQL, the transaction is the following:

```
UPDATE ORCL
SET BALANCE = BALANCE - 200
WHERE NAME     = 'MONEY GRABBERS'
AND     ACCOUNT   = '5002300';
```

Table 5-3 shows what values exist in these same three areas after running the **update**.

3. Money Grabbers is told that the machine is working, and then it asks, "Do you want to commit the changes you have made? Y". She responds YES, and the SQL issued is the following:

```
COMMIT_WORK;
```

Table 5-4 now shows the values held in these three locations after the transaction is commited.

LOCATION	ACCOUNT	NAME	BALANCE	UNDO/ REDO INFO
SGA	5002300	Money Grabbers	500	null
Rollback	null	null	null	null
Redo Log	null	null	null	null

TABLE 5-2.   *Current Account Status at Start*

LOCATION	ACCOUNT	NAME	BALANCE	UNDO/ REDO INFO
SGA	5002300	Money Grabbers	300	null
Rollback	null	null	null	500
Redo log	null	null	null	null

TABLE 5-3. *Values Stored in Three Locations After Update*

As you can see in Tables 5-2 through 5-4, your rollback segment contains your undo information. Had the machine crashed during the update in Table 5-3, the database would have recovered itself by rolling back or undoing based on what was in the rollback segment. Had the computer crashed after the complete transaction was committed, the database would have recovered using the redo log and rollback segments. What is important here is that the update statement is broken into two distinct phases. The update is no longer a bottleneck affecting system performance. Because the commit was recorded in the redo log, the database doesn't have to record the bank account balance for Money Grabbers immediately back to the database file.

Another benefit of this approach is the fact it allows *hot blocks* (blocks containing data in the midst of being changed) to stay current in memory, because among the rollback segment, the REDO LOG, and the database files, Oracle is able to remain consistent. So if another transaction happened against the same data block, that block would still be in memory even though the database file itself still contains the initial balance. The database maintains its integrity because issuing the statement commit_work; caused Oracle to record the transaction on disk. Oracle uses this mechanism to protect you and your data!

Another benefit of rollback segments has to do with read consistency. Until the rollback segments are overwritten, Oracle has a copy of the database blocks before

LOCATION	ACCOUNT	NAME	BALANCE	UNDO/ REDO INFO
SGA	5002300	Money Grabbers	300	null
Rollback	null	null	null	null
Redo log	null	null	null	–200

TABLE 5-4. *Values Stored in Three Locations When Transaction Completed and Saved*

the update. So a long-running transaction that started before the update would be able to present you a read-consistent view of the database.

ISSUES RULE #13
Always name your rollback segments in the initialization parameter file. Rollback segments named in this file are private.

ISSUES RULE #14
Always place your rollback segments in their own tablespace.

ISSUES RULE #15
Always create a special rollback segment designed to handle your large transactions (commonly referred to as "the update from hell"). See Chapter 8 for a discussion of SET TRANSACTION USE ROLLBACK SEGMENT.

NOTE
COMMIT means that Oracle has written sufficient information to disk to be able to recreate your transaction.

SEQUENCE_CACHE_ENTRIES
This parameter is the total number of sequence numbers that are cached in the SGA at one time. Setting this number correctly greatly reduces the overhead spent in obtaining sequence numbers. If you create a sequence with the NOCACHE option, setting this parameter will have no effect on the sequence.

SESSIONS
This parameter is the number of user and system sessions allowed at one time. This parameter is derived from the value you chose in the initialization parameter file for PROCESSES. Oracle sets this value to 1.1 times the value in PROCESSES to account for recursive processes. Unless your applications create concurrent recursive sessions, the derived value should be sufficient.

Individual User/Process Parameters

The following initialization parameter file entries affect an individual user process. As an example, let's say you have 100 users and you give them 1MB of sort space. Then potentially if every user is sorting, you would need an additional 100MB of O/S memory above and beyond what the SGA was using.

OPEN_CURSORS

This parameter is the maximum number of cursors a user can have open at one time. Both implicit and explicit cursors are used by processes. Oracle Forms uses cursors constantly to fetch multiple rows into blocks and to do list_values. The setting for OPEN_CURSORS determines the amount of memory a user allocates on an operating system level for handling SQL statements. It's best to have this value set high and let the operating system control the actual amount of real memory a user acquires. If this value is set too low, it will stop Oracle processing. When the operating system controls a user's memory, processing usually does not stop when a user hits the limit. In the VAX/VMS system, the user's memory is paged out. We have found that the VAX/VMS handling of memory allocation is more efficient than setting limits within the Oracle database.

ISSUES RULE #16
Be generous with the OPEN_CURSORS parameter, especially in an Oracle Forms application environment. This will be a show stopper for your application if it is set too low in the initialization parameter file.

SORT_AREA_SIZE

This is the amount of memory per user process that is allocated for sorting. When Oracle cannot acquire enough memory to complete the sort in memory, it completes the process on disk; thus, an inadequate value for this parameter causes excessive sorts on disk (disk access is very slow compared to the alternative). Be very careful, however, when being generous, because the sort area in memory is allocated on a per user basis.

If you are in the process of a full database import, substantial gains can be made by increasing the value in SORT_AREA_SIZE. Operations such as index creations require a great deal of sort work space. If your installation does a lot of nightly batch processing, we recommend increasing this parameter when there are less demands on system memory. Remember, if you change the SORT_AREA_SIZE setting, you must restart the database for it to take effect.

The v$sysstat table holds information on your sort utilization. Of particular interest are rows with sorts(memory) and sorts(disk) in the NAME column. These two statistics should be examined on a periodic basis when the system has been up and running for a while. By comparing the results from different observations and different times, you can determine if a significant number of sorts are being done on disk and not in memory. If this is the case, then the size of the sort area should be increased.

ISSUES RULE #17
Size your SORT_AREA_SIZE to fit the need of the users. This is a big user of memory and also a big help with performance.

UTLBstat.SQL and UTLEstat.SQL

Without your spending any additional money, Oracle supplies you two of the most useful scripts ever created for tuning an Oracle database. They are called UTLBstat.SQL and UTLEstat.SQL (commonly referred to as UTLBstat and UTLEstat). For those of you who have used Oracle version 6, these were previously known as Bstat.SQL and Estat.SQL. With these two scripts, you will be able to gather a snapshot of Oracle performance over a given period of time.

UTLBstat—An Introduction

UTLBstat gathers the initial performance statistics. It should not be run immediately after your database has started, or it will skew your results. When a database is first started, none of the system caches are loaded, and this would not be a realistic picture of a running database. Your goal here is to determine how well your system performs during normal business operations. Statistics that UTLBstat gathers are stored in temporary tables. Table 5-5 presents these tables, their source system tables, and a general description.

UTLEstat—An Introduction

UTLEstat gathers performance statistics at the end of your observation period. The UTLEstat script must be run at the end of the period for which you want to tune performance. The results of UTLEstat are placed in the temporary tables. Table 5-6 presents these tables, their source system tables, and a general description.

When UTLEstat has finished gathering statistics, it then does a comparison of the information that was stored in both sets of temporary tables (UTLBstat and

UTLBSTAT TABLE	DERIVED FROM	DESCRIPTION
STATS$DATES	SYSTEM	Start and end date/time for statistics gathering
STATS$BEGIN_ROLL	V$ROLLSTAT	Rollback segment information
STATS$BEGIN_FILE	V$FILESTAT, TS$, V$DATAFILE	Database file information
STATS$BEGIN_STATS	V$SYSSTAT	System statistics
STATS$BEGIN_DC	V$ROWCACHE	System data dictionary information
STATS$BEGIN_LIB	V$LIBRARYCACHE	System library cache information
STATS$BEGIN_LATCH	V$LATCH	System latch information
STATS$BEGIN_EVENT	V$SYSTEM_EVENT	Wait events information

TABLE 5-5. *UTLBstat Tables*

UTLEstat) and stores the differences in another set of temporary tables. Table 5-7 presents the tables that are used for the differences and their source.

The table of differences as shown in Table 5-7 is then used for UTLBstat/UTLEstat to generate a report of very useful information. An example of this report is gone over section by section later in this chapter. Before we go into details, let's give an example of how to use UTLBstat/UTLEstat.

UTLESTAT TABLE	DERIVED FROM	DESCRIPTION
STATS$END_EVENT	V$SYSTEM_EVENT	Wait event information
STATS$END_LATCH	V$LATCH	System latch information
STATS$END_ROLL	V$ROLLSTAT	Rollback segment information
STATS$END_FILE	V$FILESTAT, TS$, V$DATAFILE	Database file information
STATS$END_STATS	V$SYSSTAT	System statistics information
STATS$END_DC	V$ROWCACHE	System data dictionary statistics
STATS$END_LIB	V$LIBRARYCACHE	System library cache information

TABLE 5-6. *UTLEstat Tables*

UTLESTAT DIFFERENCE TABLE	SOURCE TABLES
STATS$STATS	V$STATANAME, STATS$BEGIN(END)_STATS
STATS$LATCHES	V$LATCHNAME, STATS$BEGIN(END)_LATCHES
STATS$EVENTS	STATS$BEGIN(EDN)_EVENTS
STATS$ROLL	STATS$BEGIN(END)_ROLL
STATS$FILES	STATS$BEGIN(END)_FILES
STATS$DC	STATS$BEGIN(END)_DC
STATS$LIB	STATS$BEGIN(END)_LIB

TABLE 5-7. *UTLEstat Difference Tables*

UTLBstat/UTLEstat Example

Here are the five steps needed to obtain information and arrive at some tuning recommendations:

1. Choose the correct time slice.
2. Check the initialization parameter file.
3. Turn on UTLBstat at the appropriate time.
4. Run UTLEstat at the end of the time period.
5. Interpret the output.

Choose the Correct Time Slice

The time period you choose must be representative of your work load, or you may corrupt your statistics and make poor tuning choices. For example, if your system is in the process of a major data conversion that would never normally run, then gathering results at that point in time is not going to give you an accurate portrayal of your system's resource needs. On the other hand, running UTLBstat/UTLEstat during recurring peak processing times will give you an excellent view of your performance needs.

Check INIT.ORA File

In order for all the statistics to be populated during a UTLBstat/UTLEstat session, you must set TIMED_STATICTICS = TRUE in the initialization parameter file.

Turn on UTLBstat at the Appropriate Time

You must run UTLBstat from sqldba, because it does a connect internal to start the collection of statistics. Only some operating system accounts can do connect internal. Use the following command:

```
sqldba @utlbstat.sql
```

Don't forget that the database must have been active for a while, or the results you receive will be skewed. Because the statistics are gathered from the time UTLBstat is run until the time UTLEstat is run, statistics gathered while the Oracle memory structures are being initially populated throws off the statistics. All information must be loaded into memory when you first start an Oracle database, and this action would show up in the statistics. Therefore, this utility should be run after a system has been up for a while and has reached some type of equilibrium. Remember, never run UTLBstat/UTLEstat right after the database starts.

Run UTLEstat at the End of the Time Period

Run the following command to invoke UTLEstat:

```
sqldba @utlestat
```

The output from UTLBstat/UTLEstat is placed in an ASCII file called report.txt.

NOTE
If the database went down between running UTLBstat and UTLEstat, then your results are no good, because everything that was in memory before the system went down needs to be reloaded after the system comes back up.

What is unique about these utilities is there is no performance hit on your database except for the few minutes it takes to run each program. All these programs do is gather a snapshot of the system at the start and a snapshot of the system at the end. The results reported in the output are derived from these two points of activity. Without further ado, let's interpret.

Interpret the Output

The output from UTLBstat/UTLEstat contained in the O/S file report.txt will now be gone over a section at a time. We will be highlighting only those areas that in our experience have made a difference.

Library Cache
The following output shows us information about the different types of objects in the library cache.

LIBRARY	GETS	GETHITRATI	PINS	PINHITRATI	RELOADS	INVALIDATI
BODY	0	1	0	1	0	0
CLUSTER	0	1	0	1	0	0
INDEX	0	1	0	1	0	0
OBJECT	0	1	0	1	0	0
PIPE	0	1	0	1	0	0
SQL AREA	49538	.89	177179	.924	1628	4
TABLE/PROCED	16204	.85	49261	.926	1443	0
TRIGGER	0	1	0	1	0	0

8 rows selected.

The question that most DBAs have is "How do I tune it?" Well, this is quite easy. First, you want to minimize reloads. In fact, you should strive to have zero RELOADs. Remember the golden rule: Parse once, execute many times.

Oracle manages the library cache in much the same way as it does the data cache. When a user issues a new statement, Oracle first determines that it is already in the library cache (Oracle uses a special hashing routine to determine if the statement is already present in the library cache). For example, **commit** would more than likely already be in the cache. In this case, Oracle would just execute the command. In the situation where the procedure is not in the library cache, Oracle attempts to parse the statement and place it into the cache. If there is not enough room in the library cache, then Oracle makes room for the procedure by removing an existing entry. A RELOAD means the removed entry is then re-requested. So, RELOADs are very bad. It's like doing a job twice that you hated to do the first time. They should never happen in a well-tuned system.

The second situation you look for is low hit ratios on the PINHITRATIO column and the GETHITRATIO column. Any ratio less than 80 percent is not acceptable.

To tune this cache, you just need to increase the SHARED_POOL_SIZE in the initialization parameter file.

ISSUES RULE #18
RELOAD represents entries in the library cache that were parsed more than once. You should strive for the goal of zero RELOADs. The solution is to increase the initialization parameter file SHARED_POOL_SIZE parameter.

ISSUES RULE #19
GETHITRATIO and PINHITRATIO should always be greater than 80 percent. If you fall below this mark, you should increase the value of SHARED_POOL_SIZE in the initialization parameter file.

System Stats
This output in Figure 5-2 is for the system statistics. What's nice about this section is that you are able to get the total amount of activity for the time slice you chose and an overall average for all transactions during the time slice.

The information shown in Figure 5-2 lists total system statistics for the time period, broken down by transaction average.

Data Cache Effectiveness   Effectiveness can be measured using Figure 5-2. Remember, all data must pass through this cache before it can be accessed by Oracle. To determine the hit ratio, use these simple formulae:

```
LOGICAL READS = CONSISTENT GETS + DB BLOCK GETS
HIT RATIO = (LOGICAL READS - PHYSICAL READS)/LOGICAL READS
```

Now we apply the formulae to the information in Figure 5-2:

```
LOGICAL READS  = CONSISTENT GETS + DB BLOCK GETS
(14,237,750)   =    ( 13,477,423+ 760,327 )
HIT RATIO      = (LOGICAL READS - PHYSICAL READS)/LOGICAL READS
(90.903)       = (14,237,750 - 1,374,655)/14,237,750
```

The result of this calculation gives us a hit ratio of over 90 percent. This means that over 90 percent of all requests were resolved by information residing in the data cache. Had this result been less than 80 percent, we would need to increase the value in the DB_BLOCK_BUFFERS entry in the initialization parameter file.

ISSUES RULE #20
Your data cache should have a hit ratio greater than 80 percent.

```
Statistic                      Total        Per Transact Per Logon
----------------------------   ------------ ------------ ------------
DBWR buffers scanned               677617        265.42      1259.51
DBWR checkpoints                      822           .32         1.53
DBWR free buffers found            340129        133.23       632.21
DBWR lru scans                       4314          1.69         8.02
DBWR make free requests              2290            .9         4.26
DBWR summed scan depth             691472        270.85      1285.26
DBWR timeouts                       56223         22.02        104.5
background checkpoints comp            15           .01          .03
background checkpoints star            15           .01          .03
background timeouts                 116761         45.73       217.03
calls to kcmgas                      4045          1.58         7.52
calls to kcmgcs                       663           .26         1.23
calls to kcmgrs                    146223         57.27       271.79
cluster key scan block gets       1204766         471.9      2239.34
cluster key scans                  598768        234.54      1112.95
consistent changes                  10901          4.27        20.26
consistent gets                  13477423       5279.05     25050.97
cumulative logons                     538           .21            1
cumulative opened cursors           37027          14.5        68.82
current logons                          1             0            0
current open cursors                   32           .01          .06
cursor authentications              46067         18.04        85.63
db block changes                   670927         262.8      1247.08
db block gets                      760327        297.82      1413.25
dirty buffers inspected               136           .05          .25
enqueue conversions                  1018            .4         1.89
enqueue releases                    19946          7.81        37.07
enqueue requests                    19987          7.83        37.15
enqueue timeouts                       40           .02          .07
enqueue waits                           4             0          .01
execute count                       84649         33.16       157.34
free buffer inspected                5028          1.97         9.35
free buffer requested             1421371        556.75      2641.95
max session memory               30186442      11823.91     56108.63
messages received                   11967          4.69        22.24
messages sent                       11967          4.69        22.24
parse count                         49448         19.37        91.91
physical reads                    1374655        538.45      2555.12
```

FIGURE 5-2.   *Output of the UTL report showing system statistics*

physical writes	48757	19.1	90.63
recursive calls	429933	168.4	799.13
redo blocks written	150156	58.82	279.1
redo buffer allocation retr	36	.01	.07
redo entries	339502	132.98	631.04
redo log space requests	19	.01	.04
redo size	72984806	28587.86	135659.49
redo small copies	335654	131.47	623.89
redo synch writes	3547	1.39	6.59
redo wastage	1448176	567.24	2691.78
redo writes	7409	2.9	13.77
session logical reads	14017273	5490.51	26054.41
session max pga memory	56769968	22236.57	105520.39
session memory	6155434	2411.06	11441.33
session pga memory	56705004	22211.13	105399.64
sorts (disk)	18	.01	.03
sorts (memory)	99	.04	.18
sorts (rows)	124161	48.63	230.78
summed dirty queue length	3749	1.47	6.97
table fetch by rowid	2292819	898.09	4261.75
table fetch continued row	620	.24	1.15
table scan blocks gotten	2576238	1009.1	4788.55
table scan rows gotten	44924731	17596.84	83503.22
table scans (long tables)	10588	4.15	19.68
table scans (short tables)	15769	6.18	29.31
user calls	590853	231.43	1098.24
user commits	2553	1	4.75
user rollbacks	859	.34	1.6
write requests	8988	3.52	16.71

67 rows selected.

FIGURE 5-2. *Output of the UTL report showing system statistics* (continued)

Events
The output shown in Figure 5-3 is for system events that happen within the Oracle system.

Buffer Busy Wait Ratio   The goal is to eliminate all waits for resources. We use this ratio to determine if there is a problem. Using the statistics from Figures 5-2 and 5-3, you should perform the following calculations:

BUFFER BUSY WAITS RATIO   = BUFFER BUSY WAITS/LOGICAL READS
LOGICAL READS   = CONSISTENT GETS + DB BLOCK GETS

Now we apply these calculations to the information in Figures 5-2 and 5-3:

LOGICAL READS   = CONSISTENT GETS + DB BLOCK GETS
(14,237,750)   = (13,477,423 + 760,327)
BUFFER BUSY WAITS RATIO   = BUFFER BUSY WAITS/LOGICAL READS
(.0000002)   = (3/14,237,750)

Event Name	Count	Total Time	Average Time
rdbms ipc message	125268	52588485	419.80781205
pmon timer	58474	17541770	299.9926463
smon timer	639	17493650	27376.604069
db file scattered read	81112	369856	4.5598185225
db file sequential read	117123	320759	2.7386508201
db file parallel write	8987	88347	9.8305329921
log file parallel write	7407	36462	4.9226407452
client message	1186346	25347	.02136560498
log file sync	4208	19910	4.7314638783
control file sequential rea	692	3221	4.6546242775
free buffer waits	244	3093	12.676229508
log file space/switch	48	2198	45.791666667
control file parallel write	297	1911	6.4343434343
write complete waits	80	1889	23.6125
rdbms ipc reply	760	1029	1.3539473684
db file single write	165	467	2.8303030303
latch free	1044	389	.37260536398
log file single write	14	100	7.1428571429
log file sequential read	7	47	6.7142857143
enqueue	4	32	8
buffer busy waits	3	9	3

21 rows selected.

FIGURE 5-3. *Output of the UTL report showing Oracle system events*

A ratio of greater than 4 percent is a problem. In our example, we are close to 0 percent, which is desirable. If there is a problem, we suggest looking at the v$waitstat table to determine what kinds of waits you are experiencing. You should run the following SQL statement from the SYS account:

```
SELECT class, SUM(COUNT) 'Total Waits'
from sys.v$waitstat
where class in ('undo header', undo block', 'data block')
group by class;
```

The results of the query might look like this:

```
Class                    Total Waits
------------------       ---------------
Data block                           10
Undo segment header               1,000
Undo block                        1,200
```

Examining the preceding query, we can come to the following conclusions:

- The majority of waits concerned rollback activity.

- The 1,000 waits happening for undo segment header information were for database buffers containing rollback segment headers information.

- The 1,200 waits happening for undo block buffers were for database buffers containing rollback segment data blocks.

Remember, before an update can be completed, it must first be recorded in your rollback segment. So contention in this area affects all updates, even updates that were attempted and then aborted. The solution is to add more rollback segments.

On the other hand, if your waiting was due to data blocks, you need to modify your **freelist** setting (a *freelist* is a list of data blocks that contain free space). So before Oracle inserts rows into a table, it will go to the free lists to find data blocks that have enough free space to accept the insert. Every table has one or more free lists. The value of **freelist** is determined when you first create the table. If you do not specify a **freelist** value, the default is 1.

ISSUES RULE #21
All resource waits are bad and should be avoided. If you see "undo" rollback segment waits, then increase the number of private rollback segments your database contains.

ISSUES RULE #22
If you see data block waits, you need to increase your freelist parameter on heavily inserted tables. You must re-create the table to change an existing freelist setting. When in doubt, we recommend setting the freelist to 2 on tables you suspect may become insert bottlenecks.

Sorts   Figure 5-2 gives very good statistics on your sort usage. The sorts (disk) row tells you how many times you had to sort to disk; that is a sort that could not be handled by the size you specified for SORT_AREA_SIZE parameter in the initialization parameter file. The sorts (memory) row tells you how many times you were able to complete the sort using just memory. We feel that 90 percent or higher of all sorting should be done in memory.

To eliminate sorts to disk, you should increase the initialization parameter file entry SORT_AREA_SIZE. The larger you make SORT_AREA_SIZE, the larger the sort that can be accomplished by Oracle in memory. Unlike other parameters, this is allocated per user. This is taken from available memory, not from the Oracle SGA area of memory.

Chaining   When a row spans more than one data block, this can be detected looking at the "table fetch continued row" value. Chaining negatively affects performance. The more chaining found, the poorer the database performs. We recommend eliminating all chained rows. In Figure 5-2, a total of 620 chained data blocks were read during the UTLBstat/UTLEstat period; this number is quite small, considering how many total blocks were read. However, we still recommend eliminating all chained rows. With Oracle7 and the **analyze table list chained rows** command, you can detect chaining information in the data dictionary view USER_TABLES. (See the discussion in the "Row Chaining" section later in this chapter.)

Enqueue Waits   We like to think of enqueues as locks. When you see waits appearing, this means that Oracle needed another lock but could not obtain it. So the solution is to raise the initialization parameter file entry ENQUEUE_RESOURCES. ENQUEUE_RESOURCES represents the number or resources that can be
locked by the lock manager.

Database Writer Process   In Figure 5-2, the DBWR buffers scanned row gives you an excellent overview of the volume of information that has gone through the database writer. This DBWR (database writer process) is discussed in the "Background Processes" section of Chapter 2. The DBWR checkpoints row gives you an excellent indication of how many checkpoints you are doing. The question most DBAs have is "How do I improve the speed of the database process DBWR?" because DBWR does all the reading and writing to the database files (the checkpoint process only modifies the header of database files if it is enabled in the initialization parameter file).

If you are on an operating system that supports additional database writers, the first thing to do is increase the number of database writers that are activated. Some DBAs are under the misunderstanding that this value is constrained by the number of CPUs your processes have, and this is not correct. The initialization parameter file entry should be based on the number of datafiles your database has. We recommend setting the entry DB_WRITERS to two per database file. If you suspect that you will need more, then run UTLBstat/UTLEstat, and then slowly add more.

ISSUES RULE #23
If you are on an operating system that allows multiple DBWR processes (e.g., UNIX), then increase the number of database writers you have.

The other initialization parameter file entry that has a great effect on database writer performance is DB_BLOCK_WRITE_BATCH. The larger the value, the less often the database process is signaled to write. Adjusting this parameter affects how efficient the DBWR will perform.

Application Effectiveness　By looking at the table scans (short tables) and table scans (long tables) rows, you can determine how many full table scans your database is doing. A *full table scan* occurs when Oracle does not have an appropriate index to use, and it is forced to read every row in the table. If you intend to process the majority of records, then using a full table scan is faster. In most environments, though, we expect to see the majority of the access being done via indexes. So this ratio is used primarily to determine if there is a problem. The formula is as follows:

```
NON-INDEX LOOKUPS RATIO = Table Scans (Long Tables)/Table Scans
(Long Tables)+Table Scans (Short Tables)
```

In Figure 5-2, if we apply the formula, we see the following results:

```
Table Scans (Long Table)        =  10,588
Table Scans (Short Table)       =  15,788
Non-Index Lookups Ratio  .401   =  10,588/(10,588+15,788)
```

This ratio indicates that 40 percent of all table lookups are full table scans. This is typically not a very good situation. If this were a sample taken in the middle of the night when the batch processing took place, then it would probably be okay. If this were a sample taken during the day when lots of users were logged on, you should suspect major problems. Chapter 7 discusses in great detail how to determine what indexes you need and how effectively they are working.

Average Write Queue Length

This is the average length of the dirty buffer write queue. This should be compared to the initialization parameter file entry DB_BLOCK_WRITE_BATCH. If average write queue length is larger than the DB_BLOCK_WRITE_BATCH entry, then increase the value of DB_BLOCK_WRITE_BATCH. Also, a quick inspection of the I/O balance of your disk drives should be made. This could be an indication that one disk drive is doing most of the work.

```
Average Write Queue Length
--------------------------
.4171117044948820649755292
1 row selected.
```

Tablespace and File I/O

This section of the report gives the information about the physical reads and writes that are happening to the tablespaces and files that make them up. Because I/O is one of the slowest operations a computer can perform, Figure 5-4 should prove quite useful.

The interpretation of I/O information was covered in detail in Chapter 3. Briefly, this information is used to look at the physical reads and writes that are happening to each file to detect an uneven work load. If an uneven workload exists, you may need to do one of the following.

- Move one or more database files to another disk to balance the load.

- When a frequently accessed table shares space in a datafile with other tables, take the busy table out of the shared datafile and put it in its own datafile on another drive.

The goal is to have a database with as balanced a distribution of I/O as possible.

In looking at Figure 5-4, we see a few problems. The majority, or 90 percent, of all the reads are being done by 3 tablespaces out of 11. The tablespace TBSP_DATA002 is doing 50 percent of the work. This is not a healthy balance. In addition, we see the system tablespace getting approximately 25 percent of the load. Due to the nature of tablespaces such as system, temp, and rollback, we would not expect them to dominate the I/O stream.

In summary, use the output in Figure 5-4 as a quick way to determine your I/O load balance. Remember though, this only shows you Oracle I/O. If other operating system files are on those disks, they will not be accounted for.

TABLE_SPACE	PHYS_ FILE_NAME	PHYS_ READS	PHYS_ BLKS_RD	PHYS_ RD_TIME	PHYS_ WRITES	PHYS_ BLKS_WR	PHYS_ WRT_TIM
SYSTEM	ORA_SYSTEM	38803	75587	0	1717	1717	0
TBSP_INDEX001	INDEX.001DBS	5309	5309	0	706	706	0
TBSP_DATA001	DATA001.DBS	33723	369685	0	619	619	0
TBSP_INDEX002	INDEX002.DBS	4691	4691	0	2383	2383	0
TBSP_DATA002	DATA002.DBS	68280	792468	0	17387	17387	0
TBSP_DATA003	DATA003.DBS	28	378	0	0	0	0
TBSP_INDEX003	INDEX003.DBS	8748	8748	0	1065	1065	0
TBSP_ROLLBACK	ROLLBACK.DBS	81	81	0	20227	20227	0
TBSP_TEMP	TEMPORARY.DBS	0	0	0	3131	3131	0
TBSP_WORK	WORK.DBS	136	2006	0	0	0	0

11 rows selected.

FIGURE 5-4. *Output of the UTL report that provides information on physical reads and writes*

ISSUES RULE #24
UTLBstat/UTLEstat will only give you the Oracle I/O perspective. Be very careful you don't overlook operating system files that may be on the same device.

ISSUES RULE #25
I/O is a major bottleneck for performance. You should always distribute your I/O as evenly as possible.

Latches

This section of the report (see Figure 5-5) contains information about the latches and the statistics associated with them. Latches are Oracle's method of establishing process ownership of objects that the database needs to use. Think of a latch as a very efficient internal Oracle lock.

As can be seen in Figure 5-5, latches are used in a number of different ways. The objective is to have the HIT_RATIO as high as possible: this means that when a latch is requested, it is available. The SLEEPS should be as low as possible: this means a latch was requested and could not be supplied. The process that requested the latch went into a sleep state until the needed resource was available. Sleeps should be avoided.

LATCH_NAME	GETS	MISSES	HIT_RATIO	SLEEPS	SLEEPS/MISS
cache buffer handl	41852	0	1	0	0
cache buffers chai	27143405	757	1	335	.443
cache buffers lru	1485627	1806	.999	341	.189
dml lock allocatio	15661	0	1	0	0
enqueues	64064	13	1	1	.077
latch wait list	290	1	.997	2	2
library cache	449459	106	1	88	.83
library cache load	7216	0	1	0	0
library cache pin	577473	110	1	60	.545
messages	381867	217	.999	13	.06
multiblock read ob	184938	0	1	0	0
process allocation	538	0	1	0	0
redo allocation	429626	312	.999	120	.385
redo copy	1	1	1	0	0
row cache objects	645564	52	1	20	.385
sequence cache	3282	0	1	0	0
session allocation	21128	0	1	0	0
session idle bit	1190904	6	1	2	.333
shared pool	215114	57	1	62	1.088
system commit numb	187713	2	1	0	0
transaction alloca	12056	0	1	0	0
undo global data	8044	0	1	0	0
user lock	1071	0	1	0	0

23 rows selected.

FIGURE 5-5.   *UTL latch request output*

The section shown in Figure 5-6 also contains latch information. This information is on latches that processes are not allowed to wait for. If the process cannot get the requested latch, rather than sleep, it times out. The goal is to have the NOWAIT_HIT_RATIO as close to 1 as possible.

What's important when looking at Figures 5-5 and 5-6 is that access to the redo log buffer is regulated by latches. Two types of latches control access to the redo log buffer:

- Redo allocation latch
- Redo copy latch

```
LATCH_NAME          NOWAIT_GETS      NOWAIT_MISSES      NOWAIT_HIT_RATIO
-----------------   -----------------  -----------------  -----------------
cache buffers chai      9826355              83                    1
cache buffers lru      12932049           24230                 .998
library cache             50357              13                    1
library cache pin          4467               0                    1
redo copy                 26055               1                    1
row cache objects          2189               1                    1
6 rows selected.
```

FIGURE 5-6. *UTL latch request output—latches that will not wait*

As updates occur, space is allocated in your redo log buffer using the redo allocation latch. Because there is a single redo allocation latch, only one user can allocate space in the redo log buffer via the redo allocation latch at a time. The most information that can be copied on the redo allocation latch at a time is determined by the initialization parameter file entry LOG_SMALL_ENTRY_MAX_SIZE. If the amount of information to be copied is greater than LOG_SMALL_ENTRY_MAX_SIZE, then Oracle escalates up to a redo copy latch. While holding this redo copy latch, the user process will fill the redo log buffer with its information. When the process is done, it then releases the redo copy latch.

If you are on a computer system that has multiple CPUs, then you are allowed to have one redo copy latch per CPU. This is done through the INIT.ORA parameter LOG_SIMULTANEOUS_COPIES.

If your hit ratio starts to fall below 85 percent, then you have *latch contention*. If you are having redo allocation latch contention, then make the INIT.ORA parameter LOG_SMALL_ENTRY_MAX_SIZE smaller. By making this value smaller, you will cause more activity to happen on the redo copy latches.

ISSUES RULE #26
If you determine you have redo allocation latch contention, make the INIT.ORA parameter LOG_SMALL_ENTRY_MAX_SIZE smaller; this will cause Oracle to use more redo copy latches.

If you are having redo copy latch contention, then increase the initialization parameter file entry LOG_SIMULTANEOUS_COPIES. Another way to reduce contention on the redo copy latches is to tell Oracle to prebuild the redo entry. Many times, an Oracle user's redo activity is made up of many small pieces. It can be much more efficient to instruct the database to put all the pieces together before requesting the redo copy latch. You do this through the LOG_ENTRY_PREBUILD_THRESHOLD entry. The default setting is 0.

ISSUES RULE #27

If you have redo copy latch contention, make the initialization parameter file entry LOG_SIMULTANEOUS_COPIES larger. Another alternative is to tell Oracle to prebuild redo entry information before requesting the latch. You do this by setting a value for the LOG_ENTRY_PREBUILD_THRESHOLD entry.

Rollback Segment Information

This information gives you statistics about the rollback segments and their efficiency. Remember, all updates must first become rollback entries.

UNDO SEGMENT	TRANS TBL_GETS	TRANS TBL_WAITS	UNDO BYTES_WRITTEN	SEGMENT SIZE_BYTES	XACTS	SRINKS	WRAPS
0	639	0	0	356352	0	0	0
2	5190	0	4474650	9203712	0	0	1
3	5040	0	4254436	6234112	-1	0	1
4	7727	0	9434609	8384512	0	0	34
5	4193	0	2633827	6541312	0	0	16
6	4213	0	2613917	5517312	0	0	0
7	8113	0	9440878	10432512	1	0	53

7 rows selected.

Here, the important columns are TRANS_TBL_WAITS and TRANS_TBL_GETS. The ratio of these values should be less than 4 percent, using the following formula:

```
Rollback wait ratio  =  TRANS_TBL_WAITS/TRANS_TBL_GETS * 100
```

If you see rollback contention, you just need to create additional private rollback segments. After creating them, you must reference them in the initialization parameter file entry ROLLBACK_SEGMENTS = ( ). Then alter the new rollback segments online.

ISSUES RULE #28

If you are detecting rollback segment contention, add more rollback segments. When in doubt, add more.

INIT.ORA Parameters

The section of the report shown here presents a list of all the initialization parameter file entries that have settings other than the default. This is provided for informational purposes, because an analysis of the other information might lead to changes in one of these parameters. It is convenient to have it printed here rather than printing out the file itself.

```
NAME                              VALUE
------------------------------    ----------------------------------------
audit_trail                       NONE
control_files                     user$disk2:[oradata.prodc]ora_control1_
db_block_buffers                  3000
db_block_size                     2048
db_file_multiblock_read_count     20
distributed_transactions          16
dml_locks                         400
enqueue_resources                 420
gc_db_locks                       1000
gc_rollback_locks                 10
gc_rollback_segments              10
c_save_rollback_locks             10
gc_tablespaces                    10
global_names                      TRUE
ifile                             ora_system:initps.ora
log_buffer                        81920
log_checkpoint_interval           12000
log_simultaneous_copies           3
max_dump_file_size                10240
max_enabled_roles                 22
mts_servers                       0
open_cursors                      255
optimizer_mode                    CHOOSE
processes                         50
rollback_segments                 roll_priv1, roll_priv2, roll_priv3
sequence_cache_entries            50
sequence_cache_hash_bucket        23
sessions                          60
shared_pool_size                  4000000
sort_area_retained_size           65536
temporary_table_locks             60
transactions                      66
transactions_per_rollback_segment 18
33 rows selected.
```

Data Dictionary Statistics

This section of the report give the statistics specifically on the data dictionary cache, which is part of the shared SQL area in Oracle7.

NAME	GET_REQS	GET_MISS	SCAN_REQ	SCAN_MIS	MOD_REQS	COUNT	CUR_USAG
dc_tablespaces	1025	0	0	0	0	21	7
dc_free_extents	19784	1419	1477	0	4098	74	27
dc_segments	7778	621	0	0	1004	290	286
dc_rollback_seg	11502	0	0	0	0	11	10
dc_used_extents	1578	818	0	0	1578	70	54
dc_tablespace_q	40	2	0	0	7	2	1
dc_users	13280	71	0	0	0	23	21
dc_user_grants	11350	67	0	0	0	49	18
dc_objects	18989	2068	0	0	19	598	597
dc_tables	74490	686	0	0	11	410	409
dc_columns	221240	7405	10173	1586	39	3948	3946
dc_table_grants	55388	5835	0	0	0	2482	2478
dc_indexes	11142	302	8630	548	0	232	227
dc_constraint_d	678	184	494	76	19	46	45
dc_constraint_d	0	0	235	30	0	1	0
dc_synonyms	4595	997	0	0	0	140	139
dc_usernames	14775	70	0	0	0	35	33
dc_object_ids	5	4	0	0	0	3	2
dc_constraints	38	19	0	0	38	4	3
dc_sequences	989	13	0	0	44	11	10
dc_sequence_gra	206	52	0	0	0	13	12
dc_tablespaces	818	1	0	0	818	10	4

22 rows selected.

The meanings of these parameters and the reason to have them cached in memory was covered earlier in this chapter. Here are the major areas of interest.

The GET_REQS column shows how many times a particular dictionary type was requested. The GET_MISS column shows the number of times the requested item was not found in the cache; if it's not in the cache, then Oracle must go out and get it. The CUR_USAG is the number of entries in the cache that are being used. The object is to have GET_MISS and SCAN_MISS as low as possible.

If the miss number is over 10 percent of the gets, then it helps to increase the SHARED_POOL_SIZE entry in the initialization parameter file. Again, you must keep in mind that increasing this parameter does have a direct effect on the size of the SGA and the amount of system memory that is being used by Oracle.

Statistics Gather Times

This section of the report gives the start and stop date and time of the statistics gathering. When UTLBstat is run, the date and time is recorded; likewise for UTLEstat.

```
STATS_GATHER_TIMES
-------------------
19-jul-95 07:01:12
21-jul-95 07:44:55
2 rows selected.
```

ISSUES RULE #29
Run UTLBstat/UTLEstat often with TIMED_STATISTICS = TRUE in the initialization parameter file and examine the output and make changes to the initialization parameter file, the database, or the application, as deemed necessary.

Miscellaneous Tuning Considerations

This leaves us with four remaining areas to wrap up in our discussion of Other Database Issues. Using the rules in this chapter and the assortment of short scripts presented, attending to these last four areas should tie up these issues.

Row Chaining

Row chaining occurs when an update is done on a row in a database block that increases the length of the row so that it no longer fits in the same data block. The RDBMS is forced to find another data block, which is then chained to the original block. The problem is that it now takes two I/Os to accomplish the same amount of work of one I/O previously. This situation causes your database performance to quickly degrade.

Let's take a closer look at a database block and how chaining happens. (This is a very simple look at PCTFREE; it's covered in more detail in Chapter 3.) Following is a data block before the update. In this case, we have two records, one containing the name Mary Smith, the other containing the name Jack Smothers:

III 5-1

Data Block 1 Disk Location 123 Header 90 Bytes
Record 1: Mary Smith
Record 2: Jack Smothers
Pct Free XXXXXXXXXXXXX

Mary Smith recently got married, and her name has changed to Mary Smith-Averylongname. The problem is that the original name "Smith," which is 5 characters long, has grown to 22 characters. If enough room exists in the data block, Oracle will place the additional 17 characters of the name in the space still free in the data block. So another way to think of **pctfree** is as room reserved for future updates. Let's say there's not enough room in percent free. Then Oracle would have to link the first block to another; in the very simplest form it might look like this:

III 5-2

Data Block 1 Location 123 Header Information
Mary Smith
Jack Smothers
Pct Free XXXXXXXXXXXXX
Data Block 45 Location 300 Header Information
Record 1 -averylongname
Pct Free

ISSUES RULE #30
Chaining should be avoided at all costs, because it doubles the amount of I/Os needed to accomplish retrieving the data.

In summary, you want to avoid chained rows at all costs. In addition, the I/O stream is usually quite substantial, because chaining very rarely happens early on. The chained row is usually quite a distance from the original row on the physical device, so the disk has to do substantial thrashing to obtain the information.

Chaining can be determined by use of the **analyze** command with the **list chained rows** qualifier. This command populates a chained row table. You create the chained row table by running the script UTLCHAIN.SQL. Once the table is created, the format of the command for analyzing a table is the following (for this example, the table is called People):

```
analyze table people list chained rows;
```

This command puts into the table called CHAINED_ROWS an entry for each migrated or chained row in a table. The column for the table are the table owner, the table name, the cluster name, the ROWID of the row, and a timestamp when the **analyze** command was executed. If the number of rows that have been migrated or chained is small in comparison to the total number of rows in the table, then the following should be done:

1. Move the rows of data into an intermediate table with the same column structure as the original table by using the ROWID in the CHAINED_ROWS table.

2. Delete the moved rows of data again by using the ROWID in the CHAINED_ROWS table.

3. Insert the rows from the intermediate table back into the original table.

4. Drop the intermediate table.

5. Delete the record in the CHAINED_ROWS table.

After these steps are done, the **analyze** command should be run again. If rows are put into the CHAINED_ROWS table, these are chained because there is not sufficient room in any blocks to hold the entire row. This is caused by a long row of information.

If the number of rows of data in the CHAINED_ROWS table after the **analyze** command are a majority of the rows in the table itself, then there are two possibilities why this is happening. First, the data in a single row is too lengthy to fit in a data block and must be chained. Second, the **pctfree** factor on the table is not correct. If it is the latter, then the following steps should be taken:

1. Determine a better percent free factor for the table.

2. Export the entire table with all its dependencies (i.e., indexes, grants, constraints).

3. Drop the original table.

4. Re-create it with the new specification.

5. Import the data with its dependencies.

The **analyze** command should be run again to see if there are still chained rows. If there are chained rows, then the data in the row is too long to fit into a block and a change in the data block size should be looked into. Changing the data block size is not trivial. The block size can only be set at database creation time. Therefore, if a change of this parameter is decided on, then the database and everything in it must be created. Note: If you are using clustered tables, be very careful of chaining.

ISSUES RULE #31
Avoid chaining by using an appropriate **pctfree** parameter with table creation commands.

ISSUES RULE #32
Remove as many chained or migrated rows of data as you can after identifying them with the **analyze** command.

Database Chaining

Database chaining means that a row is too big to ever fit in one database block. So Oracle is forced to obtain a second block to hold the rest of the information. If you are experiencing database chaining, you need to look at re-creating your database with a larger block size. Re-creating the database is the only way to change the block size. If you need to recreate your database, you must do the following (please refer to Kevin Loney's *Oracle DBA Handbook*, the first in the Oracle Press series from Osborne/McGraw-Hill and Oracle, for details on creating a database).

 Perform a full database export (export is discussed in Chapter 8).

■ Make at least one copy of that export file.

■ Change the DB_BLOCK_SIZE entry in the initialization parameter file to reflect the new value (you may not have an entry now and may have to add one to override your platform's default value)—for example DB_BLOCK_SIZE = 8192.

■ Invoke a SQL script that recreates the database, and then run the following:

   1. catdbsyn.sql from the SYSTEM account

   2. catproc.sql from the SYS account

   3. catexp.sql from the SYS account

   4. Any other SQL scripts needed to support the options you are licensed to run (see Chapter 2 of the *Oracle7 Server Administrator's Guide* for details on database creation and options).

■ Perform a full database import (import is discussed in Chapter 8).

PCTFREE

To avoid chaining, a lot of people over-allocate pct free. This can be a real performance mistake. Remember, **pctfree** is room that is reserved within the data block for future updates. Let's say you have a million-row table that has **pctfree** set to 20 percent. After reviewing the application, you determine that this million-row table contains lab results that rarely if ever change. You decide to re-create the table with a **pctfree** of 1 percent. This means that on a million-row table, every I/O request you make will draw 19 percent additional rows, since this room is no longer reserved for future updates. This amounts to a substantial (I/O) performance increase.

On the flip side, you may encounter situations where it makes sense to set **pctfree** to 90 percent. Here is a situation we experienced: we built a budgeting system, and every month we would load in the detail data. The first three months, all worked well. By the fourth month, our reports ran 50 percent longer. By the sixth month, they ran 200 percent longer. Finally, just as our users were on the verge of a rebellion, we determined what was wrong.

The first month, Oracle packed all the data into the data block as tightly as possible, leaving only 10 percent of the data block free for future updates. The second month, the next data load of budget actuals arrived. Oracle placed it into the **pctfree** area of the data block. The third month, when the budget actuals arrived, Oracle was forced to chain every record, because **pctfree** would not hold the new entries.

The problem here is the dataset was not completely on the initial load. We should have instructed Oracle to set **pctfree** to 90 percent when we created the table, since we only had 1/12th of the data in the first month.

Tuning Redo Logs

Every instance of the database must have at least two redo logs. These are separate from the data files, which actually store the database data. These redo logs working in conjunction with the background process LGWR record all changes made to the database. Another way to think of redo logs is to call them transaction logs. In the event of a database failure, these redo logs can be replayed to bring the database back from a failure.

There are two basic ways you can configure databases concerning redo logs: NOARCHIVELOG mode and ARCHIVELOG mode. The first configuration, NOARCHIVELOG mode, only protects you from instance failure. In this mode, whenever a redo log fills up with a transaction, it switches to the other redo log. So in essence it writes to each one in a circular fashion. Because it could eventually write over some previous transaction log information, NOARCHIVELOG mode will not protect you from media failure. In the ARCHIVELOG mode configuration, the redo logs are still used in a circular fashion, with one basic difference: the background process ARCH. Its job is to wake up when a redo log becomes inactive and write its contents out to a system file. In the event of a media failure, you will have a record of every transaction within the database, and you can replay the event to make the database whole.

Because the redo logs have the task of recording every committed transaction (note that transactions can be written to the redo logs before they are committed), you can see what great potential redo logs have to become an impediment to good system performance. Let's take a look at how we can tune the redo logs to help your system gain great system throughput.

REDO LOGS: The I/O Perspective
Whenever you look at system performance, you must look at I/O. It is one of the most expensive operations a computer can perform. One of the major benefits of Version 6 was that it eliminated the I/O bottleneck associated with **commit**: it took the process of commit and broke it into numerous I/O streams. For example, if you run the following statement,

```
UPDATE MY_TABLE
SET COL1 = 'NEW VALUE';
```

you have three clear I/O streams:

- As the update occurs, it is recorded in the rollback segment. Remember that the rollback segment is used in case the transaction is aborted. If aborted, it will roll the database back to the way it was before you started the update.

- Once you commit the transaction, the record of the commit is recorded in the redo log. In the event of system failure, Oracle will be able to recover itself. Think of **commit** as meaning that somewhere a copy of the transaction was written to disk.

- Over time, the database will record the change back onto the datafile. Remember, Oracle does a great job of keeping hot spots (frequently accessed user and dictionary data) in memory.

ISSUES RULE #33
Always put your redo logs on a separate disk from your datafiles.

Redo Logs: Memory Issues

The problem with redo logs is that when a log switch occurs, the SGA is flushed. A log switch occurs when the redo log fills up and it must switch over to another redo log to record further transactions. Once again, the log switch forces a database checkpoint to occur, which tells Oracle to flush the SGA to ensure system integrity.

The good side of this is that if you have frequent checkpoints and your system crashes, then your recovery will be quick.

The bad side is that by flushing the SGA, you loose the benefits of keeping hot spots in memory. It is a very expensive process to retrieve information off a disk, compared to fetching information out of memory. So here's what you do: as a rule of thumb, have much larger redo logs. In fact, try to time log switches so that they only happen at lunch and off-hours. If the system were to crash, it might take the database a lot longer to recover. But let's be honest: in a stable environment, the system will very rarely crash. So if you can obtain substantial performance gains 360 days out of the year, while two to five times a year the system crashes and it takes longer to recover—we can consider that a home run. Major performance gains for minimal risk. Remember, all tuning is specific to your situation. However, here are two general rules that probably apply to 98 percent of all customers who ask, "How do I make sure my log switches happen less often?"

- Make your redo logs a lot bigger.

■ Set the initialization parameter file entry LOG_CHECKPOINT_INTERVAL
to a size greater than the redo logs file size. And set the
LOG_CHECKPOINT_TIMEOUT parameter to 0. By making these
two changes, only when the redo log files fill up and cause a
log switch will you have a checkpoint. Finally, enable the
checkpoint process.

The LOG_CHECKPOINT_INTERVAL parameter forces a checkpoint when a
predetermined number of redo log blocks have been written to disk relative to the
last database checkpoint.

The LOG_CHECK_POINT_TIMEOUT parameter can be set to force a
database checkpoint based on the number of seconds after the previous database
checkpoint started.

To enable an additional background process, set the CHECKPOINT_PROCESS
parameter to TRUE. This will invoke a process whose job it is to help with the
checkpoint process. (In normal situations, this would be done by the LGWR process.)
When you start to see checkpoints cause degradation of system performance, then
you should set this parameter to TRUE. This process will never write to datafiles,
but it will take over the task of updating the headers of all the database datafiles.
In a database with a lot of datafiles, this would probably make sense.

Here are two SQL statements that are very useful when working with redo logs:

```
Select  *  from  v$ log;
Group#   Thread#   Sequence#     Bytes   Members   ARC     Status   First_change
      1         1         273   10485760         2   YES   INACTIVE          50601
      2         1         274   10485760         2    No   Current           50601
      3         1         275   10485760         2   YES   INACTIVE          50601
```

```
Select  *  from  V$logfile;
Group    Status      Member
1                    /u01/redo/redo_log1.log
1                    /u02/redo/redo_mirror1.log
2                    /u01/redo/redo_log2.log
2                    /u02/redo/redo_mirror2.log
```

You will need these SQL statements when you are ready to change the redo log files.

Let's Tune It

This section summarizes the main points of this chapter and is designed for the
DBA who needs to tune the database quickly. Later, when you have more time,

you can go back and read the specifics presented in this chapter. Following is a number of steps to make your database perform better, based on situations we see in most environments.

- Increase the initialization parameter file entry DB_BLOCK_BUFFERS. This is your data cache. Before a database can present, manipulate, or examine a piece of data, it must first reside in this cache. The larger the data cache, the more likely the Oracle database will have what it needs in memory. The smaller the cache, the more likely Oracle will have to issue I/Os to put the information in the cache.

- Increase the initialization parameter file entry SHARED_POOL_SIZE. This is your library cache and data dictionary cache. This is where Oracle stores information it needs to manage itself. If the cache is large enough, it will greatly reduce the amount of reparsing Oracle has to do or the time it takes to manage itself.

- Distribute your I/O stream and separate data from indexes. I/O is one of the most expensive operations a computer can perform. You can't eliminate all I/O, so it is best to be wise about your I/O streams. On the data side, you should separate your data and indexes. On the update side, you should look at separating your rollback segments, redo logs, and archive logs. On the system overhead side, you should separate your system tablespace, your TOOLS tablespace, and your TEMP tablespace.

- Evaluate your index scheme. One of the quickest ways to make Oracle perform well is to add needed indexes. Be generous about this. Also look for tables that have no indexes.

- Enlarge your redo logs. If you have a very stable environment, where the computer very rarely crashes, then think about making your checkpoints occur less often (remember, a checkpoint causes your SGA to be flushed). To do this, make your redo logs a lot bigger. Then set CHECK_POINT_INTERVAL greater than your redo log size.

- Enable the CHECKPOINT_PROCESS. It never hurts to have an additional process to share the work load.

- Increase your SORT_AREA_SIZE. Sorting is a major part of life in an Oracle database; try increasing your SORT_AREA_SIZE to eliminate sorting to disk.

- Eliminate chained blocks. If you suspect chaining in your database and it is small enough, export and import the entire database. This will repack the database, eliminating any chained blocks.

CHAPTER 6

Show Stoppers

Show stoppers do just that. "Stop the show—something weird's going on! Get the users to log off NOW! The instance has to come down!" The show (your applications) starts to behave in different ways. Previously unseen error situations come up all of a sudden. Experienced DBAs (yes you and us included!) run into this from time to time. In this chapter, we will guide you through some show stopping that can be avoided with knowledge and planning.

Number of Database Files

There is a finite number of database files that can be used by an Oracle instance. You must operate Oracle within the limits imposed by your operating system. At the same time, while staying within these limits, the DB_FILES entry in your initialization parameter file limits the number of datafiles that may be acquired by your instance. As well, the **maxdatafiles** parameter used when a database is created dictates the absolute maximum number of database files whose information may be tracked in a control file.

STOPPERS RULE #1
The lowest number specified by any of these three items (operating system restrictions, DB_FILES, or **maxdatafiles**) is the one that affects the other two.

For example, if your operating system limits you to an open file limit of 48, putting

```
db_files = 60
```

in your initialization parameter file or using a **maxdatafiles** value of 54 when creating a database will permit you to have 48 files open. Likewise, if your **maxdatafiles** is set to 16, and your operating system permits 64 open files for each user, putting

```
db_files = 32
```

in your initialization parameter file will still only permit you to have 16 datafiles open at the same time.

Operating System Limits

You must operate Oracle within the limits laid out by your operating system. Keep in mind that the maximum number of files that a user can have open concurrently may impact on the database configuration some point down the road when you least expect it. As your instance (or instances) approaches that number, you will have problems adding more files without intervention by your hardware support personnel. Your database has to be down and stay down while these hardware persons do whatever has to be done to increase that number.

For scenario #1, picture a corporate development environment. There are six databases owned by a UNIX account called oracle. There are 14 control files, 18 redo log group members, and 46 datafiles all used by that user.

Suppose the maximum number of open files dictated by your UNIX operating system is 128. Table 6-1 shows the minimum number of files used by Oracle (78 open files) for this six-database configuration. With the assortment of *trace files* (files written by Oracle that track system and user activities against the database)

DATABASE NAME	CONTROL FILES	REDO LOGS	DATAFILES
dev	3	3	8
tst	2	3	8
uacc	2	3	8
case	3	3	8
proto	2	3	8
prior	2	3	6
Totals:	14	18	46

TABLE 6-1. *Number of files allocated to six Oracle instances on the same machine*

and the six instance alert files (each instance maintains its own alert file for system event logging), the 128 limit could be easily exceeded. When it is exceeded you get a show stopper:

SHOW STOPPER
concurrent open file limit needs adjusting!

For scenario #2, consider the following. An Oracle instance is shut down once a week for a full image backup. When the backup completes, the machine is rebooted and Oracle is started. The file limit quota for the process that brings up Oracle is set at 20. The current number of database files, redo logs, trace files, alert file, and control files is 18. It should be noted that as far as the operating system is concerned, an open file is an open file. Therefore all files should be accounted for when setting a limit for an operating system process. During the week three new database files were created. The operating system did not have a problem with Oracle creating the additional files. What did happen was that when the database was started after the full image backup, it would not come up. The error message was very cryptic. It stated that it could not open a file because it was locked. After about 2 hours of investigating this problem with a number of coworkers in the middle of the night, we recalled that a number of files were added. The open file quota of the Oracle start up process was checked and it was discovered to be too low. After increasing it to the operating system maximum, the instance was able to start up without any problem. This time delay can be costly, not to mention frustrating, to the end user.

SHOW STOPPER

database down an extra 2 hours after backups!

STOPPERS RULE #2

Be aware of limits that may be placed on the number of open files by your operating system. Work with your hardware personnel to ensure operating system limits are not exceeded by Oracle's requirements.

Oracle Limits

One initialization parameter file entry (DB_FILES) and one parameter (**maxdatafiles**) used with the **create database** SQL command have an effect on the number of files your instance may acquire.

DB_FILES

The most common occurrence is when you try to add a file to your configuration, and you exceed the DB_FILES initialization parameter file entry. DB_FILES can be increased (governed naturally by the operating system limits mentioned above), but the instance has to be shut down and then restarted for the new value to take effect. The need to adjust DB_FILES is a show stopper:

SHOW STOPPER

database coming down to activate new value!

Consider the following real-life scenario we have experienced. Our finance people were attempting to complete a travel claim transaction (underlying table is called TRAV_AUDIT), and is receiving error

```
ORA-01547: failed to allocate extent of size 1024 in tablespace 'PRD_IDX'
```

The application is using Oracle Forms, and the activity is creating a new index entry in the TRAV_AUDIT_1 index on the TRAV_AUDIT table. For whatever reason, there is not enough space available in the PRD_IDX tablespace to satisfy the request for 1,024 blocks of space (the instance this error message was received on has an Oracle block size of 4K or 4,096 bytes—thus, the error indicates the application is requesting 1024×4096 or 4,194,304 bytes or just over 4MB). This is the explanation and suggested resolution for this problem.

```
01547, 00000, "failed to allocate extent of size %s in tablespace '%s'"
// *Cause: Tablespace indicated is out of space
// *Action: Use ALTER TABLESPACE ADD DATAFILE statement to add one or more
//     files to the tablespace indicated or create the object in other
//     tablespace if this happens during a CREATE statement
```

The natural step to take is to add another datafile to the PRD_IDX tablespace by running the command (using UNIX as an example platform). This command returns an Oracle error. Even though the SQL in the code is syntactically correct and the filename passed to UNIX is correct, an Oracle error is raised.

```
alter tablespace prd_idx
add datafile '/usr/ora/prd/indexes_prd_2.dbf' size 10M;
alter tablespace prd_idx
                       *
ERROR at line 1:
ORA-01118: cannot add any more database files: limit of 40 exceeded
```

In this case, there was an entry in the initialization parameter file that said

```
db_files = 40
```

That entry was changed to

```
db_files = 60
```

The instance restarted and the extra file added to the PRD_IDX tablespace.

MAXDATAFILES

A value for this parameter is included when a database is created. Its value affects the size of your instance control file(s)—these control file(s) must be large enough to hold information for all database files. If and when this parameter needs to be increased, you must rebuild your control file. In Chapter 9, we discuss an Oracle7 feature where you instruct Oracle to make a text copy of the SQL statements required to rebuild the control file. The need to change the value of **maxdatafiles** is a show stopper.

SHOW STOPPER
database down to rebuild control files!

STOPPERS RULE #3
Set the **maxdatafiles** parameter in the **create database** command to a number that will permit you to double the number of database files your instance uses.

STOPPERS RULE #4
When **maxdatafiles** needs to be increased, use **alter database backup controlfile to trace**.

Recreating a Database

If the need arises to perform this activity, you need to prepare yourself beforehand to minimize down time. If you are not prepared you have a show stopper.

SHOW STOPPER
need to recreate a database delayed!

Below is a standard **create database** script. Comment text is delimited by the "#" sign since this runs in sqldba.

```
# Step 1
#
# Start the database with the nomount option.  This is the only
# mode the following create statement will run in since the database
# does not yet exist
connect internal
startup nomount pfile=?/dbs/initdevel.ora
# Step 2
#
# Create the database.  Notice how the "controlfile reuse" line
# tells Oracle to reuse the current control files if it finds them
# where they are specified in the initialization parameter file.
# Even though we ask for 2 redo log files, Orace7 will actually create
# 2 single-membered redo log groups.  The "maxdatafiles" and
# "maxlogmembers" parameters are examples of database parameters
# that can only be set in when the database is created (or a new
# control file created as we discuss in Chapter 8.
```

```
# The default for this statement is "noarchivelog",
# we put it here just as a reminder.  You do not want the database
# to archive redo logs when you do the full database import.
create database devel
        controlfile reuse
        datafile '?/dbs/dbs1devel.dbf'         size 20M
        logfile '/sys1/ora/log1devel.dbf'     size 2M,
                '/sys2/ora/log2dvel.dbf'      size 2M
      maxdatafiles 40,
      maxlogmembers 6,
      noarchivelog;
# Step 3
#
# Open the database and create the first non-system rollback
# segment.  You need at least one non-system rollback segment before
# you can create a tablespace.  We always make this rollback segment
# small - based on these storage parameters, it will never grow over
# 500K (512,000 bytes).
alter database open;
create rollback segment temp
      tablespace system
      storage (initial 100K next 100K minextents 1 maxextents 5);
alter rollback segment temp online;
# Step 5
#
# Set up the data dictionary which ends up in the SYS account.  Then
# run the script "catproc.sql" that installs the procedural option.
# Then set up the views required to run the export and import utilities
# that should end up as part of your system backups.
@?/rdbms/admin/catalog.sql
@?/rdbms/admin/catproc.sql
@?/rdbms/admin/catexp.sql
@?/rdbms/admin/catldrg.sql
# Step 6
#
# As the SYSTEM user, set up private synonyms pointing at all the
# data dictionary views prefixed with the characters "dba_".  Then
# run the script to build the PRODUCT_USER_PROFILE table.  This
# table can be used to restrict certain SQL or SQL*Plus commands
# for individual or classes of Oracle users.  Without at least
# building this table, any user other than SYSTEM that enters
# SQL*Plus is told "Warning! Product user profile information
```

```
# not loaded".
connect system/manager
@?/rdbms/admin/catdbsyn
@?/sqlplus/admin/pupbld
```

We cannot stress enough the importance of adding this skill to your skill set as a DBA. It has been our experience that less than 50 percent of the DBAs out there have ever done this. Now is the time! This leads into our next rule.

STOPPERS RULE #5
Learn how to create a database and practice before you are forced to do so during a real-life emergency.

Free List Contention

As we discuss in a number of places throughout this book, Oracle maintains data dictionary information in memory. This allows almost instantaneous access to information that resides on disk but has been loaded into memory. Some of the information in memory keeps track of the space that is available in the tablespaces for inserting new rows. When tables are created, you can instruct Oracle how much information to keep in memory for blocks that are available for creating records. This is referred to as the *freelist* for the table. When creating a table, the **create table** would look like the following SQL.

```
create table my_table (seq number,
                    my_key varchar2(10),
                    desc varchar2(40))
                    freelist 12;
```

The **freelist** setting of 12 overrides the Oracle default of 1. Whatever this parameter is set to is the number of block IDs that Oracle will maintain in memory that are candidates for record insertion. When Oracle needs space in a table to create a new record, it searches the table's free list in memory until it either finds a block that can hold the new information, or runs out of block IDs. If there are no block IDs in memory that can accommodate the new record, Oracle reads more dictionary information from disk. As multiuser applications run, there are many situations where a number of transactions are simultaneously looking for a block to insert data into. This can lead to another show stopper.

SHOW STOPPER

excessive disk I/O to satisfy requests for block IDs to create new rows!

This bottleneck is called *freelist contention*. Freelist contention occurs when multiple processes are searching the **freelist** at the same time and, when the end of the list is reached, requesting additional information from disk. Mimimizing I/O, as we have advised you throughout this book, is one of the biggest contributors to tuning.

You can assess the freelist contention that is going on in your database by looking at the v$waitstat and v$sysstat dictionary views owned by SYS. Use the following queries to compute the percent of the two figures against one another. The first query will tell you how many freelist wait situations have been detected. The second will tell you how many total requests for data have been recorded in the dictionary.

```
SQL> select class,count from v$waitstat where class = 'free list';
CLASS                   COUNT
---------------------- -----
free list                  59


SQL> select name,value from v$sysstat
  2  where name in ('db_block_gets','consistent gets');
CLASS                   COUNT
---------------------- -----------
db block gets            12850
consistent gets          10119
```

The result returned in the first query (59) is then used to compute the percent of requests for data that resulted in a wait for a resource initiated by not enough **freelist**. Using the queries' results,

```
freelist wait events = (free list count) / (db block gets +
                                            consistent gets) * 100
                  = 59 / (12850 + 10119) * 100
                  = 59 / 22969 = 0.26
```

This means that less than 1 percent of the requests for data resulted in a **freelist** wait situation.

STOPPERS RULE #6
If the number of waits for free blocks is greater than 1 percent of the total number of requests, consider increasing the **freelist** parameter on your insert and update intensive tables.

We continue to stress the importance of knowing your applications. Adjustments to the **freelist** parameters is a situation where you must know which tables are high insert and update as mentioned in the last rule. To change this parameter for a table, you need to do the following.

1. Export the data from the table with the grants and indexes.

2. Drop the table.

3. Recreate the table with an increased **freelist** parameter.

4. Import the data back into the table ensuring you code IGNORE=Y when you run the import.

Since many users may be accessing a table at the same time as your applications run, you need to ensure there are at least enough **freelist** entries to accommodate this concurrent access. This leads us into our next rule.

STOPPERS RULE #7
Have a sufficient number of **freelist** entries for a table to accommodate the number of concurrent processes that will be inserting data into that table.

Do You Really Have 999 Extents?

Space for tables and indexes is allocated in chunks of space called *extents*. Space not presently allocated to a table is used to satisfy requests for additional space by existing objects. The number of extents a table may use is determined by the **maxextents** parameter when a table is created, as shown in the following listing.

```
create table my_table (seq number,
                       my_key varchar2(10),
                       desc varchar2(40))
         storage (initial 500K next 100K pctincrease 0 maxextents 999)
         pctfree 15 pctused 85 freelist 12;
```

In fact, the maximum number of extents that may be used by a table is determined by the Oracle block size. Oracle allocates space in blocks, and the block size can be between 512 and 8192 (commonly called 8K) bytes. It is set when the database is created, and cannot be changed afterwards. The block size is determined by the initialization parameter file entry DB_BLOCK_SIZE. If you look in this file, you may not see the initialization parameter anywhere. This indicates you are using your platform's default (this may vary from hardware to hardware). Regardless of whether the entry is there, you can always see its current value in sqldba. As the following listing suggests, Oracle stores instance parameters in its data dictionary.

```
SQLDBA> connect internal

Connected.

SQLDBA> show parameters db_block_size

db_block_size                         integer    4096
```

The following table shows the actual maximum number of extents that can be allocated to a table based on the two most common block sizes we have experience with.

BLOCK SIZE	MAXIMUM # OF EXTENTS
2048	121
4096	240

As you monitor the extent allocation for your tables, keep in mind these numbers. If you don't, here's another show stopper:

SHOW STOPPER
table needs more space and more extents cannot be allocated!

When you reach the maximum number of extents, there is only one thing to remedy the situation—recreate the table with more appropriate space allocated at creation time. If you have not yet reached the maximum extents for a table, and wish to increase the **maxextents** parameter, issue the following statement.

```
alter table my_table storage (maxextents 240)
```

To monitor extent allocation, you need to look in the data dictionary table dba_extents belonging to Oracle user SYS. To see what a table's current maximum number of extents is, you look in dba_tables belonging to SYS. Inspect the following queries and their comments to see how to accomplish this.

```
rem * What is the maximum number of extents that MY_TABLE can occupy?
SQL> select maxextents from sys.dba_tables
  2 where table_name = 'MY_TABLE' and owner = 'ITSME';
MAXEXTENTS
----------
        99
rem * How many extents does it have now?
SQL> select count(*) from sys.dba_extents
  2 where segment_name = 'MY_TABLE' and
  3 segment_owner = 'ITSME';
COUNT(*)
---------
      98
```

When a request is made for the next extent, there will be no problem. When a request for the one after that is made, the request will be denied for the 100th extent. You can increase the number of extents using the **alter** statement shown in the section "Oracle Limits," earlier in this chapter.

NOTE
Even with this discussion of extents, we recommend that you track extent allocation and fix situations where tables have more that 10 extents allocated to them.

This leads us into our next few rules.

STOPPERS RULE #8
Monitor expansion of tables in your database and plan for table reorganization before you run out of extents.

STOPPERS RULE #9
Learn how to re-create your database using the SQL command **create database**. If and when you want to change the block size, re-creating your database is the only way to do it.

After this discussion about block size, we feel it is worth mentioning the following rule (actually more of a suggestion).

STOPPERS RULE #10
If you use Oracle on a platform that permits it, set your Oracle block size to 4K (4,096 bytes) or even 8K (8,192 bytes).

Runaway Size (PCTINCREASE)

The storage **pctincrease** is used when creating tables, tablespaces, indexes, and clusters. Without fully understanding usage of **pctincrease**, you can create a show stopper.

SHOW STOPPER
unpredictable and runaway amounts of space being eaten up by tables!

When speaking about this parameter, we need to mention **initial** and **next** to discuss the concept of **pctincrease** fully. Starting with version 6 of Oracle, you were given control over the fine tuning of space allocation. Consider the following **create table** statement.

```
create table my_table (seq number,
                       my_key varchar2(10),
                       desc varchar2(40))
      storage (initial 100K next 100K pctincrease 0);
```

The three keywords in the parentheses after the word **storage** and their values are as follows:

- **initial** is the amount of space allocated to a table when created—in this case, 100K (102,400 bytes) of space is reserved for data when the table is created.

- **next** is the size of the first extent allocated when the table needs additional space—here, though not always, it is the same as **initial**.

- **pctincrease** is the percent that each extent (other than the first as sized by the **next** value) exceeds the size of the previous extent.

EXTENT ID	EXTENT SIZE IN BYTES
1	12288
2	20480
3	40960
4	61440
5	81920
6	122880
7	184320
8	266240
9	389120

TABLE 6-2. *Extent sizes for initial 4K next 10K pctincrease 50*

Oracle uses 50 as the default for **pctincrease**. You need to visit that value when you create tables. The size of extents can grow exponentially—think of the doubling penny concept. If you were to start with a single penny and keep doubling it every day, you would be a very rich person in a remarkably short time period! In a mere 18 days, you would have over $10,000. Tables 6-2, 6-3, and 6-4 show the size of extents allocated to three tables with the listed storage parameters. These tables exist in a database where the Oracle block size is 4K (4,096 bytes).

EXTENT ID	EXTENT SIZE IN BYTES
1	102400
2	163840
3	245760
4	368640
5	532480

TABLE 6-3. *Extent sizes for initial 500K next 100K pctincrease 50*

EXTENT ID	EXTENT SIZE IN BYTES
1	102400
2	102400
3	102400
4	102400
5	102400
6	102400
7	102400
8	102400

TABLE 6-4.   *Extent sizes for initial 100K next 100K pctincrease 0*

If the **pctincrease** of a table needs adjusting, issue the command

```
alter table my_table storage (pctincrease 0);
```

Naturally, this will take effect with the next extent allocated. Those already used by a table stay as they are. Keep in mind that once an extent is allocated to a table, it belongs to that table for the life of the table. The only time extents are deallocated from a table is when that table is re-created.

STOPPERS RULE #11
Set the **pctincrease** to 0 when creating tables. Look at existing tables and reset this value to 0.

Situations may arise that have extraordinary space requirements. Say that, for example, according to the formula

```
next extent size = previous extent size * pctincrease / 100
```

you know that a table is going to need 1MB (one megabyte or 1,024,000 bytes) for some new records. Prior to Oracle7, you had to change the **next** value, create the new rows, then change the value back to what it was previously. You can now do the following.

```
alter table my_table allocate extent size 1M;
```

The worry about doing it the old way is if you ever forget to change the storage parameters back to what they used to be, you may continue to grab 1MB rather than the 100K (what the **next** value was before you changed it).

STOPPERS RULE #12
When you require space for a table larger than the next extent will be, use the SQL statement **alter table allocate extent** rather than adjusting the storage parameters for the table.

Free Space in Indexes

Correct sizing of indexes becomes even more crucial when we discuss how Oracle deals with index entries for rows deleted from tables. Oracle will not reuse index space in blocks whose corresponding data rows have been deleted. For example, using a 2K block size, say each index entry for a table takes up 50 bytes, and the index has **initrans** set to 2. There are 46 bytes reserved for transaction information, leaving 2,002 bytes for index entries. The index block will hold up to 40 index entries. If 50 percent of the rows a full index block points to are deleted, Oracle will not use the 1,000 bytes freed up. This could lead to another show stopper.

SHOW STOPPER
runaway space consumption on indexes pointing to tables undergoing high delete activity!

This indicates that you need to monitor the amount of index space dedicated to deleted rows. First, you need to **validate** an index, then look at statistics in the INDEX_STATS dictionary view. Use the following query.

```
SQL> validate index product_1;

Index analyzed.

SQL> select lf_rows,lf_rows_len,del_lf_rows,del_lf_rows_len
  2  from index_stats where name = 'PRODUCT_1';
```

```
LF_ROWS LF_ROWS_LEN DEL_LF_ROWS DEL_LF_ROWS_LEN
---------- ----------- ----------- ---------------
     53075     1576044        5789          164308
```

From examining this output, there are now 53,075 values in the index, whose space consumption in the index amounts to 1,576,044 bytes. There are 5,789 slots in the index that used to point to rows that have been deleted, consuming 164,308 bytes of space in the index. Thus, 10.91 percent of the space allocated to the PRODUCT_1 index is taken up by what we call "dead entries."

STOPPERS RULE #13
When the deleted row space in an index is over 20 percent of the space being used in the index, you should drop and re-create the index to reclaim unused space.

Transaction Space

The **initrans**, **maxtrans**, and **pctfree** parameters control the amount of space that keeps track of transactions against a table. The **initrans** parameter sets aside 23 bytes for each transaction slot in each data block that resides in a table. Space is reserved in a data block for data and header information. Data will be loaded into data blocks until it occupies an amount dictated by the **pctfree** entry for each table. If this **pctfree** is set to 40 for a table, Oracle will reserve 40 percent of each block (1,638 bytes of a 4,096-byte or 4K block) free for expansion of column values in existing rows. The space left over for expansion of existing records we call the pctfree space. If your applications need to support concurrent access to a table by more than one user, you should increase this **initrans** value. Oracle will allocate space in a data block for transactions in these 23-byte slices, and will allocate up to the number of slots delineated by **maxtrans**. If **maxtrans** is set too low you have a show stopper:

SHOW STOPPER
block contention—transaction space limited in data blocks!

Using a 2K (2,048 bytes) block size as an example, Oracle will initially reserve 23 bytes of transaction space in the header of the data block with the following **create index** statement

```
create index my_index on my_table (seq,my_key)
        storage (initrans 1 maxtrans 4);
```

This header is in the same physical location as the block itself. Each block is logically made up of header space and data space. If the my_index index ever needs transaction space for four concurrent transactions, Oracle will use the extra three slots, bringing the total transaction space up to 92 bytes. Those 92 bytes are taken from the free data space and, when the slots are no longer needed, they are not deallocated from the header space as unused data space. If a fifth concurrent transaction needed a transaction slot, it queues itself behind a transaction already using one of the slots. It then uses that slot when the previous transaction completes. Thus, if **maxtrans** is set too low, you will get another show stopper.

SHOW STOPPER
wait time for previous transactions to terminate!

STOPPERS RULE #14
Set **initrans** high enough at least to accommodate the expected number of concurrent transactions a table experiences.

STOPPERS RULE #15
Set **maxtrans** to the value of **initrans** + 2.

STOPPERS RULE #16
When raising **initrans** and **maxtrans** for a table, raise it for the data and index components at the same time. After all, inserting a row into a table also requires creation of an additional index entry.

Dual Table

We have experienced an odd show stopper in a few databases. The DUAL table belongs to the Oracle user SYS. Prior to the introduction of PL/SQL with version 6, all we could do to perform arithmetic, string, and conversion operations was reference this DUAL table in our applications. Table 6-5 shows the difference between using SQL and using PL/SQL to perform a few operations.

Even when using PL/SQL, some assignment statements (those in the right-hand column of Table 6-5 with the ":=" sign) access this DUAL table implicitly:

```
today := sysdate;
logged_in := user;
```

If there happens to be more than one row in DUAL, you get a show stopper:

SHOW STOPPER
applications behaving in unusual ways all of a sudden!

You may wonder how this is possible. We have no concrete recollection of how this occurs—perhaps a DBA inadvertently makes a typo when coding an **insert** statement into something other than DUAL while logged into the database as SYS and creates the row by mistake! Any user can detect the number of rows in DUAL using the following.

```
SQL> select count(*) from dual;
    COUNT(*)
------------
           1
SQL> select * from dual;
DUMMY
------------
X
```

SQL USING DUAL	PL/SQL WITHOUT USING DUAL
select 2+4 into :accumulator from dual;	:accumulator := 2+4;
select substr(char_val,1,4) into part_of_char from dual;	part_of_char := substr(char_val,1,4)
select to_char(date_val) into char_val from dual;	char_val := to_char(date_val)

TABLE 6-5. *Statements with and without DUAL*

If the output from one or both of the above queries shows more than one row, issue the following statement while logged on as SYS.

```
SQL> delete dual where rownum = 1;
1 row deleted.
```

ARCHIVELOG Destination Full

We have recommended running your production database in ARCHIVELOG mode. We discuss this concept in a number of places (see Chapter 9). Oracle makes a copy of redo logs before it reuses them and places that copy in a location specified by the two initialization parameter file entries LOG_ARCHIVE_DEST and LOG_ARCHIVE_FORMAT. It is your responsibility to monitor the space on the drive where Oracle writes archived redo logs. If the destination fills to capacity, the next time Oracle tries to archive a redo log, you have a show stopper:

SHOW STOPPER
archive process unable to complete redo log copy!

This unfortunate situation is evident in the following two ways.

- Users signing into Oracle Forms–based applications are suddenly presented with the secure database login screen, and asked to enter a username and password.

- Users entering SQL*Plus are presented with the Oracle error 00257, meaning.

```
00257, 00000, "archiver error. Connect internal only, until freed."
// *Cause:  The archiver process received an error while trying to archive
//    a log.  Unless the problem is resolved soon, the database will
//    stop executing transactions.
// *Action:  By far the most likely cause of the error is the archive
//    destination device is out of space.  Check archiver trace file
//    for detail description of the problem.
```

We have found the following reasons for the archive directory to suddenly fill up during normal operating conditions.

■ The previous night's backup routine, which is supposed to put archived redo logs out to tape and then erase them, for some reason aborted the last time it ran—the step that was supposed to erase them never ran.

■ An application has deleted a large number of rows from a very large table, and the redo log files written by that transaction alone created a very large number of archived redo logs.

■ If your archive log destination drive shares space with other Oracle database files, you may have inadvertently drastically reduced the available space by adding a datafile to a tablespace that resides on that drive.

This leads into our next few rules.

STOPPERS RULE #17
Monitor the available space on the directory that contains your archived redo logs. If its utilization climbs over 90 percent, it may require immediate intervention.

STOPPERS RULE #18
Dedicate enough space in your archive log destination to hold at least two full days of archived redo logs.

STOPPERS RULE #19
Archived redo logs should be backed up every day and deleted afterwards. Do not rely on manual purging of the archived redo log destination.

Picture the following scenario that happened to one of our clients using Oracle on HP-UX. They were having a problem with locking on a few central tables in their application and decided to shut down the database then restart it at once. Closing and subsequently reopening will cause any locks that were held to be released. When they brought the database up, the very first user that attempted to connect was presented with the secure database logon screen as mentioned previously. They looked at the space utilization on the archive destination, knowing it must be 100 percent. They had filled up this drive a number of times and felt, as we would have, smug in being so quick to recognize the situation. The UNIX *bdf* command reported the utilization of the destination drive was a mere 72 percent. Briefly, this is what had happened (it may not happen to you, but isn't is interesting how easily the show can be stopped?).

- Oracle is responsible for making the copy of a redo log in the archive destination.

- There is a UNIX concept (as with most operating systems) of file protection. When Oracle is in the midst of copying the redo log, the file protection is set to 000—this means that no processes are allowed to overwrite the archived redo log until the copying is complete.

- If the background process ARCH (as discussed in Chapter 2) does not complete the copying, the file protection is left at 000.

- When the copying completes, the protection of the file is changed to 640, meaning that Oracle can overwrite it if necessary.

- When the database was first shut down, Oracle had partially archived a redo log but, since the copy was not complete, the file protection for the archived redo log was left at 000.

- When the database was brought up, one of the first things it did was try to create a complete copy of the archived redo log it had started to create but had not finished.

- Since it could not overwrite the partially created archived redo log, the database sat in limbo until the partially copied redo log was erased manually.

- When the partially copied redo log was erased, Oracle carried on re-creating the full copy of the archived redo log and all was well once again.

Restricted Database Access

In Chapter 4, we discussed the Oracle7 feature whereby you can restrict access to the database by issuing the command

```
alter system enable restricted session;
```

When a database is operating in this mode, only users or roles explicitly granted permission to use the database in this mode are permitted to log on. If you put your database in restricted mode, you could have a show stopper:

SHOW STOPPER
DBA forgot to take database out of restricted mode and nobody can log on!

Fortunately, the database can be returned to unrestricted access by issuing the command

```
alter system disable restricted session;
```

from sqldba or SQL*Plus. If you use this restricted access feature, you may wish to do what our next rule suggests.

STOPPERS RULE #20
Take your database out of restricted access daily before all your users start logging on.

If your database was inadvertently left in restricted access mode, this will ensure access is unrestricted before your users attempt to sign on. If the database access was already unrestricted, no harm done.

Getting Locked Up by Locks

As discussed in Chapter 5, the initialization parameter file entry DML_LOCKS sets the maximum number of locks that can be placed on all objects by all users at one time. If this entry is set too low you have a show stopper:

SHOW STOPPER
applications raising Oracle errors due to too few DML_LOCKS!

We have found through our experience that the default value for this entry is too low and must be raised.

STOPPERS RULE #21
Set DML_LOCKS in your initialization parameter file to the number of concurrent users times 10.

▮ Let's Tune It

This chapter is different from others in this book. The material presented affects the ability of Oracle to run uninterrupted. We have presented the theme in a number of spots throughout this book that a down database is not a tuned database. The points we present in this chapter are relevant—they are a series of known situations to watch out for. Being aware of potential problems before they happen to you is part of the tuning approach.

- Ensure the operating system open file limit is high enough to allow Oracle to have more than enough open files to support all database operations.

- Allow enough transaction space (through setting of **initrans** and **maxtrans**) in your data blocks to support concurrent user access.

- Set **pctincrease** for tables to 0 when they are created.

- Know how to reorganize your tables using a combination of export and import.

- Track the space dedicated to deleted rows in your tables' indexes and re-create indexes when the percent is over 20.

- Monitor the disk utilization of the directory that receives your archived redo logs.

- When required, manually allocate large extents to tables that exceed the tables' current storage parameters using **alter table allocate extent** rather than adjusting these parameters beforehand and resetting them after.

- Learn how to create a database and become fluent with the series of SQL scripts that need to be run on a fresh database to set up the data dictionary.

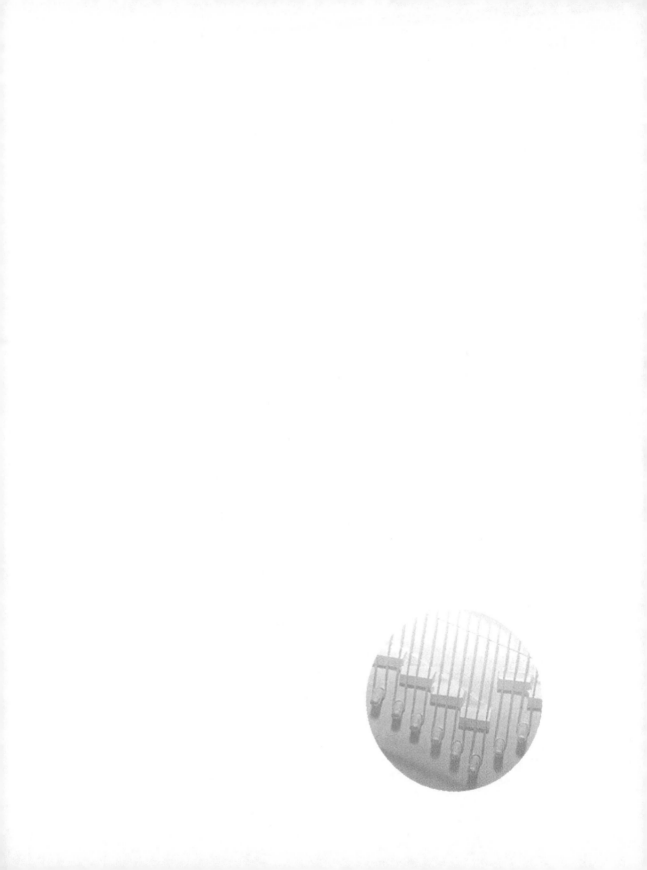

CHAPTER 7

Application Tuning

As with all computer programming languages, tuning plays an important role with Oracle. Due to added memory management enhancements with Oracle7, application and program tuning become even more crucial. You need to train yourself to optimize SQL statements, make use of central blocks of code (database triggers, procedures, functions, and packages), investigate declarative integrity, and use the off-the-shelf performance monitoring tools. Incorporating program tuning into on-going program development and maintenance allows you to code in ways that take advantage of the speed and throughput enhancing routines that Oracle continues to add to the software. DBA and hardware support personnel can tune the database and support hardware; without tuning applications, this effort may be *wasted*.

This chapter will discuss some of the tools at your disposal for tuning your applications. We will highlight some of the rules you should follow when choosing and setting up indexes to speed data retrieval. We will cover forms of generic code that you are encouraged to write to take advantage of the Oracle7 shared SQL area. Throughout this chapter are references to the *initialization parameter file,* which is a file read by Oracle whenever a database is started.

Table 7-1 shows the database objects that will be referenced in some of the application tuning examples in this chapter.

The Shared SQL Area

One of the turnkey performance enhancements with Oracle7 is the creation of an area in the SGA called the *shared pool.* This segment of memory is dedicated to holding parsed and executable SQL statements as well as the dictionary cache (see Chapter 2 for a discussion on this cache). Subsequent statements passed to Oracle are compared against statements in the shared pool. If, according to the following rules, the new statement matches an old statement already in the pool, Oracle executes the compiled statement rather than reprocessing the statement just received. In order to qualify for this matching condition, all three of the following rules must be true.

APPLICATION TUNING RULE 1
There must be a character-by-character match between the statement being examined and one already in the shared pool.

TABLE	COLUMN	DATATYPE
PEOPLE	PIN	NUMBER(6)
	POS_ID	NUMBER(2)
	LAST_NAME	VARCHAR2(20)
	FIRST_NAME	VARCHAR2(20)
PLANT_DETAIL	PLANT_ID	NUMBER(2)
	CITY_ID	NUMBER(2)
	LOCATION	VARCHAR2(20)
SAL_LIMIT	POS_ID	NUMBER(2)
	SAL_CAP	NUMBER(8,2)
	OVER_TIME	VARCHAR2(1)
WORK_CITY	CITY_ID	NUMBER(2)
	SDESC	VARCHAR2(20)
	LDESC	VARCHAR2(60)

TABLE 7-1. *Sample Database Tables*

NOTE
Before this comparison is performed, Oracle applies an internal algorithm using the new statement. It then checks the results against values of statements already in the pool. If the new value matches one already there, the string comparison outlined in Rule #1 is performed.

To illustrate Rule 1, consider the following Oracle statements and why they do or do not qualify.

1. select pin from person where last_name = 'LAU';

2. select PIN from person where last_name = 'LAU';

Statements 1 and 2 *do not* qualify because "pin" is lowercase in 1 and uppercase in 2.

1. select pin from person where last_name = 'LAU';

2. select pin from person where last_name = 'LAU';

Statements 1 and 2 *do* qualify because the case match of both statements is exactly the same.

1. select pin from person where last_name =
   'LAU';

2. select pin from person where last_name = 'LAU';

Statements 1 and 2 *do not* qualify because 1 is split over two lines whereas 2 is on a single line.

APPLICATION TUNING RULE 2
The objects being referenced in the new statement are exactly the same as those objects in a statement that has passed the comparison in Rule #1.

For this example, the users have access to the objects in Table 7-2.

NOTE
If an object referenced in SQL statement in the shared pool is modified, the statement is flagged as invalid. The next time a statement is passed to Oracle that is the same as that invalid statement, the old statement will be replaced by the new since the underlying object has been modified.

USER	OBJECT NAME	ACCESSED VIA
mcleodmg	sal_limit	private synonym
	work_city	public synonym
	plant_detail	public synonym
jproudf	sal_limit	private synonym
	work_city	public synonym
	plant_detail	table owner

TABLE 7-2. *Sample Database Objects for Two Users*

Consider the statements in Table 7-3 and why they can or cannot be shared between the two users listed in Table 7-2.

Table 7-3 shows that the objects are different. Even though both users have a private synonym sal_limit to refer to the same database table, these individual private synonyms are actually database objects themselves.

SQL STATEMENT	OBJECTS MATCHING	WHY
select max(sal_cap) from sal_limit;	NO	Each user has a private synonym **sal_limit** — these are different objects.
select count(*) from work_city where sdesc like 'NEW %';	YES	Both users reference **work_city** by the same public synonym — the same object.
select a.sdesc,b. location from work_city a,plant_detail b where a.city_id = b.city_id;	NO	User mcleodmg references **plant_detail** by a public synonym whereas user jproudf is the table owner — these are different objects.
select * from sal_limit where over_time is not null;	NO	Each user has a private synonym **sal_limit** — these are different objects.

TABLE 7-3. *Object Resolution of SQL Statements*

APPLICATION TUNING RULE 3
If bind variables are referenced, they must have the same name in both the new and existing statements.

As examples, the first two statements in the following listing are identical, whereas the next two statements are not (even if the different bind variables have the same value at run time).

```
select pin,pos_id,last_name,first_name from people where pin = :blk1.pin;
select pin,pos_id,last_name,first_name from people where pin = :blk1.pin;
select pos_id,sal_cap from sal_limit where over_time = :blk1.ot_ind;
select pos_id,sal_cap from sal_limit where over_time = :blk1.ov_ind;
```

Monitoring the Shared Pool

You may wonder what is sitting in the shared pool. Knowing what statements are already there assists you in coding SQL that matches. As mentioned in the previous section, by matching your statement to an already existing statement (according to the three rules outlined), you ensure that the one already there is reused. You can monitor the shared pool using full-screen sqldba. You must **connect internal** (log on to the database as user SYS), then issue the command **monitor sqlarea** to see the contents of the pool. Alternatively, once in sqldba and connected to the database, you can press the MENU key, select Monitor, then select the SQL Area option. The second method is shown in Figure 7-1.

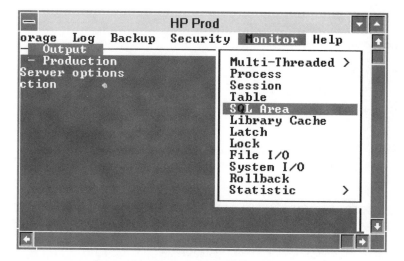

FIGURE 7-1. *Monitor sqlarea using the sqldba menu bar*

NOTE
Not all operating system accounts may be able to **connect internal**. Security is in place in most systems to make this a privileged operation. The **connect internal** command does not work anywhere else than sqldba.

The shared pool monitor display appears in Figure 7-2. Notice the shared pool contains PL/SQL blocks as well as SQL statements. The code that begins with the word **declare** is the start of a PL/SQL block. The code segments that start with the words **select** and **delete** are straight SQL. The other columns in the monitor screen are explained in Table 7-4.

The Persistent Memory row in Table 7-4 mentions cursors. According to the *Oracle7 Server Concepts Manual,* "A cursor is a handle (a name or pointer) for the memory associated with a specific statement."

One can also monitor the shared pool by querying v$sqlarea dictionary view in SQL*Plus. Figure 7-3 shows the number of users with cursors open for each statement and the number of users executing each cursor.

Tuning the Shared Pool

The shared pool holds shared SQL and PL/SQL statements (referred to as the *library cache*), the data dictionary cache, and information on sessions against the database. The size of the shared pool is dictated by the value in SHARED_POOL_SIZE in the initialization parameter file. DBAs may need to visit the size of the shared pool if they receive ORA-4031 errors (out of shared memory when allocating *num* bytes) when Oracle tries to find more space in the shared pool. Statements are placed in

```
┌─────────────────────────────────────────────────────────────────────┐
│ ▬                           HP Prod                                ▼ │
│ tatement Filter: %%                                                  │
│                                                                      │
│                              Version Sharable --Per User Memory--    │
│ QL Statement Text             Count   Memory  Persistent  Runtime    │
│                                                                      │
│               select lang_pref   1     7433      532      1440       │
│        declare                   0     4130        0         0       │
│        declare                   0     2467        0         0       │
│        declare                   0     4127        0         0       │
│        declare                   0     2995        0         0       │
│        declare                   0     2441        0         0       │
│        update chain_h            0      363        0         0       │
│ SELECT  TO_CHAR(sysdate, 'DD-MON-YY HH  1  4298   500      584       │
│ delete cww   where               0      466        0         0       │
│ commit                           0      205        0         0       │
│                                                                      │
│                                    ⟨Restart⟩  ⟨Hide⟩  ⟨Quit⟩         │
│                                                                      │
└─────────────────────────────────────────────────────────────────────┘
```

FIGURE 7-2. *Shared SQL area through sqldba*

COLUMN	MEANING
Version Count	If greater than zero, more than one user is using the statement.
Sharable Memory	Indicates the number of bytes shared by users using this statement at the same time.
Persistent Memory	Indicates the number of bytes per user while that user's cursor is open in the shared pool.
Runtime Memory	Indicates the number of bytes that is needed per user while the cursor is executing.

TABLE 7-4. *Interpreting the SQL Area Screen*

the shared pool and flushed according to an LRU (least recently used) algorithm. Even though the parsed form of statements are aged out of the pool, the SQL text remains in dictionary tables in memory for longer time periods (space permitting).

NOTE
The database must be shut down and restarted to activate a resize of the shared pool.

```
=                              HP Prod                                  ▼
SQL> select substr(sql_text,1,50)"Text",users_opening "Open",
  2         users_executing "Executing"
  3    from v$sqlarea
  4  order by 2,3 desc
  5  /

Text                                                  Open   Executing
-------------------------------------------------    ------  ---------
            select lang_pref                    f      4         2
     declare                                           4         2
     declare                                           4         2
     declare                                           4         2
     declare                                           4         2
     declare                                           3         2
     update chain_h                                    3         2
  SELECT  TO_CHAR(sysdate, 'DD-MON-YY HH:MM PM') t     3         2
  commit                                              3         2
  insert into job_his                                 3         2
  insert into job_his                                 3         2
◄                                                                    ►
```

FIGURE 7-3. *Query v$sqlarea dictionary view*

The most common way to monitor library cache activity is with sqldba in full-screen mode. After connecting to the database, issue the **monitor lcache** command. Alternatively, once in sqldba and connected to the database, you can press the MENU key, select <u>M</u>onitor, then select the Library <u>C</u>ache option. You will be presented with a screen as illustrated in Figure 7-4.

DBAs are finding that sizing the shared pool is partially a game of hit and miss. The shared pool size is coded in init.ora in the SHARED_POOL_SIZE parameter. The default is 3.5MB, and the value is in bytes. The library cache holds all shared SQL and PL/SQL statements. Rapid access to this cache is the biggest contributor to shared pool tuning. Statements are loaded and flushed from the pool using the familiar LRU (least recently used) algorithm.

The display in Figure 7-4 is 80 columns wide. The Name Space column values TRIGGER, SQL AREA, BODY, and TABLE/PROCEDURE all relate to library cache activity. When a database is up all the time, the values in the Gets Requests/Hits and Pins Requests/Hits columns will very likely overflow their respective columns; ###### appears to indicate this overflow. For this reason, you might consider querying the v$librarycache view in the data dictionary to assess the hit ratio in the library cache. You can find the hit ratio as calculated using the formula in Figure 7-5.

NOTE
To access the v$ views in the dictionary, user SYS must grant privileges to database users. The views actually start with v_$, but the public synonyms begin with v$.

```
┌──────────────────────────────────────────────────────────────┐
│ ▬                         HP Prod                        ▼ ▲  │
│ File  Edit  Session  Instance  Storage  Log  Backup  Security  Monit▲ │
│                              Output                           │
│ ┌────────────── ORACLE Library Cache Monitor ──────────────┐  │
│                                                              │
│ Name Space Filter: ░░                                        │
│                                                              │
│             ─────────Gets────────  ─────────Pins────────    │
│ Name Space   Requests  Hits Ratio Requests  Hits Ratio Reloads │
│                                                              │
│ BODY               0      0    1        0      0    1      0  │
│ CLUSTER           22      7  .32       15      5  .33      0  │
│ INDEX            233     62  .27      233      0    0     62  │
│ OBJECT             0      0    1        0      0    1      0  │
│ PIPE               0      0    1        0      0    1      0  │
│ SQL AREA       37447  35257  .94   122026 117332  .96    196  │
│ TABLE/PROCEDURE 4484   3723  .84    13663  12585  .92    286  │
│ TRIGGER            0      0    1        0      0    1      0  │
│                                                              │
│                                        ⟨Restart⟩    ⟨Hide▼  │
│ ◄                                                        ►   │
└──────────────────────────────────────────────────────────────┘
```

FIGURE 7-4.   *The Library Cache screen through sqldba*

```
━                              HP Prod                         ▼ ▲
SQL> desc v$librarycache                                        ▲
Name                                  Null?     Type
─────────────────────────────         ─────     ────
NAMESPACE                                       VARCHAR2<15>
GETS                                            NUMBER
GETHITS                                         NUMBER
GETHITRATIO                                     NUMBER
PINS                                            NUMBER
PINHITS                                         NUMBER
PINHITRATIO                                     NUMBER
RELOADS                                         NUMBER
INVALIDATIONS                                   NUMBER

SQL> select sum(pins) Hits,sum(reloads) Misses,
  2         sum(pins)/(sum(pins)+sum(reloads)) "Hit ratio"
  3*    from v$librarycache

     HITS      MISSES  Hit ratio
──────────  ──────────  ─────────
  15798545      128992 .991901322
```

FIGURE 7-5.   *Query v$librarycache dictionary view*

Oracle makes room in the shared pool for new statements when processing a statement that does not match one already there. The initialization parameter file entry CURSOR_SPACE_FOR_TIME affects when a statement in shared SQL can be deallocated from the pool. When set to FALSE (the default), Oracle deallocates space held by a statement in the shared pool even if application cursors using that statement are still open. If the amount of available memory is enough such that the shared pool can be sized to hold all application cursors, you may consider setting this parameter to TRUE. A small amount of time is saved during statement execution when the parameter is set to TRUE. Oracle does not have to search the pool to see if the statement is already there.

SQL Statement Processing

The Structured Query Language (SQL) is the basis for all interaction with data in the Oracle database. Regardless of the tool used to communicate with Oracle (SQL*Plus, Oracle Reports, Oracle Forms, or others), SQL statements are passed to Oracle. After syntax checking, object resolution, and the selection of the most efficient access path, data is fetched and modified and/or displayed for the user.

The processing of statements involves three phases:

■ During the parse phase, the syntax of the SQL statement is checked and object resolution is determined. Any errors are encountered during this phase. Objects mentioned in a statement must exist in the user's schema or be accessible in a schema belonging to another user.

- During the execute phase, the necessary reads and writes are performed to support the statement being processed.

- During the fetch phase, data (if any) that qualifies based on the SQL statement being processed is retrieved, assembled, sorted (if necessary), and displayed as statement output.

Parse is the most expensive (time-consuming and resource-intensive) of the three phases because (1) the most effective execution plan for each SQL statement is constructed, and (2) a search for an identical statement already in the shared pool is performed.

By avoiding the expensive parse phase, your application will run faster. This is why it is important to code SQL statements to take advantage of those already parsed and sitting in the shared pool. This is a large contributor when tuning applications written to interact with the Oracle7 database.

Using Generic Code

Generic code refers to SQL statements that are stored in the database. Since it is stored in the database, every user who needs to process the code while running an application uses a copy of this centralized code. When generic code is processed, it is first fetched from the database and passed to Oracle for processing. Allowing Oracle to process matching SQL statements enhances performance. Oracle7 triggers and procedures are the most common implementation of central shared code. *Declarative integrity* (building predefined relationships into the dictionary at object creation time) is a form of shared generic code, because the routines initiated by Oracle are always the same. The nature and execution of declarative integrity routines at run time are determined by Oracle and are always identical each time they are invoked.

Declarative Integrity

With declarative integrity, you are encouraged to start using and experimenting with data-dictionary–enforced constraints. Data integrity ensures that relationships between values in different database objects are enforced. You code rules for these relationships using SQL during object creation and modification. For example, a business rule may require that when entering a new plant definition into the plant_detail table, the CITY_ID entered must already exist in the work_city table. Doing this programmatically is fine, but to use generic code, you should use declarative integrity. Enforcement of declarative integrity is done by non-SQL internal Oracle code, not by SQL in the shared pool. Thus, in a way, it is a form of generic code.

TIP
When converting existing application objects to take advantage of declarative integrity, try disabling the constraints while doing the conversion. Sudden implementation at run time may cause applications to "stop working"! Applications not designed to work with database enforced integrity constraints need careful evaluation before turning this feature on.

With Version 6 of Oracle, we sometimes coded declarative integrity when tables were created. With Version 6, when applications ran against tables containing declarative integrity definitions, the constraints they defined were not enforced automatically as they ran. Enforcement of constraints was done by you when writing applications— they were implemented programmatically. When we speak of converting existing applications, we refer to an exercise you may go through to move the programmatic enforcement of constraints into Oracle's hands by using declarative integrity. To illustrate this point, consider the following table definition.

```
create table plant_detail  (
        plant_id      number(2),
        city_id       number(2) check (city_id < 90),
        location      varchar2(20));
```

Against a Version 6 database, the syntax of the declarative integrity in this statement was checked when the table was created. However, as your application ran, it was your responsibility to ensure a CITY_ID of 95 was not saved in the database. With Oracle7, a form of generic code is invoked that does the check for you. When you convert existing applications, you take the program segment that does the checking out of your applications and let Oracle do the enforcement.

Database Triggers

Database triggers are event-driven routines that run transparent to applications. They are stored in the data dictionary and are created using the SQL **create trigger** command. They cannot be invoked manually, unlike some other forms of triggers you may be familiar with in Oracle Forms. Triggers are commonly used for auditing purposes. Some applications write a before-update image of a row when it is changed; prior to database triggers, this procedure had to be done manually. As well, some triggers are used to do activity logging. For example, the update activity on a restricted screen can be logged using a database trigger. Using triggers contributes to efficient use of generic code.

> **NOTE**
> Developers and object owners need the system privilege CREATE TRIGGER to successfully write database triggers. To execute triggers, you need privileges on the objects upon which the trigger performs operations.

Procedures and Packages

Procedures accomplish specific tasks for you, and they are a group of SQL and/or PL/SQL statements; they must be invoked manually. *Packages* group related procedures and functions together and allow their storage as a single unit in the database; their SQL text and compiled code is stored in the data dictionary, and executable copies reside in the shared pool. It is possible that frequently used procedures may reside in the SGA forever (so to speak). A number of packages belong to the Oracle user SYS that are automatically loaded when the database is started. For example, the package STANDARD is referenced implicitly by Oracle during processing of most PL/SQL blocks and will always be in the shared pool. A frequently used application that contains many database procedures will more than likely find these procedures always in memory.

Cost-Based Optimizing

An *optimization approach* is an internal mechanism used by Oracle to figure out the most efficient access path to the data required to satisfy an SQL statement. Previous versions of Oracle used a rule-based approach to optimization to establish this path. Based on a set of 15 access paths, the rule-based approach inspects the SQL statement and chooses an access path, selecting the one with the lowest rank. Accessing a single row by ROWID is rank 1, and accessing by a full table scan is rank 15. The *cost-based optimizer* chooses an execution plan based on the access path that would produce the best throughput. When working with cost-based optimizing, you may find that its execution plan compared to the rule-based approach is drastically different. The execution plan can be made up of several access paths. Using the rule-based approach, one or more access paths are chosen that have the lowest rank. Using the cost-based approach, access paths are chosen that have the lowest cost.

NOTE
The dreaded full table scan may appear more often with the cost-based approach—this is not necessarily a performance bottleneck. The cost-based optimizer may deem, in certain cases, full table scans to be more efficient.

The cost-based optimizer should be looked at and incorporated into programs where appropriate. Features such as *transitivity* (the decomposition of some forms of syntax into more standard wording) help process SQL statements faster and more efficiently. Transitivity exists in rule-based optimization, and it can speed statement processing even more with cost-based. For example, the statement

```
select * from sal_limit where sal_cap between 100000 and 200000;
```

will be transformed into

```
select * from sal_limit where sal_cap >= 100000 and sal_cap <= 200000;
```

Likewise, the statement

```
select sdesc from work_city where city_id in (1,15,67);
```

will be transformed into

```
select sdesc from work_city where city_id = 1 or city_id = 15 or city_id = 67;
```

Refer to the sections later in this chapter that deal with **tkprof** and **explain plan** where optimizer modes and hints are discussed.

Using Hints

Hints, the comment text placed immediately after **select**, **update**, or **delete** keywords, can be useful when deciding how to instruct cost-based optimization. SQL statements that contain hints will be treated according to the hint text. You can use either form of SQL comment conventions: the text bounded on either end by the **/*** and ***/** characters or preceded by a double dash (--). For example, the comment

```
/*+ first_rows */
```

is the same as

```
--+ first_rows
```

Table 7-5 lists the most commonly used hints. In this table, throughput means optimizing to retrieve *all rows* that satisfy the query as quickly as possible. When we speak of the best response time, we mean optimizing to present the *first row* that qualifies for the query as quickly as possible. A query against a view rather than a table is an example of a statement that assembles all rows before returning the first.

Other possible hints are FULL, ROWID, CLUSTER, HASH, INDEX, INDEX_ASC, AND_EQUAL, USE_NL, and USE_MERGE. An exhaustive discussion with examples of using hints can be found in Chapter 5 of the *Oracle7 Server Application Developer's Guide.* Programs may contain many SQL statements that use different approaches. Your SQL may end up looking like any of the following:

```
select   /*+RULE  */ ...

select   /* there is no hint in this statement */ ...

select   /*+ALL_ROWS  */ ...
```

The first statement forces use of the rule-based optimizer. The second uses the optimizer mode as defined in the initialization parameter file. The third statement uses the cost-based optimizer and chooses the most efficient access path for retrieval of all rows that satisfy the selection criteria.

TYPE	HINT(S)	MEANING/CAVEATS
Goal	ALL_ROWS	Optimizes for the best throughput
	FIRST_ROWS	Optimizes for the best response time; ignores in delete and update statements (they return no rows) and select statements that require assembly of all rows before returning the first
	RULE	Uses the rule-based approach; ignores any other hints
Join order	ORDERED	Joins tables in order they appear in FROM rather than allowing optimizer to choose
Access	INDEX_DESC (table index_name)	Index scans in descending order (opposite of the default ascending scan)

TABLE 7-5.   *The Five Most Commonly Used Hints*

Optimizer Mode by Session

The OPTIMIZER_MODE entry in the initialization parameter file decides the instance-wide default mode for query optimization. To override this default for a complete session in SQL*Plus, at the top of your program code put the statement

```
alter session set optimizer_goal= {mode_of_desire};
```

This statement remains in effect until the termination of that session or you issue a similar statement that resets to another value. The {mode_of_desire} can be any of the modes listed in Table 7-6.

You can use a combination of session statements and hints in your SQL programs. Your code may look like the following:

```
alter session set optimizer_goal = ALL_ROWS;
select /*+ RULE  : uses rule-based approach */ ...
select /* there is no hint in this statement */ ...
select /*+ FIRST_ROWS */ ...
alter session set optimizer_goal = RULE;
select /* uses rule-based approach for remainder of statements without hints */ ...
```

When to Use the Cost-Based Approach

Applications that have run well using the rule-based approach should be either left as is or tested, using the cost-based approach and comparing the results. Get users to participate in an exercise with both approaches and report their findings. Oracle

OPTIMIZER MODE	MEANING
RULE	Use the rule-based approach.
ALL_ROWS	Use the cost-based approach with the goal of best throughput for all rows that satisfy selection criteria.
FIRST_ROWS	Use the cost-based approach with the goal of the best response time for the first row that will be retrieved.
CHOOSE	Use the cost-based approach with the goal choice decided by the optimizer at execution time.

TABLE 7-6. *Goals for Alter Session Command*

feels that you do not need to tune SQL statements with the cost-based approach. Using rule-based, you must ensure that SQL is prepared based on what you know about access path ranking. After collecting statistics on your data, Oracle can optimize your statements by examining the results in the data dictionary at run time. When room is available in the SGA, the dictionary cache will contain some statistics alleviating the need for a recursive data dictionary call.

explain plan

The **explain plan** tool can prove useful when determining access paths to your data. Using the SQL*Plus command

```
EXPLAIN PLAN SET STATEMENT_ID
```

you insert rows into an object called the PLAN_TABLE. When running this command, you specify an identifier in single quotes to store the explained statement in this table. To accomplish this, perform the following steps:

1. Load the statement. If the statement contains any substitution variables, you will be prompted for them when the statement is run. The word "Explained" appears to indicate successful completion.

2. Run a script to report on the execution plan.

3. Assess the execution plan.

These three steps should be repeated until you are happy with the access path. In the following code, notice the **delete** statement at the top of the script. This ensures that any other statements that may have been loaded into the PLAN_TABLE are not left lying around when you report on the statement you have just loaded. The tmdt_pin, tmdt_weekending, and tmdt_product columns in the TIME_DETAIL table are indexed. The pin column from the PERSON table is indexed. The **select** statement reports on persons whose PIN values are between 1720 and 1730 and who worked on time codes TC210 and TC680 during the period between April 1, 1994, and March 31, 1995.

```
delete plan_table where statement_id = 'ZZ';
explain plan set statement_id = 'ZZ' for
  select t.tmdt_pin pin,b.last_name surname,b.first_name given,
```

```
    t.tmdt_product prod,
    sum(nvl(t.tmdt_orig_sat,0)+nvl(t.tmdt_orig_sun,0) +
    nvl(t.tmdt_orig_mon,0)+nvl(t.tmdt_orig_tue,0) +
    nvl(t.tmdt_orig_wed,0)+
    nvl(t.tmdt_orig_thu,0)+nvl(t.tmdt_orig_fri,0) +
    nvl(t.tmdt_transfer_sat,0)+nvl(t.tmdt_transfer_sun,0) +
    nvl(t.tmdt_transfer_mon,0)+nvl(t.tmdt_transfer_tue,0) +
    nvl(t.tmdt_transfer_wed,0)+
    nvl(t.tmdt_transfer_thu,0)+nvl(t.tmdt_transfer_fri,0) +
    nvl(t.tmdt_adjustment_sat,0)+nvl(t.tmdt_adjustment_sun,0) +
    nvl(t.tmdt_adjustment_mon,0)+nvl(t.tmdt_adjustment_tue,0) +
    nvl(t.tmdt_adjustment_wed,0)+
    nvl(t.tmdt_adjustment_thu,0)+nvl(t.tmdt_adjustment_fri,0)) acc
 from  time_detail t,person b
 where tmdt_pin = b.pin
 and tmdt_pin between 1720 and 1730
 and tmdt_weekending between '940401' and '950331'
 and tmdt_product IN ('TC210','TC680')
group by t.tmdt_pin,b.last_name,b.first_name,t.tmdt_product;
```

The statement now resides in the PLAN_TABLE and can be extracted using the following code:

```
set echo off term off feed off ver off
spool xpl
select decode(id,0,'',
    lpad(' ',2*(level-1))||level||'.'||position)||' '||
    operation||' '||options||' '||object_name||' '||
    object_type||' '||
    decode(id,0,'Cost = '||position) Query_plan
  from plan_table
connect by prior id = parent_id
and statement_id = upper('&1')
start with id = 0 and statement_id = upper('&1');
spool off
set term on
prompt
prompt Output from EXPLAIN PLAN is in file called "xpl.lst" . . .
prompt
```

The resulting output from running this code is as follows:

```
QUERY_PLAN
------------------------------------------------------------------------

SELECT STATEMENT    Cost = 902
  2.0 SORT GROUP BY
    3.1 NESTED LOOPS
      4.1 VIEW  TIME_DETAIL
        5.1 SORT GROUP BY
          6.1 NESTED LOOPS
            7.1 TABLE ACCESS BY ROWID TRS_TIMESHEET
              8.1 INDEX RANGE SCAN TRS_TIMESHEET_IDX1 UNIQUE
            7.2 TABLE ACCESS BY ROWID TRS_TS_STATUS
              8.1 INDEX RANGE SCAN TRS_TS_STATUS_IDX1 UNIQUE
      4.2 TABLE ACCESS BY ROWID PEOPLE_MASTER
      5.2 INDEX UNIQUE SCAN PEOPLE_MASTER_1 UNIQUE
```

This output seems cryptic on first examination. Most of this output can be explained by the names of the operations, which are listed in Table 7-7.

Keep in mind that EXPLAIN PLAN is a valuable off-the-shelf tuning aid provided by Oracle. It is useful throughout the development cycle. Programs that have bottlenecks at certain spots can be tuned using this facility. You must own a PLAN_TABLE or have access to one in someone else's schema. When figuring out what indexes to set up based on the requirements of an application, you can see if indexes are actually getting used and check the efficiency of the access path Oracle chooses based on the indexes in place. The first row returned from an ordered query on an execution plan (if explained using a cost-based approach) is the *cost* estimated by Oracle to execute according to those existing indexes. Comparing that cost relative to ones with a different set of indexes helps you make tough indexing decisions. The following difficult decisions about indexing can become readily clear after such an exercise.

■ Are the existing indexes being used?

■ What columns should be put together in composite (concatenated) indexes?

■ Would it be more efficient to break up a composite index into multiple single-column indexes?

LINE	OPERATION	MEANING
2.0	SORT GROUP BY	An operation that sorts a set of rows into groups for a query with a **group by** clause.
3.1	NESTED LOOPS	An operation that accepts two sets of rows, an outer set and an inner set. Oracle compares each row of the outer set with each row of the inner set and returns those rows that satisfy a condition.
4.1	VIEW	An operation that performs a view's query and then returns the resulting rows to another operation.
5.1	See 2.0	
6.1	See 3.1	
7.1	TABLE ACCESS BY ROWID	A retrieval of a row from a table based on its ROWID.
8.1	INDEX RANGE SCAN	A retrieval of one or more ROWIDs from an index. Indexed values are scanned in ascending order.
7.2	See 7.1	
4.2	See 7.1	
5.2	See 8.1	

TABLE 7-7. *Operations and Explanations, from Oracle7 Server Application Developer's Guide (reprinted by permission of Oracle Corporation)*

NOTE
A script called utlxplan.sql creates the PLAN_TABLE table. Its location is usually rdbms/admin, but it can differ on different machines.

The Hints and EXPLAIN PLAN Toolbox

While investigating the use of the cost-based optimizer, most installations will find the DBA wants to leave the initialization parameter file entry OPTIMIZER_MODE set to RULE. Hints are the way to go while tuning SQL statements for the cost-based optimizer. To do this, load a SQL statement into the PLAN_TABLE with hints in place. Run the script and inspect the output. This is an iterative process until the **cost =** value is a minimum. The hints used with Figures 7-6 and 7-7 are explained in Table 7-5.

The cost figures (3018 versus 18) are significant. They are the results from using different hints with the same SQL statement. This means that the FIRST_ROWS hint execution plan bore less than 1% of the cost of the plan used to execute the query using the ORDERED hint alone. The 19-line execution plan in Figure 7-6 and the 16-line plan in Figure 7-7 suggest that the fewer the number of lines in the plan, the more efficient the plan may be.

Notice the drastic difference in the cost = value between Figures 7-6 and 7-7. These amounts must be interpreted relative to one another on the same statement; they cannot be compared across statements. Note as well that the step values of both statements are the same (up to 9.1), whereas the total number of lines in Figure 7-6 is 19 and in Figure 7-7 it's 16.

tkprof and SQL trace

Closely related to EXPLAIN PLAN is the tkprof facility. With tkprof you can produce output that shows the three phases of SQL statement processing in hundredths of a second. To use tkprof, you (on a per-session basis) or the DBA (on an instance-wide basis) must enable tracing. To enable SQL trace by session, issue the following SQL statement:

```
alter session set sql_trace = true;
```

To disable SQL trace by session, issue the following SQL statement:

```
alter session set sql_trace = false;
```

Regardless of session or instance tracing, the entry

```
timed_statistics = true
```

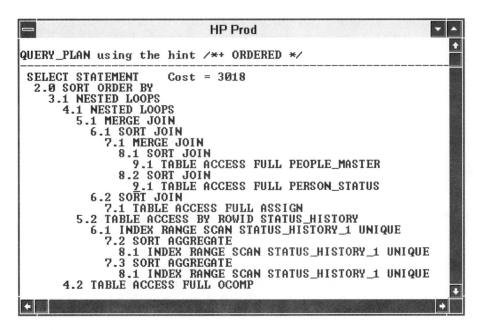

FIGURE 7-6. *Output using the hint ORDERED*

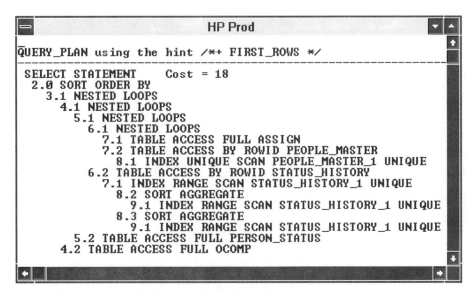

FIGURE 7-7. *Output using the hint FIRST_ROWS*

must be set in the initialization parameter file. This permits the collection of statistics on the CPU and elapsed time. Instance enabling is set in the initialization parameter file with the parameter

```
sql_trace = true
```

NOTE
Setting sql_trace=true in the initialization parameter file causes every session to produce a trace file. This can amount to a one-percent to five-percent performance decrease on most systems.

The trace files accumulate in the USER_DUMP_DEST directory (specified in the initialization parameter file with different default locations based on the operating system). They usually have the prefix ora_ and the extension .trc. The following listing shows a sample of the output from tkprof. Notice how the column headings above the parse, execute, and fetch statistics are defined at the top of the output. As well, when tkprof is called with the EXPLAIN option, the EXPLAIN PLAN for the statement comes after the statistics for the statement.

```
******************************************************************************
count   = number of times OCI procedure was executed
cpu     = cpu time in seconds executing
elapsed = elapsed time in seconds executing
disk    = number of physical reads of buffers from disk
query   = number of buffers gotten for consistent read
current = number of buffers gotten in current mode (usually for update)
rows    = number of rows processed by the fetch or execute call
******************************************************************************

select userid
from assign,person where assign.pin = person.pin and assign.home_base_ind =
  'Y'

call      count      cpu    elapsed     disk    query current        rows
-------  -------  -------  ---------  -------  ------- -------  ----------
Parse          1     0.01       0.01        0        4       0           0
Execute        1     0.00       0.00        0        0       0           0
Fetch        141     0.26       1.09      207    12812       3        2113

Misses in library cache during parse: 0
Parsing user id: 678   (JPROUDF)
```

```
Rows       Execution Plan
-------    --------------------------------------------------
      0    SELECT STATEMENT
   2113    NESTED LOOPS
   2706       TABLE ACCESS (FULL) OF 'PEOPLE_MASTER'
   2255       TABLE ACCESS (BY ROWID) OF 'ASSIGN'
   4961          INDEX (RANGE SCAN) OF 'ASSIGN_1' (NON-UNIQUE)
```

If the trace file contains any *recursive calls* (reads of data dictionary information from disk that is not in the SGA), Oracle displays their statistics as well. These statistics are included in the statistics for your SQL statement processing. They should not be added in again when adding times together. For example, if your statement took 0.26 seconds of CPU time, and a recursive call initiated by your statement took 0.05 seconds, the total CPU time would be 0.26, not 0.31.

Since tkprof is an executable run from the operating system prompt, be sure that your DBA has it somewhere where you can run it. Invoke tkprof using the command

```
tkprof [name_of_trace_file] output=[output_file_name]
explain=[userid_password] sort=[sort_options]
```

Using the sort option with tkprof, you can get a better picture of the most troublesome statements. The following listing shows the options you may sort on.

```
prscnt   number of times parse was called
prscpu   cpu time parsing
prsela   elapsed time parsing
prsdsk   number of disk reads during parse
prsqry   number of buffers for consistent read during parse
prscu    number of buffers for current read during parse
prsmis   number of misses in library cache during parse
execnt   number of execute was called
execpu   cpu time spent executing
exeela   elapsed time executing
exedsk   number of disk reads during execute
exeqry   number of buffers for consistent read during execute
execu    number of buffers for current read during execute
exerow   number of rows processed during execute
exemis   number of library cache misses during execute
fchcnt   number of times fetch was called
fchcpu   cpu time spent fetching
fchela   elapsed time fetching
fchdsk   number of disk reads during fetch
```

```
fchqry   number of buffers for consistent read during fetch
fchcu    number of buffers for current read during fetch
fchrow   number of rows fetched
userid   userid of user that parsed the cursor
```

Indexing Columns

Indexes are separate data segments used by Oracle for quick access to data blocks. They store values for fields in a table and pointers to the location of the actual data. You may find yourself setting up indexes during program development and going through a process of investigating their usage, dropping some, and perhaps setting up new ones. Indexes are created on one column (single-column indexes) or multiple columns (composite or concatenated indexes).

The big question is: What columns to index? Following are six guidelines to help make this difficult decision.

APPLICATION TUNING RULE 4
Know your data. Figure out the columns with good selectivity. Selectivity is the percent of rows in a table that have the same value. Columns with low selectivity are good candidates for indexing.

Our experience dictates that if a column contains few distinct values, then even in a table with 250,000 rows, the performance using an index and doing a full table scan can be just about the same. In some instances, the performance using an indexed column that perhaps should not be indexed may even be worse than the dreaded full table scan. If you do not know what your data will look like, use EXPLAIN PLAN and constantly run a sample of your application SQL statements to see the indexes that are being used.

APPLICATION TUNING RULE 5
The only candidates for indexing are columns that are mentioned after WHERE and AND in SQL statements.

Mentioning column names in these clauses causes Oracle to use indexes when they exist. The order of the columns mentioned in the *predicate* (that part of the coding of the SQL statement following the object name(s) and preceding any **group by** or **order by** portions) may become an issue when using the cost-based optimization approach. It is possible that the order of the columns, during your experimentation, may affect the access path.

APPLICATION TUNING RULE 6
Even if a column's contents contain a wide range of values, do not index if it is always mentioned using a function (e.g., FLOOR or ABS) or string manipulation and conversion (e.g., SUBSTR or TO_CHAR).

The query

```
select substr(location,1,10) from plant_detail;
```

would be an example of this type of column usage.

APPLICATION TUNING RULE 7
When looking at and using the cost-based optimizer, ensure that your tables are analyzed to gather important column statistics that aid in the selection of indexes to create.

Gather these column statistics using the SQL*Plus **analyze** command. Most of the useful output from **analyze table** is stored in the data dictionary in user_tables and user_indexes (see Figure 7-8).

```
                                    HP Prod
select distinct_keys, avg_leaf_blocks_per_key,
       avg_data_blocks_per_key, clustering_factor
  from user_indexes
 where table_name = 'TIME_DETAIL';

 select num_rows, blocks, empty_blocks, avg_space, chain_cnt, avg_row_len
   from user_tables
 where table_name = 'TIME_DETAIL';

DISTINCT_KEYS AVG_LEAF_BLOCKS_PER_KEY AVG_DATA_BLOCKS_PER_KEY
------------- ----------------------- -----------------------
CLUSTERING_FACTOR
----------------
       559104                       1                       1
       537768
          842                       4                      20
       455382


   NUM_ROWS    BLOCKS EMPTY_BLOCKS  AVG_SPACE  CHAIN_CNT AVG_ROW_LEN
   --------    ------ ------------  ---------  --------- -----------
     559944     15554          375        450          0          98
```

FIGURE 7-8. *Statistics from user_tables and user_indexes when a table is analyzed*

After placing an index on a table, the information stored in the USER_TABLES and USER_INDEXES views shown in Figure 7-8 can be quite helpful. Examining the output leads to the following conclusions:

- For the first index: Of the over 500,000 rows in the table, the columns have distinct values except for 840 rows (the column is highly selective and therefore this is a good index). This 840 is the difference between the NUM _ROWS (559,944) returned from USER_TABLES and the DISTINCT_KEYS (559,104) returned from USER_INDEXES.

- For the second index: Less than one percent of the columns have distinct values (this index is a candidate for performance monitoring—it may be creating a bottleneck rather than helping execution of SQL statements that use it). This one percent is the number of DISTINCT_KEYS (842) per NUM_ROWS (559,104).

- Since the clustering factor of both indexes is closer to the number of rows than the number of blocks, it is unlikely that index entries in the same index block point to data that resides in the same block (thus I/O is performed for the index block information with a separate I/O for the data block).

APPLICATION TUNING RULE 8
When choosing candidate columns for composite indexes, look at those columns that are used in **where** and **and** together during your application. If they are retrieved in **where** and **and** separately as well as together, two single-column indexes may be better.

From time to time, you may find, based on your applications, that maintaining a composite index as well as multiple single column indexes may be the way to proceed. This reinforces the need to know your data and your applications when making indexing decisions.

APPLICATION TUNING RULE 9
A composite index will only be used to satisfy a query when the leftmost column in that composite index is mentioned in WHERE or AND.

If there is a composite index on cola and colb on a table (and neither column has a single column index in place), the first query in the following will use that index whereas the second will not:

```
select colc, substr(cold,1,30) from taba where cola >= 'ABC';

select colc, substr(cold,1,30) from taba where colb >= 'ABC';
```

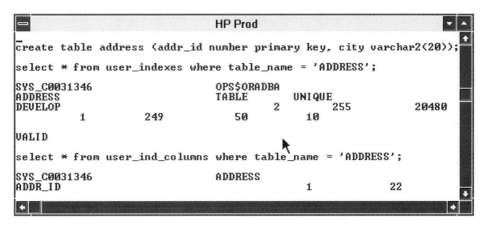

FIGURE 7-9. *Index(es) set up by UNIQUE and PRIMARY KEY constraints*

Some syntax you may use in defining declarative integrity in tables will cause Oracle to maintain an index automatically. Notice the index called SYS_C0031346 on the ADDRESS table in Figure 7-9. Using a **unique** or **primary key** constraint implicitly creates one of these internal indexes. If you try to manually create an index on one or more columns that Oracle has created for enforcement of integrity constraints, you will receive an error. These indexes cannot be dropped manually.

Oracle provides two SQL scripts to help you assess the candidate columns for indexing. They are usually found in rdbms/admin. Run utloidxs.sql followed by utldidxs.sql to produce output similar to that below. In this listing, the ORG_COMP_TYPE column has been considered as a candidate for an index in the OCOMP table. The output was produced using the following two commands:

    @utloidxs OCOMP ORG_COMP_TYPE
    @utldidxs OCOMP ORG_CCOMP_TYPE

TABLE_NAME	COLUMN_NAME	STAT_NAME	STAT_VALUE
OCOMP	ORG_COMP_TYPE	Rows - Null	0.00
OCOMP	ORG_COMP_TYPE	Rows - Total	205.00
OCOMP	ORG_COMP_TYPE	Rows per key - avg	51.25
OCOMP	ORG_COMP_TYPE	Rows per key - dev	77.94
OCOMP	ORG_COMP_TYPE	Rows per key - max	166.00
OCOMP	ORG_COMP_TYPE	Rows per key - min	1.00
OCOMP	ORG_COMP_TYPE	Total Distinct Keys	4.00

```
OCOMP              ORG_COMP_TYPE     db_gets_per_key_hit
70.07
OCOMP              ORG_COMP_TYPE     db_gets_per_key_miss
140.14


9 rows selected.
```

TABLE_NAME	COLUMN_NAME	BADNESS	KEYS_COUNT	ROW_PERCENT	KEY_PERCENT
OCOMP	ORG_COMP_TYPE	166	1	80.98	25.00
OCOMP	ORG_COMP_TYPE	34	1	16.59	25.00
OCOMP	ORG_COMP_TYPE	4	1	1.95	25.00
OCOMP	ORG_COMP_TYPE	1	1	0.49	25.00

```
4 rows selected.
```

The listing displays statistics on the table and column reported. The second part can help make the indexing decision. Note that the badness factor for 80.98 percent of the rows is 166. Comparing that badness factor for that percent of rows against the badness factor for the remaining 19.02 percent of the rows shows that the ORG_COMP_TYPE column of the OCOMP table is not a good candidate for an index.

Both scripts are looking for a table name followed by a column in that table to inspect. The first script creates the tables INDEX$INDEX_STATS and INDEX$BADNESS_STATS and a view INDEX$BADNESS. You may want to drop these objects when you are done using them. Examining the output from above, the term *badness* refers to the selectivity of a column in a table. Those with high badness relative to badness counts for the same column are not good candidates for indexes.

NOTE
These scripts are intended to be an aid to the selection of columns to index. Actual experimentation with indexing and inspection of the results may clash with some of the scripts' recommendations.

In the next listing, the PIN column has been considered as a candidate for an index in the STATUS_HISTORY table. The output was produced using the following two commands:

```
@utloidxs STATUS_HISTORY PIN
@utldidxs STATUS_HISTORY PIN
```

```
TAB_NAME                          COL_NAME
-----------------------------     ----------------------------------------------
STATUS_HISTORY                    PIN

1 row selected.


TABLE_NAME        COLUMN_NAME     STAT_NAME                             STAT_VALUE
---------------   -------------   -----------------------------        -------------
STATUS_HISTORY    PIN             Rows - Null                                  0.00
STATUS_HISTORY    PIN             Rows - Total                             2,288.00
STATUS_HISTORY    PIN             Rows per key - avg                           1.87
STATUS_HISTORY    PIN             Rows per key - dev                           1.21
STATUS_HISTORY    PIN             Rows per key - max                           9.00
STATUS_HISTORY    PIN             Rows per key - min                           1.00
STATUS_HISTORY    PIN             Total Distinct Keys                      1,222.00
STATUS_HISTORY    PIN             db_gets_per_key_hit                          1.59
STATUS_HISTORY    PIN             db_gets_per_key_miss                         2.65

9 rows selected.


TABLE_NAME        COLUMN_NAME      BADNESS    KEYS_COUNT  ROW_PERCENT KEY_PERCENT
---------------   -------------   ---------- ----------  ----------- ----------
STATUS_HISTORY    PIN                 9           2          0.79        0.16
STATUS_HISTORY    PIN                 8           1          0.35        0.08
STATUS_HISTORY    PIN                 7           9          2.75        0.74
STATUS_HISTORY    PIN                 6          10          2.62        0.82
STATUS_HISTORY    PIN                 5          30          6.56        2.46
STATUS_HISTORY    PIN                 4          68         11.89        5.57
STATUS_HISTORY    PIN                 3         125         16.39       10.23
STATUS_HISTORY    PIN                 2         365         31.91       29.87
STATUS_HISTORY    PIN                 1         612         26.75       50.08

9 rows selected.
```

By examining the output, you can see that the highest badness is 9 and the lowest is 1. This column is a good candidate for an index, as 31.91 percent of the PIN column values in the table have two rows for that PIN. The first part of this output shows less than two percent (1.87 percent) average rows per key. Thus, of the 2,288 rows in the table there is an average of less than two rows per PIN value.

Locking

Oracle establishes different forms of locking to ensure consistency, concurrence, and integrity of its data. *Data consistency* ensures that users selecting data are not affected by changes to that data while the query is running. *Data concurrency* ensures that users reading data blocks do not wait for users changing those blocks and vice versa. You should allow Oracle to take care of locking resources. Oracle will acquire the least prohibitive lock necessary to accomplish a task. *Exclusive* locks do not permit sharing of the locked resource, whereas *share* locks support this sharing. Locks are released by one of the following events:

- An explicit commit by the user or program

- An implicit commit by Oracle (e.g., leaving SQL*Plus with uncommitted transactions)

- An explicit session rollback by user or program

- An implicit session rollback by Oracle (e.g., an import aborting on lack of adequate rollback segment extents)

- A rollback to a savepoint issued by the user

The PMON (process monitor) background process discussed in Chapter 2, "Memory," does user process abort cleanup and will cause locks from that process to be released. Oracle issues row and table locks to protect data where necessary. Data dictionary locks protect object definition in the data dictionary. You can expect Oracle to issue lock requests in an efficient unrestrictive manner. Any locks issued manually during application operations should be handled likewise. Full-screen sqldba and a number of SQL*Plus queries can be used to monitor locking activity and detect abnormal or unnecessary locking situations and requests. The output in Figure 7-10 was displayed using the **monitor lock** command in full-screen sqldba.

Oracle provides utllockt.sql to produce a report on lock wait situations. Prior to running this, run catblock.sql to set up objects to be used by utllockt. If there are no lock wait occurrences when the report is run, it will return "no rows selected."

NOTE
Your catblock.sql program may have an error in the SQL statement that creates the DBA_LOCK view. There may be a comment on the last line of the code that creates the view, delimited by the /* comment */ indicator. Either take the semicolon (;) off the line with the comment and put the forward slash (/) on the next line, or remove the comment.

HP Prod							
Session	Instance	Storage	Log	Backup	Security	Monitor	

Output

ORACLE Lock Monitor

Filter: %%

	Session ID	Serial Number	Lock Type	Resource ID 1	Resource ID 2	Mode Held	Mode Request
A	13	31366	TM	6155	0	RS	NONE
A	13	31366	TX	131100	12133	X	NONE
NMD	15	-24283	TM	5520	0	RS	NONE
NMD	15	-24283	TX	196670	12297	X	NONE
LLJ	57	31358	TM	4425	0	RS	NONE
LLJ	57	31358	TX	131129	12147	X	NONE

〈Restart〉 〈Hide〉 〈Quit

FIGURE 7-10. *SQLDBA monitor lock*

An alternative to using sqldba for lock monitoring is to query the v$lock dictionary view as shown in Figure 7-11. The lock mode in SQL*Plus from v$lock is a number instead of a two-character lock code. Table 7-8 translates the numbers from the LMODE column into a lock type for the most common locks.

HP Prod							
ADDR	KADDR	SID	TY	ID1	ID2	LMODE	REQUEST
C408FFC4	C408FFD4	2	MR	19	0	4	0
C4090200	C4090210	2	MR	7	0	4	0
C4090258	C4090268	2	MR	5	0	4	0
C409022C	C409023C	2	MR	6	0	4	0
C40903B8	C40903C8	2	MR	20	0	4	0
C4090074	C4090084	2	MR	16	0	4	0
C408FFF0	C4090000	4	RT	1	0	6	0
C30B7824	C30B78B8	18	TX	196650	12324	6	0
C309A52C	C309A540	18	TM	5580	0	2	0
C309A270	C309A284	35	TM	5580	0	2	0
C30B7ED0	C30B7F64	35	TX	131093	12151	6	0

FIGURE 7-11. *Querying V$LOCK in SQL*Plus*

VALUE	LOCK TYPE
1	No lock.
2	Row share: Locks rows in a table with the intent to perform **update** to those rows. Others may row share lock other rows. Others may **select** all rows in table, even those with the row share lock acquired by others.
3	Row exclusive: Locks rows while applying changes to those rows. Others may row exclusive lock other rows. Others may **select** all rows in table, even those with the row exclusive lock acquired by others.
4	Share table: Locks rows in a table for **insert update** or **delete**. Others may still **select** rows in that table and acquire their own share table locks (this is the lock acquired by **lock table in share update mode** seen in older SQL*Plus programs).
5	Share row exclusive: Similar to share table, except this prevents other users from obtaining a lock that requires acquiring a share table lock while this lock is in effect.
6	Exclusive: Locks the table and permits others to only **select** data. Prevents others from successfully issuing *any type* of lock on the table.

TABLE 7-8. *Lock Mode Types in v$lock*

Note that the TYPE column values when using SQL*Plus rather than sqldba will also include listings of Oracle internal locks. In Figure 7-11, the *MR* refers to a lock associated with media recovery and the *RT* to a lock associated with a redo log operation. You have no control over these locks.

Let's Tune It

This chapter introduced techniques for monitoring access paths during the execution of SQL statements, using tools delivered with Oracle. Discussion also covered the shared SQL area, what is in it, and how to make maximum use of parsed and executable statements. The use of centralized generic code, the use of hints with the cost-based optimizer, indexing considerations, and locking considerations were also discussed. In conclusion, here's some further advice:

- Develop coding conventions for the SQL statements in your installation. Decide issues such as keyword case, keyword placement, alignment of statements, and object aliasing.

■ Using database triggers and procedures helps standardize code. Using generic code avoids repetition of the costly parse phase of SQL statement processing.

■ Analyze database objects at night as part of backup routines. Analyzing will cause any parsed SQL statements in the shared pool to be flushed.

■ You will find the screen refreshes in sqldba using **monitor sqlarea** to be sluggish. Use a query against v$sqlarea—it's faster.

■ When sizing for the shared pool, Oracle refers to small, medium, and large databases, which means the expected number of concurrent users and NOT the sum of the size of all the database files. Rule of thumb suggests 1 to 15 users is small, 16 to 25 users is medium, and anything above 25 is large.

■ Become fluent with usage of the cost-based optimizer. Experiment with it, inspect the results, and incorporate it into your applications where they may benefit from it most.With subsequent releases, Oracle has stated that the rule-based approach may disappear. Familiarize yourself with the cost-based approach *now,* rather than rushing to learn it when you have no choice.

■ Do not rule out using the cost-based optimizer.

■ Setting SQL_TRACE=TRUE in the initialization parameter file causes every SQL session to produce a trace file. These trace files require manual cleanup and can occupy unpredictable amounts of disk space. Do not set SQL_TRACE=TRUE in the initialization parameter file for that very reason. Do tracing on a per session basis. Remember to check programs for **alter session set sql_trace=true** before they go to production.

■ Assess efficiency of indexes using EXPLAIN PLAN. See what indexes are being used for common queries, and drop any that are not used. Over-indexing a table can cause added overhead. All indexes must be updated during record creation, modification, and deletion.

■ Remove all unnecessary **lock table** statements in scripts brought up from Oracle Version 5. With Version 6 and Oracle7, the default locking mode is SHARE UPDATE (see value 4 in Table 7-8 earlier in this chapter). Explicit issuing of this type of lock statement is no longer required.

■ When using SQL*Plus for non-**select** statement work, issue commit statements after all **update**, **delete**, and **insert** statements to release resource locks. If this is not possible according to application logic, so be it.

■ When testing and coding for the cost-based optimizer, use EXPLAIN PLAN and optimizer hints to get the cost to a minimum.

■ Familiarize yourself with the contents of the shared pool during program development. You may find something there that you can match rather than coding your own statement.

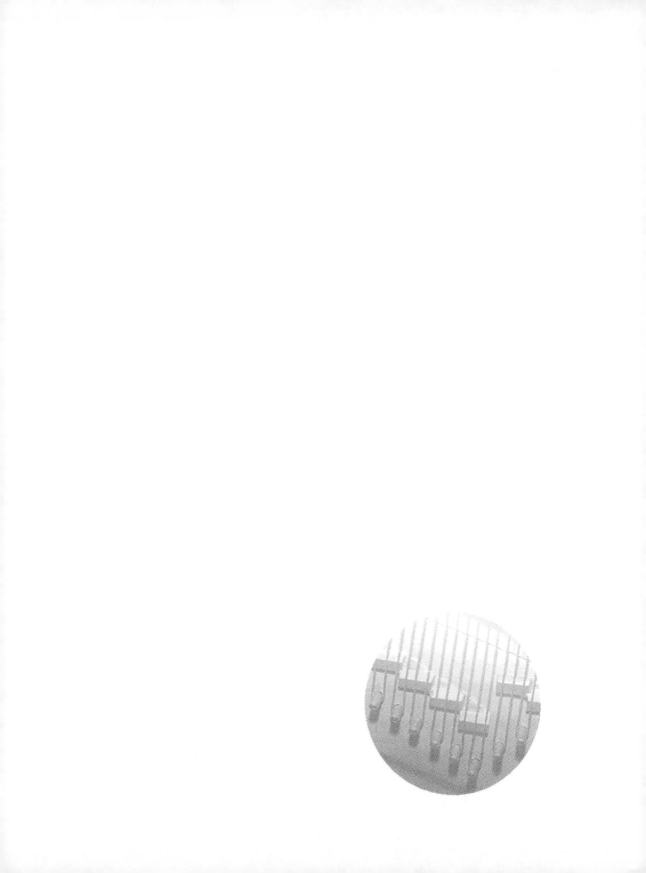

CHAPTER 8

Putting It All Together: A Wholistic Approach

We have discussed many issues on tuning the Oracle database. In this chapter, we will put it all together. To have a healthy operating Oracle environment, you need to tend to all the issues we have discussed, using a planned, methodical approach. We call the discussions here a *wholistic approach*. When tuning Oracle, you must look at the whole picture, not just the usual three-tiered approach: memory, I/O, and important applications. Yes, the Big Three are the most and they give the most noticeable results. Throughout this book, though, we have looked at many issues that require your attention during the tuning process; no stone can be unturned.

When your complete tuning exercise is done, you will have touched on most aspects of your database that require day-to-day attention. Think of your database as one of your loved ones:

- It craves your attention when you neglect it.

- It sends you messages when there is something wrong with it.

- It refuses to cooperate when you ask it to do too much.

- It confuses you when you tend to one problem when another actually needs fixing.

- It gets you up at all hours of the night.

- It sends you mixed messages.

- It thrives on TLC (tender loving care).

But above all, you must provide it with the resources that enable it to succeed on its own! We believe that tuning Oracle is a process applied to all components of the software. Providing a stable, dependable operating environment is fundamental to a regimen that minimizes database downtime and data loss potential. A down database is not a tuned database. We will discuss mechanisms you can put in place to care for and protect your database in the following areas:

- Backup: The process whereby you make copies of your data from your database at fixed time intervals. Backup protects you against the assortment of hardware, software, and user-based errors that may occur.

- Recovery: The restoration of a backup of your database from a previous time period and rolling it forward using redo log files (roll forward is discussed in the "Tuning Database Recovery" section later in this chapter).

- Error routines: DBA-defined mechanisms that you implement to alert you when predefined error situations happen with your database.

- Transaction control tuning features.

- Efficient overall resource management.

- Clusters and their potential performance gains.

Tuning Database Backups

Tuning database backups is one of the ongoing responsibilities of the DBA. You need to create and maintain adequate system backup procedures to ensure a minimum of data loss when problems occur. Backup routines use a combination of Oracle utilities and operating system programs. Sufficient attention to detail in this area will have enormous payoffs if and when something goes wrong. Backup procedures need to include a tested recovery plan. The optimal backup routines include the following two components. Tuning suggestions are included with each step.

- The EXPort and IMPort utilities (see the following section) help protect against loss of the most granular of Oracle segments: the single table (segment types are discussed in Chapter 3).

- Online backups (discussed in the "Tuning Online Backups" section) permit uninterrupted access and allow programs to run during the precious off-hours.

Tuning EXPort and IMPort

EXPort is a utility that creates an operating system file with a copy of specified data. This file is usually referred to as the dmp (pronounced "dump"). IMPort reads files created by EXPort and brings data into the database. Consult the *Oracle7 Server Utilities Guide* for a complete discussion on using these two handy utilities.

You incorporate these utilities into your backup procedures to permit object recovery. It is your job to educate your developers on the use of this utility. Some of the suggested parameter values affect the speed of EXPort and IMPort. Some of the other suggested parameter values will assist you in ensuring that they both run their work to completion. The parameters that affect EXPort performance are listed in Table 8-1; the parameters that affect IMPort performance are listed in Table 8-2.

Tables 8-1 and 8-2 both list the LOG parameter. Most error situations are going to be raised during IMPort rather than EXPort. Nothing is more frustrating than receiving the message "Import terminated with warnings" without having a log file to inspect. The PARFILE parameter in both tables can be used when either utility is run in the foreground or background.

As Table 8-1 suggests, setting the INDEXES parameter to N means no index creation statements will be written to the dump file. When performing object recovery, you usually do not want to drop the object, because any grants (privileges given out to other database users) will be lost.

The optimal way to IMPort an object is outlined in the following steps. This exercise assumes that a table called PLANT_DETAIL has been inadvertently dropped.

PARAMETER	MEANING	TUNING
BUFFER	The size of the chunk of memory in which data is assembled before it's written to the export file—asking for 10 megabytes (10,240,000) is a good place to start.	Use a large number to speed up the process—Oracle will acquire as much as you specify and will not return an error if it can't find that amount.
INDEXES	Controls whether the index create statements are written to the dump file.	When you already have SQL scripts that define your indexes, do not export indexes, because they will slow down when the export is read by IMPort.
LOG	Causes Oracle to write the screen I/O from the EXPort session to a disk file.	When things go wrong, you need the screen I/O saved to a file to browse and see what went wrong.
PARFILE	Name of a file that contains the parameters for the EXPort.	Run EXPort in the background using this keyword—it frees up your terminal to do other things at the same time.

TABLE 8-1. *Parameters Affecting EXPort Performance*

1. Restore a copy of the dump file from tape if it is no longer online.

2. Run IMPort using the INDEXFILE parameter to create a disk file with the table and index create statements (this will allow you to know whether enough space is free in the database to create the object).

3. Precreate the table and index(es).

4. IMPort the data, using COMMIT=Y on large objects (more than 10,000 rows), as suggested in Table 8-2.

WHOLISTIC RULE #1
Run EXPort and IMPort with a large buffer size. Precreate tables before an IMPort.

PARAMETER	MEANING	TUNING
ANALYZE	Controls whether Oracle runs the ANALYZE object statement after bringing in the data.	Set **analyze** to N and manually **analyze** the object after the IMPort—use the **estimate statistics** when you run the **analyze** in SQL*Plus.
BUFFER	The size of the chunk of memory in which data is assembled before it's written to the database—asking for 10 megabytes (10,240,000) is a good place to start.	Use a large number to speed up the process—Oracle will acquire as much as you specify and will not return an error if it can't find that amount.
COMMIT	Controls when Oracle issues a **commit** statement in the midst of inserting rows into tables.	Set COMMIT to Y when importing large tables—it may not speed up the performance, but partially importing a table, then having it abort when it runs out of rollback segments, is wasted time and energy.
LOG	Causes Oracle to write the screen I/O from the IMPort session to a disk file.	When things go wrong, you need the I/O saved to a file to browse and see what went wrong.
PARFILE	Name of a file that contains the parameters for the IMPort.	Run IMPort in the background using this keyword—it frees up your terminal to do other things at the same time.

TABLE 8-2. *Parameters Affecting IMPort Performance*

WHOLISTIC RULE #2
Use the Oracle utilities EXPort and IMPort to help protect against data loss. As a DBA, you can spend more of your time on a database performance–tuning exercise when you have reliable, tested backup systems in place.

Tuning Online Backups

When performing backups of the Oracle database (or any other vendors' databases), the database must be in a consistent state when the backup is written. An Oracle database is in a *consistent state* when all of the instance database files are online, accessible, and not damaged, and the time and date stamps in all of these files agree with those held in the instance control file(s). Prior to Oracle version 6, there was no mechanism in place to permit writing a consistent image of the database to tape while it was running. *Online backup* means backing up your database while it is open. An open database can be accessed by users and, as these backups are running in the precious quiet hours, permits you to provide 24-hour access to your users.

Oracle introduced the concept of ARCHIVELOG with version 6 in 1988. When we mention running a version 6 or Oracle7 database using ARCHIVELOG mode, we mean the following: ARCHIVELOG mode instructs Oracle to save a copy of each online redo log before it is reused. The saving of a copy, and the archiving of these copies to tape (or some other secondary storage device) leads to the name given this facility: archiving. Turning on ARCHIVELOG is done using the following steps:

1. Shut down the database.

2. Edit the initialization parameter file and set ARCHIVE_LOG_START to TRUE and ARCHIVE_LOG_DEST and ARCHIVE_LOG_FORMAT to values as discussed in the *Oracle7 Server Administrator's Guide.*

3. Enter sqldba, then log into Oracle as the SYS user (i.e., **connect internal**).

4. Start up the database with the MOUNT option.

5. Issue the following statements:

```
alter database archivelog;
```

```
alter database open;
```

When these steps are accomplished, you will have another background process supporting the database with the text "arch" embedded in its name. You will notice that the archived redo log files appear in the destination specified in your ARCHIVE_LOG_DEST. The name used for archived redo logs is a combination of the ARCHIVE_LOG_DEST and the ARCHIVE_LOG_FORMAT entries. Oracle takes these two parameters and builds a filename. For example, suppose ARCHIVE_LOG_DEST is set to

```
/data/oracle_prd/arc_logs/arch
```

and ARCHIVE_LOG_FORMAT is set to

`_%s.prd`

The %s in the parameter instructs Oracle to put the log sequence number in the filename. Thus, log sequence number 1287 will end up written as the following:

`/data/oracle_prd/arc_logs/arch_1287.prd`

and will become an archived redo log.

You are now ready to perform online backups, which, as we mentioned before, involve making a copy of one or more of your database files while the database is open. It is a three-step process for each tablespace; the following steps use the tablespace *personnel* as an example:

1. Inform Oracle that the tablespace is being backed up (i.e., the tablespace is in backup mode) by issuing the following command:

`alter tablespace personnel begin backup;`

2. At the operating system, make a copy of the one or more datafiles that make up the PERSONNEL tablespace.

3. Inform Oracle that the tablespace backup is complete (i.e., the tablespace is out of backup mode) by issuing the following command:

`alter tablespace personnel **end** backup;`

NOTE
If you neglect to do steps 1 and 3, step 2 will still work, but the copy you made of the datafile(s) will not be usable for recovery, as discussed in the following section.

NOTE
If any tablespace is still marked as being in backup mode, you will not be able to shut down your database.

WHOLISTIC RULE #3
Do online backups of all or part of your database when running in ARCHIVELOG mode. Do the backup one tablespace at a time, to reduce the overhead. This will minimize the impact on your online systems.

WHOLISTIC RULE #4

Ensure that your control file is part of an online backup. Copy it to the same destination as your archived redo logs at the END of your tablespace backup.

The drain on system resources during an online backup is small with a well-tuned database. However, every contributor to requests on system resources must be taken into account, using our wholistic approach.

NOTE

Oracle needs at least two single-membered redo log groups to run. Oracle writes information about transactions performed on the database to the online redo logs, and it uses the redo log groups in a cyclical fashion: it writes to one redo log group and, when the redo log files in that group are full, it switches to the other group.

Tuning Database Recovery

There are two types of recovery when running an Oracle instance. Every time an Oracle instance is started, automatic instance recovery is performed. When the need arises and your database is in ARCHIVELOG mode, you can also perform media recovery to rebuild a component of your database (e.g., a missing data file or rollback segment) from an image backup. Both types of recovery are a three-step process:

1. Rolling forward applies transactions recorded in the redo logs to recover data that may not have been written to the database.

2. Rolling back undoes transactions that had been rolled back by users or by Oracle.

3. Resources are freed up that had been in use during active user sessions.

Oracle refers to the term "media failure" during discussions of recovery. *Media failure* involves an assortment of hardware problems, such as a disk failure or damage to a read/write head on a disk drive.

WHOLISTIC RULE #5

Run your database in ARCHIVELOG mode. This allows protection against a wide range of problems with hardware and user error. It helps minimize instance downtime.

Tuning of the recovery process emphasizes our theme that a down database is not a tuned database. The recovery speed is a function of the speed of your disk drives, coupled with the amount of transaction data in the redo logs to be applied. Recovery reads redo log files and applies their changes to the database restored from your image backup. To help speed up the process, try to keep 48 hours of archived redo log files on line, i.e., those written for the full two days prior to the current day. As well, keep as much of the image backup online as possible. The most time-consuming part of the recovery exercise is reading massive amounts of data from tape.

You can perform recovery on the whole database, one or more tablespaces, or one or more datafiles that make up a tablespace. The options available and the interactive routines used to perform recovery are the subject of a chapter in the *Oracle7 Server Administrator's Guide*, and the manuals discuss what to do when parts of your database configuration is damaged.

WHOLISTIC RULE #6

Make an operating system text copy of your control file using the `alter database backup controlfile to trace` statement. Incorporate this into your backup routines.

WHOLISTIC RULE #7

A recovery procedure is only good if `TESTED`! Run a number of mock recovery situations when first putting recovery mechanisms into place. The documentation explains recovery and what-to-do-when very well, but there could be some surprises when recovering from a real-life disaster.

DBA Error-Trapping Routines

Throughout this book, we have discussed where error situations occur and what to do about them. We will now discuss ways to contribute to the tuning process by flagging error conditions and dealing with them before they get worse.

Background Process Trace Files

Each of the Oracle support processes creates a trace file. Oracle writes to these trace files to help debug system problems if and when they occur. Use these files for their intended purpose. The location of these files is operating system dependent, but they are usually in $ORACLE_HOME/rdbms/log. On any system, you can get Oracle to tell you where these trace files are written by logging into sqldba, connecting to the database, and then issuing the command

```
show parameters dump_dest
```

On most systems, the output will be the directory suggested above. The trace file name is built using the four-character process name (e.g., pmon or smon), the underscore character (_), and the process identifier. Use whatever operating system commands you wish, and ensure that you look for the following situations. Table 8-3 shows some common error situations that can be alleviated using a rigid tuning methodology. For Table 8-3, we use process identifier 1287 in the examples.

WHAT TO DO	WHAT IT MEANS AND WHAT MAY BE WRONG
Look in the instance alert file for waits during the allocation of sequence numbers for online redo log switches.	You need larger or more redo log groups—Oracle is unable to switch the redo log group because the current group is still in use.
Look in the instance alert file for ORA-04031 errors.	This error is raised when Oracle is trying to allocate more memory for a SQL statement in the shared pool, and no memory is available.
Search all trace files for the series of ORA-00600 error messages.	1. Consult your own notes—there are up to six separate arguments after the error enclosed in [ ] brackets. 2. Look for the meanings of the argument(s). 3. If new argument(s), call Oracle support. 4. Fix the situation that caused the error, if possible.
Search all trace files for ORA-01547 error messages.	This indicates a session needed to acquire more space in a data file and enough space could not be found—this typically happens without any application messages and needs your intervention.
Search all trace files for ORA-03113 error messages.	Applications that use SQL*Net to read remote databases get disconnected from Oracle periodically—the trace file may contain further information that could prove helpful to Oracle support. This does *not occur often*, but it should be watched for.
Inspect file smon_1287.trc looking for clean-up activities on aborted processes.	The system monitor is signaled by the process monitor when Oracle user processes abort and there has to be some post-abort cleanup work performed.

TABLE 8-3. *Common Error Conditions to Monitor*

NOTE
If you initiate a session via SQL*Net using a database that resides on another machine, the trace file for that session will be on the host, not on the local machine.

WHOLISTIC RULE #8
Inspect your database trace files daily using an automated process. Oracle writes these files for your information—use them.

Database Free Space

Using the two queries in the following listings, you can assess the total amount of free space in all your tablespaces and the largest chunk of free space in each tablespace. The first lists the amount of free space in each tablespace. The second displays the largest chunk of contiguous free space by tablespace. As we discussed in Chapter 3, Oracle allocates space in blocks, and adjacent chunks of blocks are referred to as *contiguous space*.

```
select tablespace_name,sum(bytes) from sys.dba_free_space
    group by tablespace_name;
select tablespace_name,max(bytes) from sys,dba_free_space
    group by tablespace_name;
```

The following listing shows the output from the code.

TABLESPACE_NAME	SUM(BYTES)
AUDIT_APPS	2678784
COMMON	18423808
DESIDERATA	10932224
FINANCIAL	40550400
ALL_INDEXES	4861952

TABLESPACE_NAME	MAX(BYTES)
AUDIT_APPS	1331200
COMMON	13897728
DESIDERATA	5734400
FINANCIAL	40550400
ALL_INDEXES	4505600

COLUMN NAME	COLUMN TYPE/LENGTH
TABLESPACE_NAME	VARCHAR2(30)
ALLOCATED	NUMBER
FREE_TODAY	NUMBER
FREE_YESTERDAY	NUMBER
PERCENT_CHANGED	NUMBER
SYSTEM_DATE	DATE

TABLE 8-4. *Table to Hold Daily Free Space Output*

Examining the output, using the DESIDERATA tablespace as an example, there are now 10,932,224 free bytes based on the first part of the output, and of that amount, the largest chunk of contiguous space is 5,734,400 bytes based on the second part of the output. A *contiguous chunk* is defined as space that is free in adjacent Oracle blocks. Because a block identifier (e.g., 4310 or 280) is assigned to each block in each tablespace in the database, if blocks 4000 through 4020 were free, we would have 21 blocks of contiguous free space.

What is even more useful is knowing the total space allocated to each tablespace, and the change in free space since the previous day. We recommend the following routine when inspecting database free space as part of the tuning exercise.

1. Create a table to hold free space information daily, as described in Table 8-4.

2. Run a script to create free space statistics for the current day.

3. Compare that amount against free space from the previous day.

4. Calculate a percentage (plus or minus) that the free space has changed since the previous day.

Using the table described in Table 8-4 (called FSPACE), the following code will populate the table with free space rows daily.

```
rem *  Create rows in FSPACE for today

insert into fspace
select a.tablespace_name,
       sum(a.bytes),            /* Allocated from DBA_DATA_FILES */
       round(sum(b.bytes)),     /* Free bytes from DBA_FREE_SPACE */
       '','',sysdate
```

```
  from sys.dba_data_files a,sys.dba_free_space b
 where a.tablespace_name = b.tablespace_name
 group by a.tablespace_name,'','',sysdate;

rem *  Yesterday's free space is in the rows from yesterday FREE_TODAY
rem *  column.  The FREE_TODAY column values from yesterday are moved into the
rem *  FREE_YESTERDAY columns for today's rows.

update fspace a
set free_yesterday =
    (select free_today
       from fspace b
      where a.tablespace_name = b.tablespace_name
        and to_char(b.system_date) = to_char(sysdate - 1))
where to_char(system_date) = to_char(sysdate);

rem *  The PERCENT_CHANGED is set to represent the following:
rem *  % change = free_today - free_yesterday / free_yesterday expressed
rem *  as a percentage.  The calculation has to use a DECODE in case the amount
rem *  of free space has not changed.  This avoids dividing by 0.

update fspace
   set percent_changed = round(decode(free_today-free_yesterday,
                            0,0,   /* If no change, set PERCENT_CHANGED to zero  */
                            100*(free_today-free_yesterday)/
                            (free_yesterday)),2)
 where to_char(system_date) = to_char(sysdate);

rem *  Print changed free space report for today.

col tablespace_name heading 'Tablespace'
col allocated heading 'Allocated' 999,999,990
col free_today heading 'Free today' form 999,999,990
col free_yesterday heading 'Yesterday form 999,999,990
col percent_changed heading 'Pct Ch' form 90.00

select tablespace_name, allocated, free_today, free_yesterday, percent_changed
  from fspace
 where to_char(system_date) = to_char(sysdate);
```

The output from this code looks like the report shown in the following listing. Negative numbers in the Pct Ch column indicate less free space today than yesterday. Positive numbers mean more free space today than yesterday.

Tablespace	Allocated	Today	Yesterday	Pct Ch
AUDIT_APPS	73,400,320	2,678,784	2,678,784	0.00
COMMON	209,715,200	18,423,808	18,423,808	0.00
DESIDERATA	209,715,200	10,932,224	7,245,824	50.88
FINANCIAL	104,857,600	40,550,400	40,796,160	-6.25
ALL_INDEXES	15,728,640	4,861,952	4,861,952	0.00

WHOLISTIC RULE #9
Examine database free space as part of the tuning process, using an automated process.

User Temporary Segment

As discussed in Chapter 3, users are pointed at a tablespace where they do sort work, when sort work space in memory is inadequate to support their sort operation. As new users are created, it is your job to ensure they do not use the SYSTEM tablespace for sorting to disk. Using the code following, report on any users that are still pointed at this forbidden tablespace.

```
select username from sys.dba_users where temporary_tablespace = 'SYSTEM';
```

WHOLISTIC RULE #10
Ensure that users are not using the SYSTEM tablespace as a work area for sorts that use disk space as well as memory.

Runaway Processes

In some environments, when users disconnect abnormally, there is a chance they could leave one or more orphan processes lying around. An orphan process is most common when a user (accessing the system using a PC with terminal emulation) does a warm boot to get out of a session that seems to be frozen. After CTRL-ALT-DEL, there is a possibility that the user's server process may not go away. In cooperation with your hardware support personnel, you must constantly look for these processes and clean up after them. Terminal emulation is an ideal candidate for this problem.

Now that more and more sites are using GUI (graphical user interface) front-ends, such as MS Windows and NT, this problem is even more common.

NOTE
We are not suggesting that the orphan process problem occurs frequently. We mention it to alert you of the situation and suggest you look out for it on your machine.

It is not unheard of that one of these orphan processes is consuming an unusually high amount of CPU (up to 85 percent at a time). It is your job to seek out these processes and remove them from your machine. These processes rob your machine, its CPU, and all other resources of precious processing time.

WHOLISTIC RULE #11
Monitor the processes on your machine for orphans that should be stopped. You will need the assistance of your installation's hardware superusers to remove unwanted processes that do not belong to you.

WHOLISTIC RULE #12
If you are using a multithreaded server (see Chapter 2 for details), watch out for runaway dispatcher processes. They can consume massive amounts of CPU time.

Two-Task Considerations

Most UNIX hardware runs Oracle using two-task architecture: a user process (e.g., SQL*Plus) and a database communication process called the *shadow process*. It is possible to build copies of most Oracle programs using what is referred to as single-task, which means the user process and the shadow process are one in the same. Oracle tools that are run in single-task have less overhead, because the interprocess communication necessary to support two-task is not needed for single-task. Oracle supplies programs to rebuild your application executables such as sqlplus and *runform30*. In HP-UX, for example, is a program called oracle.mk in the $ORACLE_HOME/rdbms/lib directory. In the midst of tuning Oracle, you may wish to experiment with single-task and examine the results.

NOTE
Client-server applications are not candidates for single-task.

The steps in a test case are as follows:

1. Using a two-task program, run a routine that accomplishes your predefined scenario.

2. Examine the statistics: elapsed time and CPU consumption.

3. Restore the data to a pre–two-task state.

4. Using a single-task program, run the same routine.

5. Compare the results.

You may find the performance of the single-task executable as high as 15 to 20 percent faster than the two-task program.

WHOLISTIC RULE #13
If your operating system supports both two-task and single-task architecture, investigate using Oracle programs in single-task.

NOTE
There can be a significant ripple effect when looking at single-task. BE CAREFUL and especially have a look at any applications in your systems that produce disk file output while running.

■ Transaction Control Features

Oracle7 introduces two time-saving features, called **truncate table** and **truncate cluster**. When rows are removed from a table, under normal circumstances, the rollback segments are used to hold undo information; if you do not commit your transaction, Oracle restores the data to the state it was in before your transaction started. With truncate, no undo information is generated. Removing rows from very large tables or clusters completes in a matter of seconds. Use **truncate** rather than **delete** for wiping the contents of small or large tables when you need no undo information generated. You may not qualify a truncate as you may be familiar with doing with delete. The following two statements illustrate using **truncate**.

```
truncate table plant_detail;
```

```
truncate cluster plant_clust;
```

Be aware that, because no undo is created with **truncate** once the "Table truncated" message is returned by Oracle, the rows in the table cannot be recovered. You cannot code any qualifiers (e.g., AND or WHERE) with the **truncate** statement. A more restrictive lock is acquired, as discussed in Chapter 7, when **truncate** is used instead of **delete**. You may find some Oracle lock errors returned that are similar to those you get from time to time performing an operation such as index creation. The secret with **truncate** is that because it requires fewer resources, it helps tune your applications.

WHOLISTIC RULE #14
Use **truncate table** and **truncate cluster** where appropriate. It is faster (allows more CPU time for other database activity) and needs fewer resources (no undo is generated) to complete.

Another transaction control feature is the following statement:

```
set transaction use rollback segment
```

This statement appeared in Oracle version 6. The name of a rollback segment is mentioned in the statement, and that rollback segment is used until the next **commit** statement is issued explicitly (by the user) or implicitly (by Oracle when disconnecting from SQL*Plus or issuing a DDL statement, such as **create**, **grant**, or **alter**). You will aid the performance of large transactions using this feature. Because the transaction is pointed at a large rollback segment, the likelihood of encountering extent errors (when the rollback segment needs more space and cannot acquire it) in the rollback segment is reduced.

WHOLISTIC RULE #15
To tune the performance of large SQL transactions, use
`set transaction use rollback segment`.

Efficient Resource Management

Of course, a finite amount of resources are available to manage the Oracle database as well as everything else your environment supports. You should incorporate a number of conventions into your applications and database management routines to minimize resource requirements and permit the sharing of these resources among more users doing more tasks. This contributes to the *wholistic* approach to tuning Oracle.

Frequency of commit Statements

During all database activity, the performance of your program is enhanced and its resource requirements are minimized by issuing frequent **commit** (i.e., saving work) statements. After all **update**, **delete**, and **insert** statements, a **commit** frees up the following resources:

- Information held in the rollback segments to undo the transaction, if necessary
- All locks acquired during statement processing
- Space in the redo log buffer cache (as described in Chapter 2)
- Overhead associated with any internal Oracle mechanisms to manage the resources in the previous three items

WHOLISTIC RULE #16
Issue frequent **commit** statements in your programs to free up resources.

Cursor Management Using PL/SQL

You may use PL/SQL with other SQL statements in SQL*Plus and most other tools that work with the Oracle database. With the emergence of new products, Oracle has adopted PL/SQL as the standard language for the new generation of tools— for example, Oracle*Card and Oracle*Glue. There are two ways to use *cursors* (the terminology Oracle uses to refer to a segment of memory acquired for SQL statement execution). The first way is to explicitly define a cursor, as illustrated in the following code:

```
procedure get_items is
cursor my_cursor is
  select count(*)
    from plant_detail
   where city_id = 12;
   temp_buffer number;
```

```
begin
  open my_cursor;
  fetch my_cursor into temp_buffer;
  close my_cursor;
end;
```

Notice how the code manually closes the cursor at the end. The second way is to allow Oracle to handle more of cursor management by implicitly defining the cursor, as shown in the following listing:

```
procedure get_items is
the_cnt number;
begin
  select count(*)
    into the_cnt
    from plant_detail
  where city_id = 12;
end;
```

There is no direct coding of any text mentioning a cursor, so Oracle handles it itself. We prefer using explicit cursors: they are easier to read, and they play a part in our wholistic tuning approach, because they perform better than implicit cursors. The major performance gain with explicit cursors is that they only initiate *one* call to the database for data. In a well-tuned system, as we discussed in Chapters 2 and 3, this "database access" will actually be a request for information in one or more of the Oracle memory caches. With implicit cursors, *two* requests are issued: the first to get (or fail to get, in some cases) the desired data, and the second to check for any error conditions that the first request may have detected.

WHOLISTIC RULE #17
Use explicit cursors in all your PL/SQL blocks.

Clusters

The wholistic approach to tuning the Oracle database must attend to using clusters. Clustering tables is an alternative way of storing Oracle data. A *cluster* is used to store data from one or more tables. Each cluster you build has a *cluster key*, which is one or more columns from the table(s) you are putting in the cluster that match one another in size and datatype. Oracle7 includes two kinds of clusters. *Indexed clusters* store data from one or more tables in the same data blocks of a tablespace; they provide a rapid access method, using indexes similar to the way they are used with unclustered tables. *Hash clusters* place rows from clustered tables in data blocks, after applying a hash function to the values in the cluster key columns. A hash table is maintained by Oracle for quick row retrieval from hash clusters. When we speak of *hash function,* consider the following example:

> Suppose a bank wants to build account numbers so that the seventh digit of each number is the units digit of the sum of all the other account number digits. This is commonly referred to as a check-digit hash formula. Using account number 2547862 as an example, the sum of the first six digits in the account number is 32. Thus, the units digit in this sum is the digit 2, which becomes the seventh digit of the full account number. We can then say a hash function is performed on the first six digits of a new account number to arrive at the seventh digit number.

You choose whether to use indexed or hash clusters by using the keyword **hashkeys** in the **create cluster** statement. Leaving out this keyword creates an indexed cluster. The keyword **hash is**, used when creating hash clusters, cannot be coded when a cluster is created, without also coding the **hashkeys** keyword at the same time. When you use clusters, you instruct Oracle to store the rows of tables in the same physical location, which can reduce the amount of I/O to retrieve the tables' data. When joins are done on clustered tables, the number of data blocks read to satisfy the query can be dramatically reduced. Candidate tables for clustering are ones that are constantly joined together and are mainly used in queries (**select** statements, as opposed to **insert**, **update**, and **delete** operations).

Clusters have been available with previous versions of Oracle, but the Oracle7 way of handling clusters further aids your efforts in tuning the performance of tables involved in joins.

Indexed Clusters

In the case of a single-table cluster, the rows sharing the same value for the cluster index column are stored in the same data blocks. In the case of multitable clusters, rows from ALL of the tables in the cluster that share column values in the cluster index are stored in the same data blocks. When creating an index cluster, it is important to pay close attention to the storage parameters even more so than when creating tables. The following steps contribute to the values you choose for some of the space parameters in a **create cluster** statement. The actual formulae used to do the calculations are not presented here. Consult the *Oracle7 Server Administrator's Guide* for the equations used for this exercise. (This summary of the steps is used with the permission of Oracle Corporation.)

1. Calculate the total block header size (the block header is a roadmap to the contents of each block in a cluster).

2. Calculate the available data space per block (the space for actual data in the block).

3. Calculate the combined column lengths of the average rows per cluster key (instructions for what to include and what to exclude from the calculations are on pages 8-45 and 8-46 of that guide).

4. Calculate the average row size of all the clustered tables (this is the minimum amount of space required by a row in a clustered table).

5. Calculate the average cluster block size (this value becomes the size parameter value when you create the cluster).

6. Calculate the total number of blocks required for the cluster (this affects the value of the **initial** parameter when you create the cluster).

If you have never worked with clusters, you will notice that the cluster index must be created before data can be inserted into the cluster. An Oracle error is raised if you try to use the cluster before making the cluster index. Oracle does not maintain index entries for indexed columns that have null values, whereas clustered tables have index entries for columns with nulls in the cluster key column(s).

WHOLISTIC RULE #18
Investigate using indexed clusters to speed up access to tables commonly joined together on a standard set of matching columns.

WHOLISTIC RULE # 19
Use documented formulae for calculating space parameters for indexed clusters based on row characteristics, volume of data, and the average number of rows per table per cluster index value.

Hash Clusters

After instructing Oracle to build a hash cluster, Oracle either performs an internal hashing routine on row cluster key values, or it bypasses the internal hashing mechanism if you use the **hash is** keyword when the hash cluster is created. Based on the result of the hash function, Oracle places rows in the hash cluster in the same data blocks as rows whose cluster key hashes to the same value. The *Oracle7 Server Administrator's Guide* includes a discussion on working with hash clusters and necessary calculations that should be made prior to defining hash clusters. If the following three conditions have been met, consider using hash clusters instead of indexed clusters.

- You are able to allocate space for tables with preallocated amounts for future growth.

- Query performance optimization is a primary goal of your tuning exercise.

- The columns that are part of the cluster key (hashed columns) are used in equality conditions in your SQL statement WHERE clause.

WHOLISTIC RULE #20
If the appropriate conditions have been met, use hash clusters to enhance the performance of applications.

Let's Tune It

The points we have made throughout this book contribute to a well-tuned database. As we have shown in this chapter, you need to monitor a wide spectrum of areas to cover all your bases. We can summarize the wholistic approach in the following high-level summary.

- Attend to the big three (I/O, memory, and CPU), but look at the bigger picture when tuning Oracle.

- Use the trace files written by Oracle to help pinpoint problem areas, and attend to them before they become more serious.

- Run your database in ARCHIVELOG mode to provide maximum protection against data loss.

- Use **truncate table** to wipe out the contents of tables—it creates no undo information and is much faster than **delete**.

- Consider using indexed and/or hash clusters when storing static data—the retrieval times for columns in clustered tables can enhance performance of some applications.

- Know your data, know your users, and know your applications.

- Use explicit cursors in PL/SQL blocks—they require less I/O than implicit cursors.

■ Whenever possible, issue frequent **commit** statements in all your programs; locks, latches, and other resources are freed up when a transaction does a commit or rollback.

■ Use EXPort and IMPort as part of your ongoing backup and recovery mechanisms.

■ Use a large buffer size (upwards of 10 megabytes, or 10,240,000 bytes) for EXPort and IMPort.

■ Always use the LOG parameter with EXPort and IMPort; partial imports especially are a nuisance when trying to figure what did not get imported, if you have no import session log file to inspect.

■ Set the COMMIT parameter to Y when importing large tables (greater than 100,000 rows).

■ Make copies of your control file in sqldba during system backups, using both of the following statements:

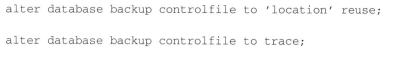

```
alter database backup controlfile to 'location' reuse;

alter database backup controlfile to trace;
```

■ Write a recovery plan and test it out on a nonproduction database to ensure the bugs are out before the real thing.

■ Run EXPort and IMPort in the background using the parameter file keyword (PARFILE=).

CHAPTER 9

Scripts and Tips

This chapter will present various scripts and tips that we have used or created from our years of working with the Oracle database. In our travel around the Oracle software over the past decade, we find ourselves armed with an assortment of tips and tricks. We have gained this knowledge from the trials and tribulations of our real-life Oracle experiences. A large number of our Oracle scripts help tune the database and contribute to efficient resource management. A great deal of experimentation with this and that has helped us to keep current with the advancing technology and to take advantage of new and better functionality as soon as it is released by Oracle.

We find the server technology that Oracle has implemented needs more information and tips disseminated than Oracle alone is capable of producing. This chapter highlights some areas we feel are high-level examples of what to look for to help you manage your Oracle databases and keep them running and running and running and running...

We will cover database backups, space management issues, accessing and using the important information in the SYS v$ and dba views, renaming a column in a table (preserving the well thought space considerations you have painstakingly put in place), and the ever-popular trick of using SQL to write SQL.

Tips on Backing Up Your Database

When deciding on a backup strategy, one of the first questions you need to ask is "If we experience hardware failure, how up to date does our database need to be after recovering from a backup?" Hardware failure is not common, but preparing a strategy to deal with problems if and when they happen is a wise decision.

ARCHIVELOG Mode

We have discussed making online backups of your database and the recovery procedures in Chapter 8.

SCRIPTS AND TIPS RULE #1
Use ARCHIVELOG mode as part of the backup strategy in your production database.

The following may convince you that there is no need to run your database in NOARCHIVELOG mode. After we present the almost bulletproof protection ARCHIVELOG offers, we know you will start using it at once. We now present four common "excuses" we hear for not using ARCHIVELOG mode, and we'll lead you through a discussion of why these (and all other reasons) should not keep you from using ARCHIVELOG.

- Our database is not used during the quiet hours, and there is no need to leave it up 24 hours a day—backing it up while it is not running is sufficient.

  1. Using the regimen described in Chapter 4, where we recommend you move reporting jobs into the quiet hours, the need to leave the database up all the time becomes obvious.

  2. As we discussed in Chapter 2 and elsewhere in this book, when the database is closed and restarted, you lose all the information held in the numerous caches that Oracle maintains as your instance operates.

These caches must be filled all over again each time the database is started. The filling of these caches leads to unnecessary disk I/O.

3. We discuss continuous monitoring that you should perform on your database (especially the UTLBstat.sql and UTLEstat.sql performance diagnostic programs in Chapter 5). The secret to monitoring is to provide the program you use with the best time slice to perform the statistics gathering. Closing your database daily for backups limits this time slice to a period always less than 24 hours.

■ Export offers us all the protection we need (refer to Chapter 8 for details on the role export can play in tuning your database), and nobody uses the instance during the night anyway.

1. You have no idea when users access your database. The only time you truly know they are not logged on is when the instance is not running. For this reason, using export alone is questionable. There is a possibility that someone may be on the machine when you least expect it.

2. Using export alone means a single point of failure. If, for example, the export does not work (the message "Import terminated with warnings" is displayed at the end) or the disk you are exporting to fills up, the file written by export may be unusable or incomplete.

■ The disk space used to store archived redo logs is just not available on our computer (refer to Chapter 8, where we discuss how this works).

1. While keeping in mind concepts such as disk striping and table/index splitting (as discussed in Chapter 3), you should consider moving database files around your disks to free up space on a dedicated drive to hold these archived redo log files.

2. When there is no disk space to be found, purchase more. Seems easier said than done, however, an $8,000 disk drive is far cheaper than running the risk of losing a full day's transactions when not running in ARCHIVELOG mode.

■ We run huge reporting jobs, which just produce so many archived redo logs that the disk holding archived redo logs would be filled to capacity.

1. Look at running those jobs on the same machine using another database that is not in ARCHIVELOG mode. Then, when using the application that accesses that data, read it from the other database using SQL*Net.

2. Move the large amount of archived redo logs to tape during the reporting job itself.

3. In UNIX, for example, compress your archived redo logs periodically during the day. They are compressed anyway as they are written to tape.

SCRIPTS AND TIPS RULE #2:
Use a combination of online backups (refer to Chapter 8 for details) and export for system backups.

SCRIPTS AND TIPS RULE #3
Test your recovery routines before you need to use them in a real emergency. Do so on a separate instance of Oracle, and go through the steps involved. Consult the Oracle7 Server Administrator's Guide for details.

Space Management Tips

Implementing routines and automated procedures to help track space allocation events in your database will help the tuning exercise. In Chapter 6, we discuss extent issues and the maximum number of extents a table may acquire. In this section, we will present a way to monitor the number of extents allocated to tables.

Part of space management for the database as a whole involves monitoring the free space by tablespace. We discuss one approach to tracking free space by tablespace in the "Database Free Space" section of Chapter 8. This chapter will discuss another way to monitor free space and present you with results that list the percentage of space free by tablespace.

Because Oracle tracks and allocates space to tables by blocks, we will discuss the concept of how Oracle7 tracks contiguous space in tablespaces. *Contiguous space* is space in adjacent blocks. In a 4K (4,096-byte) block size, if 300 blocks of free space are adjacent to one another in a tablespace, then 1,228,800 bytes of contiguous space are available.

Extent Monitoring

You need to continually inform yourself of tables in your database that are overextended or are reaching their **maxextents** limit. Bringing this information to your attention now before extent problems occur helps keep your database tuned.

Overextended Tables and Indexes (More Than Five Extents Allocated)

The following listing will inform you of the tables and indexes that are overextended. We use the term *overextended* when a table or index has more than five extents.

```
SQL> select owner "Owner", segment_name "Segment Name",
  2      segment_type "Type", tablespace_name "Tablespace",
  3      extents "#Ext", max_extents "Max"
  4      from sys.dba_extents
  5      where extents > 5
  6      and owner not in ('SYS','SYSTEM')
  7      order by owner,segment_name;
```

Owner	Segment Name	Type	Tablespace	#Ext	Max
USER1	ACC_TABLE	TABLE	TBSP_TESTONE	7	99
USER1	TBL_SECONDS	TABLE	TBSP_TESTONE	7	99
USER1	ACTORS	TABLE	TBSP_TESTONE	16	120
USER1	XFERS	TABLE	TBSP_TESTONE	6	120
USER2	HISTORY_FILE	TABLE	TBSP_TESTTWO	8	120
USER2	HISTORY_INDEX	INDEX	TBSP_TESTTWO	9	120
USER2	TEMP2	INDEX	TBSP_TESTTWO	8	120
USER3	FORM	TABLE	TBSP_TEST3	13	120
USER3	MENU	TABLE	TBSP_TEST3	21	120
USER3	REPORT	TABLE	TBSP_TEST3	8	120

The consolidation of extents into one chunk of contiguous space can be accomplished by following these steps.

1. Export the table (the grants and indexes will automatically be written to the export file with Oracle7).

2. Drop the table.

3. Import the table.

Consider the following query and its results before these three steps are performed.

```
SQL> select segment_name, extents
  2  from sys.dba_segments
  3  where table_name = 'MY_TABLE' and owner = 'USER1';
SEGMENT_NAME        EXTENTS
------------------ -------
MY_TABLE               101
```

After exporting, dropping, and importing the table, the same query results would be

```
SEGMENT_NAME        EXTENTS
------------------  -------
MY_TABLE                  1
```

This method works; however, to allow for some extra expansion, we recommend the following in our next rule.

SCRIPTS AND TIPS RULE #4

When defragmenting overextended tables, set the **initial** parameter for the table to the size of the data in the table plus an additional 25 percent.

Using the export file created for the defragmentation of the table MY_TABLE, perform the following steps to create the table with a properly sized **initial** space allocation.

1. Run import table using the following command:

```
imp userid=user1/password indexfile=my_table.sql
```

By using the INDEXFILE parameter with import, you have instructed Oracle to write table and index creation information to the file specified, rather than bring the data back into the table. The file will contain **create** statements for the table and any indexes. Any triggers and declarative integrity (refer to Chapter 7 for a brief discussion of declarative integrity) defined for the table will be brought back in step #4.

2. Edit the file my_table.sql:

■ Remove all "REM" text at the start of lines.

■ Look for and delete any rows that contain the word "Connect."

■ Look for and delete any rows that start with the word "Rows."

■ Look for the **initial** and increase it by 25 percent.

3. Run my_table.sql in SQL*Plus.

4. Import the table data using the command

```
imp userid=user1/password ignore=y tables=my_tabledata
```

This command must mention the keyword IGNORE=Y to force Oracle to bring in the table data even though the table already exists after step #3 has completed. If

IGNORE is not coded on the call to import, it defaults to N, and the import will abort because the table already exists.

SCRIPTS AND TIPS RULE #5
Always use IGNORE=Y to bring the table data in after the table has been created, when defragmenting a table using export and import.

Throughout this exercise, we have assumed that there is enough space in the tablespace where the table resides to accommodate the additional requests needed for the table. If this were not the case, you would have to either add another datafile to the tablespace or rebuild the entire tablespace with a larger datafile.

Tables and Indexes Reaching maxextents

It is wise to know when a table or index is reaching its maximum number of extents. A SQL*Plus script (we call it "withinmax.sql") that reports on this information is shown next. The report lists tables and indexes that are within "X" extents of reaching their maximum. This script first figures out the block size for the database by looking in the v$parameter data dictionary table and translates it into a maximum number of extents. As discussed in Chapter 6, this maximum is related to the Oracle block size.

```
ttitle center 'Report of Next Extent Within ' &1 ' of maxextents' skip -
       center 'Date: ' datevar skip -
       left '(T/I - Table or Index)' skip 2
column bsize new_value max_ext
column today new_value datevar format a1 noprint
select sysdate today, decode(value,2048,121,240) bsize
/* You get 121 max extents if block   */
/* size is 2048 and 240 if it is 4096 */
  from v$parameter
 where name = 'db_block_size';
select a.owner, table_name "object",
       a.tablespace_name "tablespace",
       'T' "T/I",
       a.max_extents max_extents,
       b.extents current_extent
  from sys.dba_tables a, sys.dba_segments b
 where table_name = segment_name and
       (a.max_extents < extents + &1 or &max_ext < extents + &1)
union
select a.owner, index_name, a.tablespace_name,
```

```
      'I' indicator,
        a.max_extents max_extents,
        b.extents current_extent
    from sys.dba_indexes a, sys.dba_segments b
  where index_name = segment_name and
        (a.max_extents < extents + &1 or &max_ext < extents + &1);
```

If the program is called using the following command

```
sqlplus @withinmax 10
```

the output produced is shown in the following.

```
              Report of Next Extent Within 10 of maxextents
                        DATE: 05-JAN-96
(T/I - TABLE OR INDEX)


OWNER      OBJECT             TABLESPACE          T/I MAX_EXTENTS CURRENT_EXTENT
--------   ----------------   ------------------  --- ----------- --------------
USER1      IND_BILLING        TBSP_IDX_ACTION     I            99             92
USER1      IND_SERVICE        TBSP_IDX_ACTION     I            20             12
```

Contiguous Space Monitoring

You may remember the exercise you had to go through with version 6 of Oracle, using the DBA_FREE_SPACE dictionary view, to monitor contiguous free space. The following listing is the output from a query using version 6 with the 4K (4,096 bytes) block size.

```
SQL> select * from sys.dba_free_space
  2 where tablespace_name = 'USERS7'
  3 order by block_id;

TABLESPACE_NAME     FILE_ID    BLOCK_ID        BYTES      BLOCKS
----------------  ----------  ----------   ----------  ----------
USERS7                    16         817        49152          12
USERS7                    16         829       356352          87
USERS7                    16        •5359      1024000         250
USERS7                    16        5609       409600         100
USERS7                    16        5709       565248         138
USERS7                    16        8463     13897728        3393

6 rows selected.
```

By examining Table 9-1, we used to have to assess the true amount of contiguous free space. For each row, you had to take the starting block ID and add the number of blocks free. If that equaled the block ID of the next row, then the two rows contained contiguous space even though Oracle did not present the output that way.

With Oracle7, the management of adjacent chunks of free space as reported by dba_free_space is handled in the following manner. The first step is similar to the way version 6 handled merging of adjacent free space chunks. Merging of free space chunks is referred to as *coalescing* of free space. The second step is new to Oracle7.

1. When Oracle finds contiguous chunks of free space, it will lump them together to satisfy a larger space request. If Oracle needs 40 blocks to satisfy the allocation of an extent, and it finds 30 blocks (let's call this chunka) adjacent to a 20-block chunk (let's call this chunkb), it will use all of chunka and 10 blocks of chunkb to allocate space for the 40-block extent. After the extent allocation is complete, 10 blocks will still be free—these 10 blocks represent the second half of chunkb, whose first 10 blocks were allocated to the extent. This is done dynamically by Oracle.

2. Periodically, the system monitor (SMON) background process (Chapter 2 discusses the Oracle background processes) coalesces adjacent chunks of free space to make one larger contiguous chunk.

BEGIN BLOCK ID	BLOCKS OF FREE SPACE	ACTUAL CONTIGUOUS SPACE (BLOCKS)
817	12	99
829	87	(part of the 99 above)
5359	250	488
5609	100	(part of the 488 above)
5709	138	(part of the 488 above)
8463	3393	3393

TABLE 9-1. *Resolving Actual Contiguous Free Space Using Version 6*

With Oracle7, the output of the query would be a bit different. Notice how Oracle has coalesced contiguous chunks of free space.

TABLESPACE_NAME	FILE_ID	BLOCK_ID	BYTES	BLOCKS
USERS7	16	817	405504	99
USERS7	16	5359	1998848	488
USERS7	16	8463	13897728	3393

3 rows selected.

SCRIPTS AND TIPS RULE #6
Because the system monitor Oracle process coalesces free space, don't bother running reports any more that merge adjacent chunks of free space as reported by the dba_free_space dictionary table.

NOTE
There will be no entry in dba_free_space for any tablespace that has NO free blocks. This is a trojan horse to be watched for!

SCRIPTS AND TIPS RULE #7
On reports that display the free space totals by tablespace, ensure the number of rows returned is the same as the number of tablespaces in the database. This will alert you if a situation occurs where a tablespace has no free space whatsoever.

Free Space by Tablespace Monitoring

Along with monitoring the number of extents that segments have, the monitoring of the free space in a database should be done on a regular basis. This monitoring can be used to determine if too much space is allocated to a tablespace or if additional space needs to be allocated.

The following SQL script reports on the allocated space in each tablespace, the amount of free space for each tablespace, and percentage of allocated space that remains free.

```
SQL> select b.file_id "File #"
  2          b.tablespace_name "Tablespace name",
  3          b.bytes "# bytes",
  4          (b.bytes - sum(nvl(a.bytes,0))) "# used",
  5          sum(nvl(a.bytes,0)) "# free",
  6          (sum(nvl(a.bytes,0))/(b.bytes))*100 "%free"
  7    from sys.dba_free_space a, sys.dba_data_files b
  8    where a.file_id(+) = b.file_id
  9    group by b.tablespace_name, b.file_id, b.bytes
 10    order by b.tablespace_name
```

File#	Tablespace Name	# Bytes	# Used	# Free	%Free
1	SYSTEM	104857600	26503168	78354432	74.7
3	TBSP_INDEX001	83886080	78610432	5275648	6.3
9	TBSP_INDEX001	10485760	6907904	3577856	34.1
5	TBSP_PROD001	3145728	2048	3143680	99.9
6	TBSP_PROD002	5242880	3381248	1861632	35.5
7	TBSP_PROD003	52428800	50563792	1835008	3.5
8	TBSP_PROD004	5242880	2021376	3221504	61.4
2	TBSP_ROLLBACK	157286400	47310848	109975552	69.9
4	TBSP_USER_TEMP	31457280	2048	31455232	100.0
10	TBSP_WORK	31457280	11300864	20156416	64.1

This listing shows that in tablespace TBSP_INDEX001, a mere 6.3 percent of space allocated is not being used. As well, in tablespace TBSP_PROD003, only 3.5 percent of space allocated is not in use. The SYSTEM tablespace is only using 25.3 percent of the space allocated to it. The following recommendations from this report may help you make the sizing decisions that help tune your database.

1. The INDEX001 and PROD003 tablespaces have too low a percent of space not in use.

2. If the database is in a production mode (persons use the database daily to undertake the business of your installation), the SYSTEM tablespace is using too little of its space to be sized at 102.4 megabytes.

3. Tablespace PROD001 may have too much space allocated, unless it has been preallocated for a large load of data.

SCRIPTS AND TIPS RULE #8
If the free space in a tablespace containing tables that experience high insert and update activity falls below 15 percent, add more space to the tablespace.

SCRIPTS AND TIPS RULE #9
If a tablespace holds static table data, reduce the amount of file space allocated to it if there is more than 20 percent free space.

SCRIPTS AND TIPS RULE #10
Increasing the amount of free space in a tablespace may not always involve adding an additional datafile. Tablespace reorganization using export and import may free up large quantities of space, alleviating the need to add another datafile.

SCRIPTS AND TIPS RULE #11
The only way to decrease the amount of space allocated to the SYSTEM tablespace is to re-create the database.

Table and Index Sizing

As mentioned in Chapter 3, we have developed a two-table small system of calculating estimates for table and index sizing. The two tables contain the table information in one and index information in the other. The next listing gives the create table scripts for these objects.

```
rem     Table sizing table.
create table table_sizing (
     table_pk           number primary key,
     table_name         varchar2(30),
     owner              varchar2(20),
     adj_row_size       number(4),
     row_count          number,
     tspace             varchar2(30),
     pct_free           number(3),
     initrans           number(2),
     free_lists         number(2));
rem     Index sizing table.
create table index_sizing (
```

```
table_pk                    number references (table_sizing),
index_pk                    number primary key,
index_name                  varchar2(30),
uniqueness                  number(1),
number_col_index            number(2),
total_col_length            number(3),
percent_free                number(2),
initrans                    number(2),
tspace                      varchar2(30));
```

Each of these two tables has its own sequence number associated with it, which serves as the primary key for each. The next listing gives the create sequence number statements. The sequence numbers are the primary keys for each table.

```
create sequence table_pk;
create sequence index_pk;
```

The table_sizing and the index_sizing tables are related by the relationship that a table may have one or more indexes and that an index must be for one and only one table. You may notice that the table_pk column defines the relationship between the table_sizing and the index_sizing tables.

We have developed a screen using Oracle Forms to populate these sizing tables. Figure 9-1 shows the first screen of the form, which is used to input the specifications for the table and indexes that are being sized. The second screen, shown in Figure 9-2, accepts a percent factor as input. This factor provides the ability to calculate the size of objects at different percentages of full load of the table and indexes entered in the first screen. By pressing the COMMIT key (usually mapped to the "Do" key on a VT terminal) on the second screen, the form calculates the estimated size in kilobytes for the table and indexes.

Most of the code for the form is the standard Oracle Forms code, using table_sizing as the master table and index_sizing as the detail table with the relationship of

```
table_sizing.table_pk = index_sizing.table_pk
```

The second screen contains two different blocks without a base table connected to either. The top block contains the % (percent) of full load field as the only enterable field. The bottom block contains a one-character enterable, non-echo field at the beginning of each row, so the user can enter the block and row through the rows.

```
+----------------------------------------------------------------------+
|PDD0269___                   Table / Index Sizing             05-AUG-95|
+-TABLE----------------------------------------------------------------+
|OWNER    USER1_____   TABLE NAME DATA_TABLE_1_____  |
|ROW COUNT 10000_____       TABLESPACE NAME TBSP_DATA_____  |
|ROW SIZE  240___            % FREE 10___   INITRANS 1___   FREE LIST 12__|
+-INDEXES--------------------------------------------------------------+
|                        UNIQUENESS  NUMBER OF  INDEX     %             |
|            INDEX NAME   (1-YES,0-NO) COLUMNS  LENGTH FREE INITRANS     |
|  INDX1_____    1__        4___    12__  10__  12__        |
|  TABLESPACE NAME TBSP_INDEX_____                       |
|  _____        __        ___     ___  ___   ___          |
|  TABLESPACE NAME _____                        |
|  _____        __        ___     ___  ___   ___          |
|  TABLESPACE NAME _____                        |
|  _____        __        ___     ___  ___   ___          |
|  TABLESPACE NAME _____                        |
|  _____        __        ___     ___  ___   ___          |
|  TABLESPACE NAME _____                        |
|  _____        __        ___     ___  ___   ___          |
|  TABLESPACE NAME _____                        |
+----------------------------------------------------------------------+

Count: *0                                                 <Replace>
```

FIGURE 9-1.   *The first screen of the Table/Index Sizing Form*

```
+----------------------------------------------------------------------+
|PDD0269___                   Table / Index Sizing       .     05-AUG-95|
+-TABLE----------------------------------------------------------------+
| TABLE NAME : DATA_TABLE_1_____   % OF FULL LOAD : 100__  |
|                    SIZE (IN K) : _____2,858_                     |
|(Press <CRTL>P to spool to a file)       (Press <Do> to Calculate Size)|
+-INDEXES--------------------------------------------------------------+
|              TOTAL SIZE FOR INDEXES : _____367_                |
|                                                                      |
| INDEX NAME : _INDX1_____  SIZE (IN K) : _____367_ |
|                                                                      |
|           _____    _____      |
|                                                                      |
|           _____    _____      |
|                                                                      |
|           _____    _____      |
|                                                                      |
|           _____    _____      |
|                                                                      |
|           _____    _____      |
+----------------------------------------------------------------------+

Count:*0                                                  <Replace>
```

FIGURE 9-2.   *The second screen of the Table/Index Sizing Form*

The core of this form is the KEY-COMMIT trigger on the top block of the second screen. The next listing gives the code for the KEY-COMMIT trigger.

```
Trigger Name: key-commit                      Style: V3   Hide: No
      Text: DECLARE
          I_NAME CHAR(30);
          I_SIZE integer;
          ITOTAL INTEGER;
          BEGIN
          if :load_percent is null then
              message('Load Percent is required.');
              bell;
          else
              if round(((1958 - (:tables.initrans * 23)) *
                    ((100-:PCT_FREE)/100))/:adj_row_size) = 0 then
              :TSIZE_K := greatest(4, ceil((:ROW_COUNT * (:LOAD_PERCENT/100)) /
                          ((((1958 - (:tables.initrans * 23)) *
                          ((100-:PCT_FREE)/100)) /
                          :ADJ_ROW_SIZE)))) * 2);
           else
              :TSIZE_K := greatest(4, ceil((:ROW_COUNT * (:LOAD_PERCENT/100)) /
                          ((round(((1958 - (:tables.initrans * 23)) *
                          ((100-:PCT_FREE)/100)) /
                          :ADJ_ROW_SIZE)))) * 2);
           end if;
          ITOTAL := 0;
          GO_BLOCK('INDEXES');
          FIRST_RECORD;
          GO_BLOCK('SIZE_INDEX');
          FIRST_RECORD;
          LOOP
              GO_BLOCK('INDEXES');
              IF :INDEX_NAME IS NULL THEN
                 EXIT;
              END IF;
              I_NAME := :INDEX_NAME;
              I_SIZE := greatest(4, ( 1.01 ) *
                      (( (:row_count * (:load_percent/100.)) /
                      (( floor(((2048 - 113 - (:indexes.initrans * 23)) *
                      (1-(:percent_free/100.))) / ((10+:uniqueness)+
                      :number_col_index+(:total_col_length)))))))*2));
              ITOTAL := ITOTAL + I_SIZE;
              NEXT_RECORD;
```

```
        go_block('size_index');
        :sindex_name := I_name;
        :isize_k := i_size;
        NEXT_RECORD;
    END LOOP;
    GO_BLOCK('Indexes');
    FIRST_RECORD;
    GO_BLOCK('SIZE_INDEX');
    FIRST_RECORD;
    :ITOT_K := ITOTAL;
    end if;
    end;
```

Following is a description of what the trigger does:

1. Checks to make sure that a value has been entered into the Percent of Full Load field.

 `if :load_percent is null...`

2. The number of records per blocks is then calculated and it is determined if the record will span more than one block or not.

 `if round(((...)=0...`

3. The size of the table in kilobytes is then calculated using the information entered into the TABLES block. The calculation is slightly different depending on whether a record will span more than one block.

 `:tsize_k :=...`

4. A local variable that will be used to sum up the total size of all the indexes is initialized and the current record for both the INDEXES block and SIZE_INDEX block is set to be the first record in each.

 `Itotal := 0...`

5. A loop is established that will continue until the current record on the INDEXES block is blank.

 `Loop...`

6. The index name is held in a local variable, the size of the index is put into a local variable, and its size is added to the total size local variable.

```
I_NAME := ... ITOTAL := ITOTAL + I_SIZE
```

7. The next record in the INDEXES block is made the current record, the index name and size are entered into the appropriate fields in the SIZE_INDEX block, and the next record in the SIZE_INDEX block is made the current record.

```
NEXT_RECORD; ...NEXT_RECORD;
```

8. End of the loop.

```
END LOOP;
```

9. When all records have been processed, the total index size field is populated and the trigger ends.

```
:TOT_K :=ITOTAL; ... end
```

Once the information is entered into the table_sizing and index_sizing table by way of the Oracle Forms, reports can be produced that calculate and print out the estimated sizing for the tables and indexes. Next is an SQL*Plus script that produces a listing of the estimated sizing.

```
rem      Table sizing report.
rem
set pagesize 60
set newpage 0
column initial format 999,999,999
column next format 99,999,999
break on report
compute sum of "INITIAL" on report
compute sum of "NEXT"  on report
column pct new_value percent noprint;
ttitle center -
    'Table Storage Calculations for Initial and Next Extents (in kilobytes)' -
    skip center 'Percent of Total ' percent skip 2
select &3 pct from dual;
spool &4
```

```
select owner,table_name ,
        decode (round(((1958 - (initrans * 23)) *
                          ((100-pct_free)/100))/adj_row_size),0,
          greatest(4, ceil((row_count*(&3/100)) /
          (((((1958 - (initrans * 23)) *
          ((100-pct_free)/100)) /
          adj_row_size)))) * 2),
          greatest(4, ceil((row_count*(&3/100)) /
          ((round(((1958 - (initrans * 23)) *
          ((100-pct_free)/100)) /
           adj_row_size)))) * 2)) "INITIAL",
  decode (round(((1958 - (initrans * 23)) *
                          ((100-pct_free)/100))/adj_row_size),0,
          greatest(4, (ceil((row_count*(&3/100)) /
          (((((1958 - (initrans * 23)) *
          ((100-pct_free)/100)) /
          adj_row_size)))) * 2) * .1),
          greatest(4, (ceil((row_count*(&3/100)) /
          ((round(((1958 - (initrans * 23)) *
          ((100-pct_free)/100)) /
           adj_row_size)))) * 2) * .1)) NEXT
  from table_sizing
 where table_name like upper('&1')
   and owner like upper('&2')
 order by 1,2;
rem
rem        Index sizing report.
rem
set pagesize 60
set newpage 0
ttitle center 'Index Storage Calculations (in kilobytes)' -
        skip center 'Percent of Total ' percent skip2 2
column index_size format 999,999
column table_name format a20
column index_name format a20
break on report
compute sum of index_size on report
select owner, table_name, index_name,
       greatest(4, ( 1.01 ) * (( (row_count*(&3/100)) / (( floor(((2048 - 113 -
               (a.initrans * 23)) *
               (1-(percent_free/100))) /
               ((10+uniqueness)+ number_col_index+(total_col_length))))))*2))
               index_size
```

```
  from index_sizing a, table_sizing b
 where index_name is not null
   and a.table_pk = b.table_pk
   and table_name like upper('&1')
   and owner like upper('&2')
 order by owner, table_name,index_name;
spool off
exit;
```

The script takes four parameters. The first parameter is a table name qualifier that will be used in a **like** command. The second parameter is the owner qualifier that will be used in a **like** command. The third parameter is the percent of full load to be used for the calculations. The fourth parameter is an operating system file name to which the output will be directed. The following gives an example of running this script from an operating system prompt. The name of the file that contains the script is sizing.sql.

```
sqlplus / @sizing "%" "USER1" "100" "sizing.rpt"
```

This command will produce a table and index sizing report for all tables ("%") that were entered with an owner of USER1 at 100 percent of full load. As a standard practice we set the **next** parameter in **create table** to 10 to 15 percent of the value coded for **initial**. The listing report from the above specifications is shown as follows.

```
Table Storage Calculations for Initial and Next Extents (in kilobytes)
                    Percent of Total          100


OWNER                 TABLE_NAME                       INITIAL        NEXT
-------------------   -----------------------------  ------------  -----------
USER1                 DATA_TABLE_1                        2,858          286
                                                     ------------  -----------
sum                                                       2,858          286
                     Index Storage Calculations (in kilobytes)
                          Percent of Total      100


OWNER                 TABLE_NAME            INDEX_NAME             INDEX_SIZE
-------------------   --------------------  ---------------------  ----------
USER1                 DATA_TABLE_1          INDX1                         367
                                                                  ----------
sum                                                                      367
```

The output from this report can then be used in the **create table** and **create index** commands to specify the **initial** and **next** size for the objects.

SCRIPTS AND TIPS RULE #12
Go through a sizing exercise similar to the one presented when planning for new tables.

User Information

There will come times, either for auditing purposes or user requests, that user information will need to be gathered. We have used Oracle Reports to create a report that gives the username, the date it was created, roles that have been granted to the user, the user's default and temporary tablespaces, and if the username is assigned a role in Oracle Forms. We use the parent/child query relationship in Oracle Reports to see if any Oracle Forms menu role has been given to each user. In Oracle Reports (as was the case with its predecessor, SQL*Reportwriter), you worded a top-level query (called the parent query), such as

```
select username, id, promo_date, name
  from sys_users;
```

and caused a lower-level query (called the child query), such as

```
select cumulative_logons, screens_accessed, username
  from sys_activities;
```

to be executed for each row returned to the parent. You tell Oracle Reports to suppress displaying the username from the child query. A few lines of the output are shown next.

Username	ID	Due promo	Name	Logons	Screens
ABBFLAB	213	12-DEC-95	Boris Abbflantro	289	29
BESDESN	198	11-MAR-97	Nancy Besdesmith	812	102
NADROJN	23	09-FEB-96	Norman Nadrojian	34	2345
DEFWAYF	721	11-MAR-95	Francis Defwayno	321	1189

The following two queries are set up to produce the Oracle Forms report.

<u>Parent query</u>
```
select username "Username", created "Created",
       substr(granted_role,1,15) "Roles",
       default_tablespace "Default TS",
       temporary_tablespace "Temporary TS"
  from sys.dba_users, sys.dba_role_privs
 where username = grantee (+)
 order by username
```
<u>Child query</u>
```
select unique '#' "#", user_name
from menu_v_user
```

An example of the output that is produced from this report follows. The last column just has a # indicator in it if the username is granted at least one menu role.

```
                            USER LIST
PAGE: 1                                          DATE: 24-AUG-97


Username        Created   Roles            Default TS       Temporary TS    #
--------------  --------  ---------------  ---------------  ---------------  -

ADAMS           03/18/94  CONNECT          TBSP_WORKDEV     TBSP_TEMPORARY
FORMS30         03/18/94  CONNECT          TBSP_WORKDEV     TBSP_TEMPORARY
FORMS30         03/18/94  RESOURCE         TBSP_WORKDEV     TBSP_TEMPORARY
OPS$USER1       03/18/94  CONNECT          SYSTEM           SYSTEM          #
OPS$USER1       03/18/94  DBA              SYSTEM           SYSTEM          #
OPS$USER1       03/18/94  RESOURCE         SYSTEM           SYSTEM          #
OPS$USER002     03/18/94  CONNECT          TBSP_WORKDEV     TBSP_TEMPORARY  #
OPS$APPLIC1     03/18/94  CONNECT          TBSP_DATA001     TBSP_TEMPORARY
OPS$APPLIC1     03/18/94  RESOURCE         TBSP_DATA001     TBSP_TEMPORARY
SYS             03/17/94  CONNECT          SYSTEM           SYSTEM          #
SYS             03/17/94  DBA              SYSTEM           SYSTEM          #
SYS             03/17/94  EXP_FULL_DATABA  SYSTEM           SYSTEM          #
SYS             03/17/94  IMP_FULL_DATABA  SYSTEM           SYSTEM          #
SYS             03/17/94  RESOURCE         SYSTEM           SYSTEM          #
```

As can be seen, the users are listed alphabetically by their username and appear multiple times if they have been assigned multiple Oracle roles.

SCRIPTS AND TIPS RULE #13
Gather user information as part of your daily backups—it will assist you when trying to set up new users or groups of users.

Accessing all v$ and dba_ Dictionary Views

Throughout this book, we make continual reference to the assortment of v$ views owned by Oracle user SYS. The assortment of views prefixed by the characters dba_ prove useful to the DBA and application developers as well. Regardless of what is done at installation time, our experience dictates that you should manually give access to these views. A script that will grant select access to PUBLIC on all v$ and dba_ views is shown next. It must be run connected to the database as Oracle user SYS.

```
set echo off feed off pages 0
spool veedollar_dba.sql
select 'grant select on '||table_name||' to public;'
  from user_views
 where view_name like 'V_$%'
    or view_name like 'DBA_%;
set echo on feed on
@veedollar_dba
```

After this script completes, all database users will be able to access the desired dictionary views. Public synonyms are in place for the v$ tables. None are in place (unless you put them there) for the dba_views. When using these dba_ views, simply qualify the view name with the SYS account qualifier.

SCRIPTS AND TIPS RULE #14
Do not create public synonyms for the dba_ views. Developers who need to use them can use the account qualifier syntax (e.g., the dba_free_space view is referenced using the name sys.dba_free_space).

Sizing the Shared Pool

Finding the optimal size for the shared pool can be an elusive exercise. As DBAs and application programmers, we are all too familiar with Oracle error ORA-04031.

```
04031, 00000, "out of shared memory when trying to allocate %s bytes (%s,%s)"
// *Cause:  More shared memory is needed than was allocated in the shared
//          pool.
```

```
// *Action: Reduce your use of shared memory, or increase the amount of
//          available shared memory by increasing the value of the
//          init.ora parameter "shared_pool_size".
```

Using the code that follows, that figure can be calculated. There are a few points worth noting in the listing. They are embedded in the code as remarks.

```
set echo off ver off feed off pages 0

rem * You are prompted for the Oracle ID of someone currently
rem * logged on. That person's memory consumption will be used
rem * as a sample amount. You are also asked for the # of
rem * concurrent users to base this calculation on.

accept username prompt 'User to use?? '
accept numusers prompt '# of users ?? '

rem * Get that user's session identifier by joining v$process
rem * and v$session matching the ADDR column from v$process
rem * against the PADDR column from v$session, and matching
rem * the USERNAME column from v$session against the username
rem * entered before

set term off
col a new_value snum
select sid a
  from v$process p, v$session s
 where p.addr = s.paddr
   and s.username = 'OPS$'||upper('&username');

rem * Now that we have the sample user's session
rem * ID, we can go to v$sesstat for the amount of memory
rem * that user is consuming.  We use STATISTIC# = 16 which is
rem * the MAX SESSION MEMORY per user maintained in
rem * v$sesstat for each user connected to the database.

col b new_value pumem
select value b
  from v$sesstat
 where statistic# = 16
   and sid = &snum;
```

```
rem * Get the amount of memory in the shared pool that is
rem * currently in use (i.e., the size of the SQL sitting in the
rem * shared pool).
col c new_value spl
select sum(sharable_mem) c
  from v$sqlarea;
rem * Using the following formula, make the optimal shared
rem * pool size calculation.
rem * optimal size = 1.3 * (per_user_memory * number _users +
                            size_of_sql_in_pool)
col d new_value size1
col e new_value size2
select (&pumem*&numusers+&spl) d,
       (&pumem*&numusers+&spl)+3/10*(&pumem*&numusers+&spl) e
  from dual;

col pmem form 99,999,990
col nu    like pmem
col sss   like pmem
col tmu   like pmem
col s1    like pmem
col s2    like pmem
set term on
prompt
prompt
prompt
prompt ====================================================
select 'Per user memory requirement:  ', &pumem pmem
  from dual;
select 'Number of users              :  ', &numusers nu
  from dual;
prompt ====================================================
select 'Total memory for users    :  ', &numusers*&pumem tmu
  from dual;
select 'Size of stuff in shared SQL:  ', &spl sss
  from dual;
prompt ====================================================
select 'Base shared pool size      :  ', &size1 s1
  from dual;
select 'Pool size with 30% free    :  ', &size2 s2
  from dual;
prompt ====================================================
```

You will receive output similar to that shown next when you run this code.

```
SQL> @pool
User to use?? ops$jonespg
# of users ?? 30
==================================================
Per user memory requirement:      198,116
Number of users           :            30
==================================================
Total memory for users    :     5,943,480
Size of stuff in shared SQL:    10,360,432
==================================================
Base shared pool size     :    16,303,912
Pool size with 30% free   :    21,195,086
==================================================
```

SCRIPTS AND TIPS RULE #15
Run this script to estimate optimal shared pool size at regular intervals during the business day and NEVER within 24 hours of instance startup.

Notice the figure "30%" as free space in the shared pool. We believe that shared pool sizing is the single activity you are responsible for that has the biggest payback in the tuning exercise. Fine-tuning the SHARED_POOL_SIZE entry in the initialization parameter file can be assisted using this script. Watch out for more help with this job as Oracle provides more and more tools with each new release of the software.

SCRIPTS AND TIPS RULE #16
When sizing the shared pool, allow an extra 30 percent free space. If and when the concurrent user load increases, revisit shared pool sizing programs.

Use of Database Block Buffers in the SGA

It is handy to know whether all the buffers specified in the initialization parameter file entry DB_BLOCK_BUFFERS are being used during day-to-day operations. The next script must be run as the Oracle user SYS.

```
select decode(state,0,'FREE',
                     1,'Read and Modified',
                     2,'Read and Non-Modified',
                     4,'Current Block Read','Other'),count(*)
  from x$bh
 group by decode(state,0,'FREE',
                        1,'Read and Modified',
                        2,'Read and Non-Modified',
                        4,'Current Block Read','Other');
```

The figure to pay the most attention to is the FREE buffers. This is the number of database block buffers in the cache that are not in use. They can be unused for one of two reasons. It can be due to a very small concurrent use of the database (as in quiet off-hours). It could also be that the entry for DB_BLOCK_BUFFERS in the initialization parameter file is set too high. The former reason requires no intervention. For the latter, you may want to decrease the value of this parameter.

SCRIPTS AND TIPS RULE #17
If the FREE buffer count is non-zero over an extended sampling period (e.g., after running script once an hour between 9:00 and 5:00 and inspecting the results), consider lowering the value DB_BLOCK_BUFFERS and restarting the instance.

Creating an Instance Control File

When backing up the database, we recommend creating a text copy of the code required to re-create a control file. This is done in sqldba or SQL*Plus using the command

```
alter database backup controlfile to trace;
```

Oracle will respond with "Database altered" when the command successfully completes. The SQL script written by the command is placed in the directory specified by the USER_DUMP_DEST entry in the initialization parameter file. Most systems put them in $ORACLE_HOME/rdbms/log by default. Through our experience, this copy of the control file can be a lifesaver. The output is shown in the next listing. As you can see, part of it is a bona-fide SQL script that could be used to create a control file. The code would be run in sqldba—hence the # character is used as the comment indicator.

```
# The following commands will create a new control file and use it
# to open the database.
# No data other than log history will be lost. Additional logs may
# be required for media recovery of offline data files. Use this
# only if the current version of all online logs are available.
STARTUP NOMOUNT
CREATE CONTROLFILE REUSE DATABASE PRD NORESETLOGS ARCHIVELOG
     MAXLOGFILES 20
     MAXLOGMEMBERS 4
     MAXDATAFILES 30
     MAXINSTANCES 1
     MAXLOGHISTORY 100
LOGFILE
   GROUP 1 (
     '/disk2/prd_log/log1prd_g1.dbf',
     '/data/log_shadow/log2prd_g1.dbf',
     '/disk1/log_shadow/log3prd_g1.dbf'
   ) SIZE 2M,
   GROUP 2 (
     '/oracle/dbs/log1prd_g2.dbf',
     '/disk3/log_shadow/log2prd_g2.dbf',
     '/disk1/log_shadow/log3prd_g2.dbf'
   ) SIZE 2M,

DATAFILE
   '/disk1/oracle_prd/dbs1prd.dbf' SIZE 30M,
   '/oracle/dbs/finance.dbf' SIZE 120M,
   '/disk1/oracle_prd/audit.dbf' SIZE 20M,
   '/disk2/oracle_prd/dba_stats.dbf' SIZE 18M;
# Recovery is required if any of the datafiles are restored backups,
# or if the last shutdown was not normal or immediate.
RECOVER DATABASE
# All logs need archiving and a log switch is needed.
ALTER SYSTEM ARCHIVE LOG ALL;
# Database can now be opened normally.
ALTER DATABASE OPEN;
```

This script can be used to change some of the database creation parameters that previously could only be given a new value by re-creating the database. For example, the **maxlogmembers** entry in the **create database** indicates the maximum number of redo log group members. As we have discussed throughout this book, redo log files are written by Oracle and contain transaction and rollback information about activities against the database. Redo log files are used for database recovery. With Oracle7, you can instruct Oracle to write simultaneously to a number of redo logs. This facility is called using *multiplexed redo logs*. The redo log files that are written to at the same time are referred to as a *redo log group*. Each group of redo logs can have up to the value specified in **maxlogmembers** members written to at the same time.

SCRIPTS AND TIPS RULE #18
Incorporate **alter database backup controlfile to trace** into your system backup routines. Use the output to change database parameters that cannot be altered using the SQL command **alter database**.

Renaming a Column in a Table

There is no SQL statement to accomplish this. Time and time again, it has been suggested to Oracle that there be an **alter table modify** where the name of a column can be changed. Oracle, as other database vendors, has no plans to implement this functionality. There are strict rules set out by ANSI (American National Standards Institute) that do not allow this operation for databases that conform to the SQL standards ANSI controls. The best way to do it is using the SQL statement

```
create table as select
```

with a column list. For example, consider the following table definition for the JOBS table.

```
Name                Null?     Type
------------------- --------  ----
FY_CODE             NOT NULL  VARCHAR2(5)
JOB_NUM             NOT NULL  VARCHAR2(6)
PROJ_NUM            NOT NULL  NUMBER(2)
SDESC_E                       VARCHAR2(30)
SDESC_F                       VARCHAR2(30)
LDESC_E                       VARCHAR2(60)
LDESC_F                       VARCHAR2(60)
BUDGET_HOURS                  NUMBER(7,2)
STATUS                        VARCHAR2(2)
```

Suppose you wanted to change the name of the BUDGET_HOURS column to BUD_HOURS. The first suggestion would be to issue the SQL statements that follow.

```
rem * Create a temp table with the new column name.
create table jobs_temp (fy_code, job_num, proj_num, sdesc_e, sdesc_f,
                        ldesc_e, ldesc_f, bud_hours, status)
as select * from jobs;
rem * swap names of tables.
rename jobs to jobs_old;
rename jobs_temp to jobs;
```

This exercise seems to complete the task. However, the following problems may have been introduced.

1. Any indexes that existed on the old jobs table are not present in the new table.

2. Any grants on the jobs object have been lost.

3. Any views built on the old column names in the jobs table are invalid if the view definition included the old column name.

4. The storage parameters of the new jobs table may not match those of the old table.

The following steps will ensure that indexes, grants, and storage parameters will be preserved.

1. Export the existing table definition using the following command. This will create a file called jobs.dmp, which will be input to the next step.

```
exp userid=user/password tables=jobs rows=n compress=n file=jobs
```

2. Using import with the INDEXFILE option, create an SQL script using the following command. This will create a file called jobs.sql with the existing table and index definitions with all their existing storage parameters.

```
imp userid=/ indexfile=jobs.sql file=jobs
```

3. Run the following script in SQL*Plus to preserve the grants on the old jobs table. The script will produce a file called regrant_jobs.sql that can be run in SQL*Plus against the new jobs table. Notice the **decode** that is done on the values in the GRANTABLE column in USER_TAB_PRIVS_MADE. This is necessary to preserve the **with grant option** grants given out on the existing jobs table.

```
set echo off feed off pages 0
spool regrant_jobs.sql
select 'grant ' || privilege || ' on ' || table_name || ' to ' ||
         grantee  || decode (grantable,'YES',' with grant option;',';')
   from user_tab_privs_made
  where table_name = 'JOBS';
spool off
```

4. Create a SQL script to drop any indexes on the old jobs table. Using the following, a script called jobs_idrop.sql will be created.

```
set pages 0 feed off echo off
spool jobs_idrop.sql
select 'drop index ' || index_name || ';'
   from user_indexes
  where table_name = 'JOBS';
spool off
```

5. Issue the following statement to rename the jobs table to jobs_old.

```
rename jobs to jobs_old;
```

6. Run jobs_idrop.sql to drop indexes on the jobs_old table. With version 6 and Oracle7 you may only have one object, regardless of object type, by the same name. If you left the indexes in place on the jobs_old table, the index creation in the next step would fail, because like-named indexes still exist on jobs_old.

7. Precreate the new jobs table by running the jobs.sql script that was created in step 2 of this exercise. Before running the script, edit jobs.sql and change the old column name in the table create script BUDGET_HOURS to BUD_HOURS. Also, remove all the REM text from the start of any lines, remove any lines that start with the text CONNECT, and remove any lines that contain a number followed by the word "rows".

```
CREATE TABLE "OPS$SLOANKJ"."JOBS" ("FY_CODE" VARCHAR2(5) NOT NULL,
"JOB_NUM" VARCHAR2(6) NOT NULL, "PROJ_NUM" NUMBER(2, 0) NOT NULL,
"SDESC_E" VARCHAR2(30), "SDESC_F" VARCHAR2(30), "LDESC_E"
VARCHAR2(60), "LDESC_F" VARCHAR2(60), "BUD_HOURS" NUMBER(7, 2),
"STATUS" VARCHAR2(2)) PCTFREE 40 PCTUSED 60 INITRANS 1 MAXTRANS 255
STORAGE(INITIAL 5242880 NEXT 1064960 MINEXTENTS 1 MAXEXTENTS 240
```

```
PCTINCREASE 20 FREELISTS 1 FREELIST GROUPS 1) TABLESPACE "USERS" ;

CREATE INDEX "OPS$SLOANKJ"."JOBS_1" ON "JOBS" ("FY_CODE" , "JOB_NUM",
"PROJ_NUM" ) PCTFREE 10 INITRANS 2 MAXTRANS 255 STORAGE (INITIAL 835584
NEXT 81920 MINEXTENTS 1 MAXEXTENTS 240 PCTINCREASE 20 FREELISTS 1)
TABLESPACE "INDEXES" ;
CREATE INDEX "OPS$SLOANKJ"."JOBS_3" ON "JOBS" ("PROJ_NUM" ) PCTFREE
10 INITRANS 2 MAXTRANS 255 STORAGE (INITIAL 565248 NEXT 40960 MINEXTENTS 1
MAXEXTENTS 240 PCTINCREASE 20 FREELISTS 1) TABLESPACE "INDEXES" ;
CREATE INDEX "OPS$SLOANKJ"."JOBS_2" ON "JOBS" ("JOB_NUM" ) PCTFREE
10 INITRANS 2 MAXTRANS 255 STORAGE (INITIAL 589824 NEXT 61440 MINEXTENTS 1
MAXEXTENTS 240 PCTINCREASE 20 FREELISTS 1) TABLESPACE "INDEXES" ;
```

8. Move data from jobs_old to jobs by issuing the statement

```
insert into jobs select * from jobs_old;
```

9. Run regrant_jobs.sql to put back the grants as they existed on the old table.

10. Drop the jobs_old table.

You will now have a properly indexed and properly sized jobs table that has the BUDGET_HOURS column renamed to BUD_HOURS. The last task is looking in the data dictionary for any view built using the old BUDGET_HOURS column. These views, if any, are now flagged as invalid and must be re-created. The following query will list the names and owners of any views mentioning the BUDGET_HOURS column.

```
select owner, table_name, column_name
  from sys.dba_tab_columns
 where column_name = 'BUDGET_HOURS';
```

There is no way to automatically re-create any views that use the old BUDGET_HOURS column name. You must manually intervene and rebuild these views.

Using SQL to Write SQL

If you are not familiar with this technique, now is the time! With the spooling capabilities of SQL*Plus and the correct wording of SQL statements, it is possible to create a spool file from a SQL command that is SQL itself. Suppose you wanted to drop all objects belonging to a user (OPS$FRANCISL in this example), but did not have enough privileges to issue the SQL command

```
drop user ops$francisl;
```

The following code will accomplish this for you. When you are done, there will be a script called nukeuser.sql with the drop statements.

```
set echo off pages 0 feed off
spool nukeuser.sql
select 'drop ' || object_type || ' ' || owner || '.' || object_name || ';'
  from sys.dba_objects
 where object_type in ('TABLE','VIEW','SEQUENCE','SYNONYM') and
       owner = 'OPS$FRANCISL';
spool off
```

Taking this one step further, let's rebuild the tablespace quotas given out to your users using this technique. The following will do this for you and create a SQL script as output called ts_quotas.sql.

```
spool ts_quotas.sql
select 'alter user quota ' || max_bytes || ' on ' || tablespace_name || ';'
  from sys.dba_ts_quotas
 where nvl(max_bytes,0) > 0;
spool off
```

Why not use SQL to dynamically build a parameter file for use with export? Let's create a parameter file to export all the data for any user that has objects in the tablespace YR_TRANS. This script, unlike the two previous, uses a combination of SQL and SQL*Plus statements.

```
set pages 0 feed off echo off
spool yr_trans.parfile
prompt userid=system/manager
prompt file=yr_trans
prompt buffer=10240000
prompt indexes=y
prompt grants=y
prompt owner=(
select unique owner || ','
  from sys.dba_tables
 where tablespace_name = 'YR_TRANS'
    and  owner <>
    (select max(owner)
     from sys.dba_tables
    where tablespace_name = 'YR_TRANS');
select max(owner) || ')'
```

```
   from sys.dba_tables
where tablespace_name = 'YR_TRANS';
spool off
```

The sky's the limit. Once you get started with this technique, you will end up finding a host of situations where you can use it. Why not use the information stored in the data dictionary to assist your backup procedures by creating a SQL script to rebuild your rollback segments?

```
select 'create rollback segment ' || segment_name || chr(10),
        '          tablespace ' || tablespace_name || chr(10),
        '          storage ( initial     ' || initial_extent || chr(10),
        '                     next        ' || next_extent || chr(10),
        '                     minextents  ' || min_extents || chr(10),
        '                     maxextents  ' || max_extents || chr(10) ||
        '                     optimal     ' || optsize || ');'
   from sys.dba_rollback_segs a,v$rollstat b,v$rollname c
 where segment_name <> 'SYSTEM'
   and b.usn = c.usn
   and a.segment_name = c.name;
```

Let's Tune It

We have provided you with some food for thought in this chapter, drawing your attention to some issues (and their resolution) that you will wrestle with tomorrow (if not today) or have already visited. In this book, we repeatedly state that the tuning process is ongoing—and you need to attend to every facet of managing the resources to get the best return from your tuning investment.

- Run your database in ARCHIVELOG mode—you provide yourself with almost bulletproof protection against data loss due to a variety of emergencies (e.g., disk drive headcrash or mistaken erasure of a database file).

- Monitor and report on extent allocations to tables and indexes to help you manage space effectively.

- Keep up-to-date user information at your fingertips to assist you if you need to prepare reports for auditors or reset privileges for users or a class of users.

- Grant access to the assortment of v$ and dba_ data dictionary tables to allow your developers and co-DBAs to allow them to access a wide assortment of performance information they need to make tuning decisions.

- Compute the optimal setting for the SHARED_POOL_SIZE entry in your initialization parameter file that will turn on the light at the end of the shared-sql-area-sizing tunnel.

- Monitor the activity of the buffers in the database buffer cache—if some buffers are not being used steadily, consider adjusting the DB_BLOCK_BUFFERS entry in your initialization parameter file.

- When renaming a column in a table, use our method—it preserves grants, indexes, and storage parameters.

APPENDIX A

Describes of Tables Referenced Throughout This Book

The following data dictionary tables and miscellaneous Oracle objects are referenced throughout *Tuning Oracle*. These commands are extracted from the Oracle 7.0.16.4 data dictionary. Column names may change in subsequent releases of the Oracle RDBMS. These views are owned by Oracle user SYS. You may have to connect to the SYS account and grant **select** on these objects to allow others to use them. Note that user SYS will not be able to grant anything on the two x$ views—you will get the following error if you try to make grants as SYS on these views.

```
02030, 00000, "can only select from fixed tables/views"
// *Cause:  An attempt is being made to perform an operation other than
//    a retrieval from a fixed table/view.
// *Action:  You may only select rows from fixed tables/views.
```

We have included them here for reference and to keep the reader from having to balance *Tuning Oracle* on one hand and the *Oracle7 Server Administrator's Guide* on the other. At the end of the appendix are the views and tables used by utlbstat.sql and utlestat.sql that are discussed in Chapters 2 and 5. These objects only exist during the time between which these two scripts are run.

Describes of Miscellaneous Tables

DBA_DATA_FILES

Name	Null?	Type
FILE_NAME		VARCHAR2(257)
FILE_ID		NUMBER
TABLESPACE_NAME		VARCHAR2(30)
BYTES		NUMBER
BLOCKS		NUMBER
STATUS		VARCHAR2(9)

DBA_EXTENTS

Name	Null?	Type
OWNER		VARCHAR2(30)
SEGMENT_NAME		VARCHAR2(81)
SEGMENT_TYPE		VARCHAR2(17)
TABLESPACE_NAME		VARCHAR2(30)
EXTENT_ID	NOT NULL	NUMBER
FILE_ID	NOT NULL	NUMBER
BLOCK_ID	NOT NULL	NUMBER
BYTES		NUMBER
BLOCKS	NOT NULL	NUMBER

DBA_FREE_SPACE

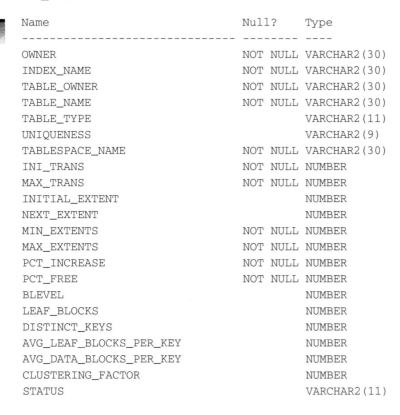

```
Name                            Null?     Type
------------------------------- --------  ----
TABLESPACE_NAME                 NOT NULL  VARCHAR2(30)
FILE_ID                         NOT NULL  NUMBER
BLOCK_ID                        NOT NULL  NUMBER
BYTES                                     NUMBER
BLOCKS                          NOT NULL  NUMBER
```

DBA_INDEXES

```
Name                            Null?     Type
------------------------------- --------  ----
OWNER                           NOT NULL  VARCHAR2(30)
INDEX_NAME                      NOT NULL  VARCHAR2(30)
TABLE_OWNER                     NOT NULL  VARCHAR2(30)
TABLE_NAME                      NOT NULL  VARCHAR2(30)
TABLE_TYPE                                VARCHAR2(11)
UNIQUENESS                                VARCHAR2(9)
TABLESPACE_NAME                 NOT NULL  VARCHAR2(30)
INI_TRANS                       NOT NULL  NUMBER
MAX_TRANS                       NOT NULL  NUMBER
INITIAL_EXTENT                            NUMBER
NEXT_EXTENT                               NUMBER
MIN_EXTENTS                     NOT NULL  NUMBER
MAX_EXTENTS                     NOT NULL  NUMBER
PCT_INCREASE                    NOT NULL  NUMBER
PCT_FREE                        NOT NULL  NUMBER
BLEVEL                                    NUMBER
LEAF_BLOCKS                               NUMBER
DISTINCT_KEYS                             NUMBER
AVG_LEAF_BLOCKS_PER_KEY                   NUMBER
AVG_DATA_BLOCKS_PER_KEY                   NUMBER
CLUSTERING_FACTOR                         NUMBER
STATUS                                    VARCHAR2(11)
```

DBA_OBJECTS

Name	Null?	Type
OWNER		VARCHAR2(30)
OBJECT_NAME		VARCHAR2(128)
OBJECT_ID		NUMBER
OBJECT_TYPE		VARCHAR2(13)
CREATED		DATE
LAST_DDL_TIME		DATE
TIMESTAMP		VARCHAR2(75)
STATUS		VARCHAR2(7)

DBA_ROLE_PRIVS

Name	Null?	Type
GRANTEE		VARCHAR2(30)
GRANTED_ROLE	NOT NULL	VARCHAR2(30)
ADMIN_OPTION		VARCHAR2(3)
DEFAULT_ROLE		VARCHAR2(3)

DBA_ROLLBACK_SEGS

Name	Null?	Type
SEGMENT_NAME	NOT NULL	VARCHAR2(30)
OWNER		VARCHAR2(6)
TABLESPACE_NAME	NOT NULL	VARCHAR2(30)
SEGMENT_ID	NOT NULL	NUMBER
FILE_ID	NOT NULL	NUMBER
BLOCK_ID	NOT NULL	NUMBER
INITIAL_EXTENT		NUMBER
NEXT_EXTENT		NUMBER
MIN_EXTENTS		NUMBER
MAX_EXTENTS		NUMBER
PCT_INCREASE		NUMBER
STATUS		VARCHAR2(16)
INSTANCE_NUM		VARCHAR2(40)

DBA_SEGMENTS

Name	Null?	Type
OWNER		VARCHAR2(30)
SEGMENT_NAME		VARCHAR2(81)
SEGMENT_TYPE		VARCHAR2(17)
TABLESPACE_NAME		VARCHAR2(30)
HEADER_FILE		NUMBER
HEADER_BLOCK		NUMBER
BYTES		NUMBER
BLOCKS		NUMBER
EXTENTS		NUMBER
INITIAL_EXTENT		NUMBER
NEXT_EXTENT		NUMBER
MIN_EXTENTS		NUMBER
MAX_EXTENTS		NUMBER
PCT_INCREASE		NUMBER
FREELISTS		NUMBER
FREELIST_GROUPS		NUMBER

DBA_TAB_COLUMNS

Name	Null?	Type
OWNER	NOT NULL	VARCHAR2(30)
TABLE_NAME	NOT NULL	VARCHAR2(30)
COLUMN_NAME	NOT NULL	VARCHAR2(30)
DATA_TYPE		VARCHAR2(9)
DATA_LENGTH	NOT NULL	NUMBER
DATA_PRECISION		NUMBER
DATA_SCALE		NUMBER
NULLABLE		VARCHAR2(1)
COLUMN_ID	NOT NULL	NUMBER
DEFAULT_LENGTH		NUMBER
DATA_DEFAULT		LONG
NUM_DISTINCT		NUMBER
LOW_VALUE		RAW(32)
HIGH_VALUE		RAW(32)
DENSITY		NUMBER

DBA_TABLES

Name	Null?	Type
OWNER	NOT NULL	VARCHAR2(30)
TABLE_NAME	NOT NULL	VARCHAR2(30)
TABLESPACE_NAME	NOT NULL	VARCHAR2(30)
CLUSTER_NAME		VARCHAR2(30)
PCT_FREE	NOT NULL	NUMBER
PCT_USED	NOT NULL	NUMBER
INI_TRANS	NOT NULL	NUMBER
MAX_TRANS	NOT NULL	NUMBER
INITIAL_EXTENT		NUMBER
NEXT_EXTENT		NUMBER
MIN_EXTENTS		NUMBER
MAX_EXTENTS		NUMBER
PCT_INCREASE		NUMBER
BACKED_UP		VARCHAR2(1)
NUM_ROWS		NUMBER
BLOCKS		NUMBER
EMPTY_BLOCKS		NUMBER
AVG_SPACE		NUMBER
CHAIN_CNT		NUMBER
AVG_ROW_LEN		NUMBER

DBA_TABLESPACES

Name	Null?	Type
TABLESPACE_NAME	NOT NULL	VARCHAR2(30)
INITIAL_EXTENT		NUMBER
NEXT_EXTENT		NUMBER
MIN_EXTENTS	NOT NULL	NUMBER
MAX_EXTENTS	NOT NULL	NUMBER
PCT_INCREASE	NOT NULL	NUMBER
STATUS		VARCHAR2(9)

DBA_TS_QUOTAS

```
Name                             Null?     Type
------------------------------   --------  ----
TABLESPACE_NAME                  NOT NULL  VARCHAR2(30)
USERNAME                         NOT NULL  VARCHAR2(30)
BYTES                                      NUMBER
MAX_BYTES                                  NUMBER
BLOCKS                           NOT NULL  NUMBER
MAX_BLOCKS                                 NUMBER
```

DBA_USERS

```
Name                             Null?     Type
------------------------------   --------  ----
USERNAME                         NOT NULL  VARCHAR2(30)
USER_ID                          NOT NULL  NUMBER
PASSWORD                                   VARCHAR2(30)
DEFAULT_TABLESPACE               NOT NULL  VARCHAR2(30)
TEMPORARY_TABLESPACE             NOT NULL  VARCHAR2(30)
CREATED                          NOT NULL  DATE
PROFILE                          NOT NULL  VARCHAR2(30)
```

INDEX_STATS

```
Name                             Null?     Type
------------------------------   --------  ----
HEIGHT                                     NUMBER
BLOCKS                           NOT NULL  NUMBER
NAME                             NOT NULL  VARCHAR2(30)
LF_ROWS                                    NUMBER
LF_BLKS                                    NUMBER
LF_ROWS_LEN                                NUMBER
LF_BLK_LEN                                 NUMBER
BR_ROWS                                    NUMBER
BR_BLKS                                    NUMBER
BR_ROWS_LEN                                NUMBER
BR_BLK_LEN                                 NUMBER
```

```
DEL_LF_ROWS                        NUMBER
DEL_LF_ROWS_LEN                    NUMBER
DISTINCT_KEYS                      NUMBER
MOST_REPEATED_KEY                  NUMBER
BTREE_SPACE                        NUMBER
USED_SPACE                         NUMBER
PCT_USED                           NUMBER
ROWS_PER_KEY                       NUMBER
BLKS_GETS_PER_ACCESS              NUMBER
```

PLAN_TABLE

```
Name                           Null?     Type
------------------------------ --------  ----
STATEMENT_ID                             VARCHAR2(30)
TIMESTAMP                                DATE
REMARKS                                  VARCHAR2(80)
OPERATION                                VARCHAR2(30)
OPTIONS                                  VARCHAR2(30)
OBJECT_NODE                              VARCHAR2(30)
OBJECT_OWNER                             VARCHAR2(30)
OBJECT_NAME                              VARCHAR2(30)
OBJECT_INSTANCE                          NUMBER(38)
OBJECT_TYPE                              VARCHAR2(30)
SEARCH_COLUMNS                           NUMBER(38)
ID                                       NUMBER(38)
PARENT_ID                                NUMBER(38)
POSITION                                 NUMBER(38)
OTHER                                    LONG
```

PRODUCT_USER_PROFILE

```
Name                           Null?     Type
------------------------------ --------  ----
PRODUCT                        NOT NULL VARCHAR2(30)
USERID                                   VARCHAR2(30)
ATTRIBUTE                                VARCHAR2(240)
SCOPE                                    VARCHAR2(240)
NUMBERIC_VALUE                           NUMBER(15,2)
CHAR_VALUE                               VARCHAR2(240)
DATE_VALUE                               DATE
LONG_VALUE                               LONG
```

TS$

Name	Null?	Type
TS#	NOT NULL	NUMBER
NAME	NOT NULL	VARCHAR2(30)
OWNER#	NOT NULL	NUMBER
ONLINE$	NOT NULL	NUMBER
UNDOFILE#		NUMBER
UNDOBLOCK#		NUMBER
BLOCKSIZE	NOT NULL	NUMBER
INC#	NOT NULL	NUMBER
SCNWRP		NUMBER
SCNBAS		NUMBER
DFLMINEXT	NOT NULL	NUMBER
DFLMAXEXT	NOT NULL	NUMBER
DFLINIT	NOT NULL	NUMBER
DFLINCR	NOT NULL	NUMBER
DFLEXTPCT	NOT NULL	NUMBER

V$DATAFILE

Name	Null?	Type
FILE#		NUMBER
STATUS		VARCHAR2(7)
CHECKPOINT_CHANGE#		NUMBER
BYTES		NUMBER
NAME		VARCHAR2(257)

V$LATCH

Name	Null?	Type
ADDR		RAW(4)
LATCH#		NUMBER
LEVEL#		NUMBER
NAME		VARCHAR2(50)
GETS		NUMBER
MISSES		NUMBER
SLEEPS		NUMBER
IMMEDIATE_GETS		NUMBER

```
IMMEDIATE_MISSES                      NUMBER
WAITERS_WOKEN                         NUMBER
WAITS_HOLDING_LATCH                   NUMBER
SPIN_GETS                            NUMBER
SLEEP1                              NUMBER
SLEEP2                              NUMBER
SLEEP3                              NUMBER
SLEEP4                              NUMBER
SLEEP5                              NUMBER
SLEEP6                              NUMBER
SLEEP7                              NUMBER
SLEEP8                              NUMBER
SLEEP9                              NUMBER
SLEEP10                             NUMBER
SLEEP11                             NUMBER
SLEEP12                             NUMBER
SLEEP13                             NUMBER
```

V$LATCHNAME

```
Name                              Null?    Type
-----------------------------     -------- ----
LATCH#                                     NUMBER
NAME                                       VARCHAR2(64)
```

V$LIBRARYCACHE

```
Name                              Null?    Type
-----------------------------     -------- ----
NAMESPACE                                  VARCHAR2(15)
GETS                                       NUMBER
GETHITS                                    NUMBER
GETHITRATIO                                NUMBER
PINS                                       NUMBER
PINHITS                                    NUMBER
PINHITRATIO                                NUMBER
RELOADS                                    NUMBER
INVALIDATIONS                              NUMBER
```

V$LOCK

```
Name                            Null?    Type
------------------------------- -------- ----
ADDR                                     RAW(4)
KADDR                                    RAW(4)
SID                                      NUMBER
TYPE                                     VARCHAR2(2)
ID1                                      NUMBER
ID2                                      NUMBER
LMODE                                    NUMBER
REQUEST                                  NUMBER
```

V$LOG

```
Name                            Null?    Type
------------------------------- -------- ----
GROUP#                                   NUMBER
THREAD#                                  NUMBER
SEQUENCE#                                NUMBER
BYTES                                    NUMBER
MEMBERS                                  NUMBER
ARCHIVED                                 VARCHAR2(3)
STATUS                                   VARCHAR2(8)
FIRST_CHANGE#                            NUMBER
FIRST_TIME                               VARCHAR2(20)
```

V$LOGFILE

```
Name                            Null?    Type
------------------------------- -------- ----
GROUP#                                   NUMBER
STATUS                                   VARCHAR2(7)
MEMBER                                   VARCHAR2(257)
```

V$PARAMETER

Name	Null?	Type
NUM		NUMBER
NAME		VARCHAR2(64)
TYPE		NUMBER
VALUE		VARCHAR2(512)
ISDEFAULT		VARCHAR2(9)

V$ROLLSTAT

Name	Null?	Type
USN		NUMBER
EXTENTS		NUMBER
RSSIZE		NUMBER
WRITES		NUMBER
XACTS		NUMBER
GETS		NUMBER
WAITS		NUMBER
OPTSIZE		NUMBER
HWMSIZE		NUMBER
SHRINKS		NUMBER
WRAPS		NUMBER
EXTENDS		NUMBER
AVESHRINK		NUMBER
AVEACTIVE		NUMBER
STATUS		VARCHAR2(15)

V$ROWCACHE

Name	Null?	Type
CACHE#		NUMBER
TYPE		VARCHAR2(11)
SUBORDINATE#		NUMBER
PARAMETER		VARCHAR2(32)
COUNT		NUMBER
USAGE		NUMBER
FIXED		NUMBER
GETS		NUMBER

GETMISSES	NUMBER
SCANS	NUMBER
SCANMISSES	NUMBER
SCANCOMPLETES	NUMBER
MODIFICATIONS	NUMBER
FLUSHES	NUMBER

V$SESSION

Name	Null?	Type
SADDR		RAW(4)
SID		NUMBER
SERIAL#		NUMBER
AUDSID		NUMBER
PADDR		RAW(4)
USER#		NUMBER
USERNAME		VARCHAR2(30)
COMMAND		NUMBER
TADDR		VARCHAR2(8)
LOCKWAIT		VARCHAR2(8)
STATUS		VARCHAR2(8)
SERVER		VARCHAR2(9)
SCHEMA#		NUMBER
SCHEMANAME		VARCHAR2(30)
OSUSER		VARCHAR2(15)
PROCESS		VARCHAR2(9)
MACHINE		VARCHAR2(64)
TERMINAL		VARCHAR2(10)
PROGRAM		VARCHAR2(48)
TYPE		VARCHAR2(10)
SQL_ADDRESS		RAW(4)
SQL_HASH_VALUE		NUMBER

V$SESSTAT

Name	Null?	Type
SID		NUMBER
STATISTIC#		NUMBER
VALUE		NUMBER
SQL_TEXT		VARCHAR2(1000)

```
SHARABLE_MEM                       NUMBER
PERSISTENT_MEM                     NUMBER
RUNTIME_MEM                        NUMBER
SORTS                              NUMBER
VERSION_COUNT                      NUMBER
LOADED_VERSIONS                    NUMBER
OPEN_VERSIONS                      NUMBER
USERS_OPENING                      NUMBER
EXECUTIONS                         NUMBER
USERS_EXECUTING                    NUMBER
LOADS                              NUMBER
FIRST_LOAD_TIME                    VARCHAR2(19)
INVALIDATIONS                      NUMBER
PARSE_CALLS                        NUMBER
```

V$SQLAREA

```
Name                          Null?     Type
------------------------------ -------- ----
SQL_TEXT                                VARCHAR2(1000)
SHARABLE_MEM                            NUMBER
PERSISTENT_MEM                          NUMBER
RUNTIME_MEM                             NUMBER
SORTS                                   NUMBER
VERSION_COUNT                           NUMBER
LOADED_VERSIONS                         NUMBER
OPEN_VERSIONS                           NUMBER
USERS_OPENING                           NUMBER
EXECUTIONS                              NUMBER
USERS_EXECUTING                         NUMBER
LOADS                                   NUMBER
FIRST_LOAD_TIME                         VARCHAR2(19)
INVALIDATIONS                           NUMBER
PARSE_CALLS                             NUMBER
DISK_READS                              NUMBER
BUFFER_GETS                             NUMBER
COMMAND_TYPE                            NUMBER
PARSING_USER_ID                         NUMBER
PARSING_SCHEMA_ID                       NUMBER
KEPT_VERSIONS                           NUMBER
ADDRESS                                 RAW(4)
HASH_VALUE                              NUMBER
```

V$STATNAME

```
Name                              Null?     Type
--------------------------------- --------- ----
STATISTIC#                                  NUMBER
NAME                                        VARCHAR2(64)
CLASS                                       NUMBER
```

V$SYSSTAT

```
Name                              Null?     Type
--------------------------------- --------- ----
STATISTIC#                                  NUMBER
NAME                                        VARCHAR2(64)
CLASS                                       NUMBER
VALUE                                       NUMBER
```

V$SYSTEM_EVENT

```
Name                              Null?     Type
--------------------------------- --------- ----
EVENT                                       VARCHAR2(64)
TOTAL_WAITS                                 NUMBER
TOTAL_TIMEOUTS                              NUMBER
TIME_WAITED                                 NUMBER
AVERAGE_WAIT                                NUMBER
```

V$WAITSTAT

```
Name                              Null?     Type
--------------------------------- --------- ----
CLASS                                       VARCHAR2(18)
COUNT                                       NUMBER
TIME                                        NUMBER
```

X$KCBCBH

```
Name                              Null?     Type
--------------------------------- --------- ----
ADDR                                        RAW(4)
INDX                                        NUMBER
COUNT                                       NUMBER
```

X$KCBRBH

```
Name                                Null?     Type
----------------------------------- --------  ----
ADDR                                          RAW(4)
INDX                                          NUMBER
COUNT                                         NUMBER
```

utlbstat.sql/utlestat.sql Views and Tables

In Chapters 3 and 5 views and tables created by utlbstat.sql and dropped by utlestat.sql were used. This code is included here for your convenience.

stats$begin_stats

```
Name                                Null?     Type
----------------------------------- --------  ----
STATISTIC#                                    NUMBER
NAME                                          VARCHAR2(64)
CLASS                                         NUMBER
VALUE                                         NUMBER
```

stats$end_stats

```
Name                                Null?     Type
----------------------------------- --------  ----
STATISTIC#                                    NUMBER
NAME                                          VARCHAR2(64)
CLASS                                         NUMBER
VALUE                                         NUMBER
```

stats$begin_latch

```
Name                                Null?     Type
----------------------------------- --------  ----
ADDR                                          RAW(4)
LATCH#                                        NUMBER
LEVEL#                                        NUMBER
NAME                                          VARCHAR2(50)
GETS                                          NUMBER
```

MISSES	NUMBER
SLEEPS	NUMBER
IMMEDIATE_GETS	NUMBER
IMMEDIATE_MISSES	NUMBER
WAITERS_WOKEN	NUMBER
WAITS_HOLDING_LATCH	NUMBER
SPIN_GETS	NUMBER
SLEEP1	NUMBER
SLEEP2	NUMBER
SLEEP3	NUMBER
SLEEP4	NUMBER
SLEEP5	NUMBER
SLEEP6	NUMBER
SLEEP7	NUMBER
SLEEP8	NUMBER
SLEEP9	NUMBER
SLEEP10	NUMBER
SLEEP11	NUMBER
SLEEP12	NUMBER
SLEEP13	NUMBER

stats$end_latch

Name	Null?	Type
ADDR		RAW(4)
LATCH#		NUMBER
LEVEL#		NUMBER
NAME		VARCHAR2(50)
GETS		NUMBER
MISSES		NUMBER
SLEEPS		NUMBER
IMMEDIATE_GETS		NUMBER
IMMEDIATE_MISSES		NUMBER
WAITERS_WOKEN		NUMBER
WAITS_HOLDING_LATCH		NUMBER
SPIN_GETS		NUMBER
SLEEP1		NUMBER
SLEEP2		NUMBER
SLEEP3		NUMBER
SLEEP4		NUMBER
SLEEP5		NUMBER

```
SLEEP6                               NUMBER
SLEEP7                               NUMBER
SLEEP8                               NUMBER
SLEEP9                               NUMBER
SLEEP10                              NUMBER
SLEEP11                              NUMBER
SLEEP12                              NUMBER
SLEEP13                              NUMBER
```

stats$begin_roll

```
Name                            Null?    Type
------------------------------- -------- ----
USN                                      NUMBER
EXTENTS                                  NUMBER
RSSIZE                                   NUMBER
WRITES                                   NUMBER
XACTS                                    NUMBER
GETS                                     NUMBER
WAITS                                    NUMBER
OPTSIZE                                  NUMBER
HWMSIZE                                  NUMBER
SHRINKS                                  NUMBER
WRAPS                                    NUMBER
EXTENDS                                  NUMBER
AVESHRINK                                NUMBER
AVEACTIVE                                NUMBER
STATUS                                   VARCHAR2(15)
```

stats$end_roll

```
Name                            Null?    Type
------------------------------- -------- ----
USN                                      NUMBER
EXTENTS                                  NUMBER
RSSIZE                                   NUMBER
WRITES                                   NUMBER
XACTS                                    NUMBER
GETS                                     NUMBER
WAITS                                    NUMBER
OPTSIZE                                  NUMBER
HWMSIZE                                  NUMBER
```

```
SHRINKS                         NUMBER
WRAPS                           NUMBER
EXTENDS                         NUMBER
AVESHRINK                       NUMBER
AVEACTIVE                       NUMBER
STATUS                          VARCHAR2(15)
```

stats$begin_lib

```
Name                            Null?     Type
------------------------------- --------- ----
NAMESPACE                                 VARCHAR2(15)
GETS                                      NUMBER
GETHITS                                   NUMBER
GETHITRATIO                               NUMBER
PINS                                      NUMBER
PINHITS                                   NUMBER
PINHITRATIO                               NUMBER
RELOADS                                   NUMBER
INVALIDATIONS                             NUMBER
```

stats$end_lib

```
Name                            Null?     Type
------------------------------- --------- ----
NAMESPACE                                 VARCHAR2(15)
GETS                                      NUMBER
GETHITS                                   NUMBER
GETHITRATIO                               NUMBER
PINS                                      NUMBER
PINHITS                                   NUMBER
PINHITRATIO                               NUMBER
RELOADS                                   NUMBER
INVALIDATIONS                             NUMBER
```

stats$begin_dc

```
Name                            Null?     Type
------------------------------- --------- ----
CACHE#                                    NUMBER
TYPE                                      VARCHAR2(11)
SUBORDINATE#                              NUMBER
```

```
PARAMETER                                VARCHAR2(32)
COUNT                                    NUMBER
USAGE                                    NUMBER
FIXED                                    NUMBER
GETS                                     NUMBER
GETMISSES                                NUMBER
SCANS                                    NUMBER
SCANMISSES                               NUMBER
SCANCOMPLETES                            NUMBER
MODIFICATIONS                            NUMBER
FLUSHES                                  NUMBER
```

stats$end_dc

```
Name                             Null?    Type
------------------------------   -------- ----
CACHE#                                    NUMBER
TYPE                                      VARCHAR2(11)
SUBORDINATE#                              NUMBER
PARAMETER                                 VARCHAR2(32)
COUNT                                     NUMBER
USAGE                                     NUMBER
FIXED                                     NUMBER
GETS                                      NUMBER
GETMISSES                                 NUMBER
SCANS                                     NUMBER
SCANMISSES                                NUMBER
SCANCOMPLETES                             NUMBER
MODIFICATIONS                             NUMBER
FLUSHES                                   NUMBER
```

stats$begin_event

```
Name                             Null?    Type
------------------------------   -------- ----
EVENT                                     VARCHAR2(64)
TOTAL_WAITS                               NUMBER
TOTAL_TIMEOUTS                            NUMBER
TIME_WAITED                               NUMBER
AVERAGE_WAIT                              NUMBER
```

stats$end_event

Name	Null?	Type
EVENT		VARCHAR2(64)
TOTAL_WAITS		NUMBER
TOTAL_TIMEOUTS		NUMBER
TIME_WAITED		NUMBER
AVERAGE_WAIT		NUMBER

stats$dates

Name	Null?	Type
STATS_GATHER_TIMES		VARCHAR2(100)

stats$file_view

Name	Null?	Type
TS	NOT NULL	VARCHAR2(30)
NAME		VARCHAR2(257)
PYR		NUMBER
PYW		NUMBER
PRT		NUMBER
PWT		NUMBER
PBR		NUMBER
PBW		NUMBER

stats$begin_file

Name	Null?	Type
TS	NOT NULL	VARCHAR2(30)
NAME		VARCHAR2(257)
PYR		NUMBER
PYW		NUMBER
PRT		NUMBER
PWT		NUMBER
PBR		NUMBER
PBW		NUMBER

stats$end_file

```
Name                             Null?    Type
-------------------------------- -------- ----
TS                               NOT NULL VARCHAR2(30)
NAME                                      VARCHAR2(257)
PYR                                       NUMBER
PYW                                       NUMBER
PRT                                       NUMBER
PWT                                       NUMBER
PBR                                       NUMBER
PBW                                       NUMBER
```

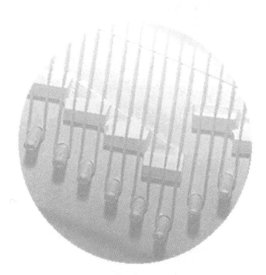

Index

T

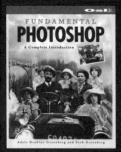

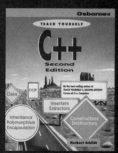

Think Fast
PASSING LANE AHEAD

ORDER BOOKS DIRECTLY FROM OSBORNE/MC GRAW-HILL.

For a complete catalog of Osborne's books, call 510-549-6600 or write to us at 2600 Tenth Street, Berkeley, CA 94710

Call Toll-Free: *1-800-822-8158*
24 hours a day, 7 days a week
in U.S. and Canada

Mail this order form to:
McGraw-Hill, Inc.
Blue Ridge Summit, PA 17294-0840

Fax this order form to:
717-794-5291

EMAIL
7007.1531@COMPUSERVE.COM
COMPUSERVE GO MH

Ship to:

Name _____

Company _____

Address _____

City / State / Zip _____

Daytime Telephone: _____
(We'll contact you if there's a question about your order.)

ISBN #	BOOK TITLE	Quantity	Price	Total
0-07-88				
0-07-88				
0-07-88				
0-07-88				
0-07-88				
0-07088				
0-07-88				
0-07-88				
0-07-88				
0-07-88				
0-07-88				
0-07-88				

Shipping & Handling Charge from Chart Below	
Subtotal	
Please Add Applicable State & Local Sales Tax	
TOTAL	

Shipping & Handling Charges

Order Amount	U.S.	Outside U.S.
Less than $15	$3.45	$5.25
$15.00 - $24.99	$3.95	$5.95
$25.00 - $49.99	$4.95	$6.95
$50.00 - and up	$5.95	$7.95

Occasionally we allow other selected companies to use our mailing list. If you would prefer that we not include you in these extra mailings, please check here: ☐

METHOD OF PAYMENT

☐ Check or money order enclosed (payable to Osborne/McGraw-Hill)

☐ AMERICAN EXPRESS   ☐ DISCOVER   ☐ MasterCard   ☐ VISA

Account No. ☐☐☐☐☐☐☐☐☐☐☐☐☐☐☐

Expiration Date _____

Signature _____

In a hurry? Call 1-800-822-8158 anytime, day or night, or visit your local bookstore.

Thank you for your order   **Code BC640SL**

About the Authors...

Michael J. Corey is Vice-President of Database Technologies, Inc., and is currently President of the International Oracle Users Group-Americas. He is also a SYSOP on the IOUG-A Oracle forum on CompuServe.

Michael Abbey, who lives and works in Ottawa, Canada, is an experienced Oracle user and is active on the Oracle forum on CompuServe. As an active user group participant, Abbey has taught at a number of International Oracle User Week conferences and regularly presents tutorials at the East Coast Oracle conference on Oracle DBA and performance issues. He is currently Vice-President of Communications and Director of Publications for the International Oracle Users Group-Americas.

Daniel J. Dechichio, Jr., an Oracle Database Administrator with the First National Bank of Boston, has over 15 years of EDP software experience with a concentration in Database Management Systems. Before joining the First National Bank of Boston, Dechichio worked for Oracle Corporation as a senior consultant implementing a Multi-National Sales Analysis System which was installed worldwide.